EVERYTHING YOU NEED TO KNOW
About Your
ASTROLOGY SIGN

*Dear Elizabeth,
Many warm wishes to a very kind + warm-hearted soul! I hope you enjoy the book.
With blessings,
Laurie Baum*

EVERYTHING YOU NEED TO KNOW
About Your
ASTROLOGY SIGN

Laurie A. Baum, M.S.W.

iUniverse, Inc.
New York Lincoln Shanghai

EVERYTHING YOU NEED TO KNOW
About Your ASTROLOGY SIGN

Copyright © 2007 by Laurie A. Baum, MSW

All rights reserved. No part of this book may be used or reproduced by any means, graphic, electronic, or mechanical, including photocopying, recording, taping or by any information storage retrieval system without the written permission of the publisher except in the case of brief quotations embodied in critical articles and reviews.

iUniverse books may be ordered through booksellers or by contacting:

iUniverse
2021 Pine Lake Road, Suite 100
Lincoln, NE 68512
www.iuniverse.com
1-800-Authors (1-800-288-4677)

The views expressed in this work are solely those of the author and do not necessarily reflect the views of the publisher, and the publisher hereby disclaims any responsibility for them.

ISBN-13: 978-0-595-42082-7 (pbk)
ISBN-13: 978-0-595-86429-4 (ebk)
ISBN-10: 0-595-42082-6 (pbk)
ISBN-10: 0-595-86429-5 (ebk)

Printed in the United States of America

Dedicated to Paramahansa Yogananda

CONTENTS

NOTE FROM THE AUTHOR xi
HOW TO USE THIS BOOK xiii
DEFINITIONS xv
HIGHLIGHTS xxiii
INTRODUCTION 1

♈ **ARIES (March 21–April 19)**
Personality Profile 11
Personal growth 17
Relationships 19
Spirituality 28
Health 30
Finances 32
Career 34

♉ **TAURUS (April 20–May 20)**
Personality Profile 39
Personal growth 45
Relationships 47
Spirituality 53
Health 54
Finances 56
Career 58

♊ **GEMINI (May 21–June 21)**
Personality Profile 61

Personal growth 67
Relationships 68
Spirituality 75
Health 76
Finances 78
Career 80

♋ CANCER (June 22–July 22)
Personality Profile 85
Personal growth 92
Relationships 94
Spirituality 103
Health 105
Finances 110
Career 112

♌ LEO (July 23–August 22)
Personality Profile 117
Personal growth 121
Relationships 124
Spirituality 132
Health 134
Finances 137
Career 139

♍ VIRGO (August 23–September 22)
Personality Profile 143
Personal growth 150
Relationships 153
Spirituality 162
Health 165

| Finances | 169 |
| Career | 171 |

♎ LIBRA (September 23–October 23)
Personality Profile	175
Personal growth	180
Relationships	181
Spirituality	191
Health	193
Finances	196
Career	197

♏ SCORPIO (October 24–November 21)
Personality Profile	201
Personal growth	209
Relationships	212
Spirituality	227
Health	229
Finances	231
Career	232

♐ SAGITTARIUS (November 22–December 21)
Personality Profile	237
Personal growth	244
Relationships	246
Spirituality	254
Health	256
Finances	259
Career	261

♑ CAPRICORN (December 22–January 19)
Personality Profile	265

Personal growth 271
Relationships 273
Spirituality 281
Health 283
Finances 286
Career 288

♒ AQUARIUS (January 20–February 18)
Personality Profile 293
Personal growth 300
Relationships 302
Spirituality 310
Health 312
Finances 315
Career 316

♓ PISCES (February 19–March 20)
Personality Profile 319
Personal growth 326
Relationships 332
Spirituality 342
Health 345
Finances 347
Career 349

NOTES 351

ENDORSEMENTS 353

NOTE FROM THE AUTHOR

It is my hope that by reading *Everything You Need to Know About Your Astrology Sign*, you will gain greater understanding of the reasons for your sojourn on Earth and ways you may ameliorate your sacred journey.

Your astrological chart is a reflection of a decision by your soul to assume a physical form at an exact time and in a specific place. There are no accidents from this perspective. The moment of your birth represents the culmination of a series of choices made by your soul prior to your incarnation, and in past lives. Astrology, through your Sun Sign, Moon Sign, and Rising Sign, describes your nature—and the best ways to manifest your destiny at this time.

As you read these pages, it is my hope that you will hear a whisper from your soul, one of the many signs from the cosmos that shines a light on your path.

Many blessings as you turn the pages of this book, and on the sacred journey of your soul.

HOW TO USE THIS BOOK

Each chapter of *Everything You Need to Know About Your Astrology Sign* shows the unfolding of human consciousness as it begins in the self-oriented first sign of the Zodiac, Aries, and progresses to the midpoint of the Zodiac, to the relationship-oriented sign of Libra, and reaches its most spiritual level in the spiritually-oriented sign of Pisces.

If you are a student of astrology, you may read each chapter as a journey through the evolution of consciousness undergone by every soul. You may see the descriptions of each sign as aspects represented in every individual's psyche, to greater or lesser degrees, depending upon the time of one's birth.

If you are a casual observer of astrology, you may read your own Sun Sign, or the Sun Sign of the people with whom you are close. You may also read the character descriptions associated with your Moon Sign or Rising Sign, or the Moon Sign or Rising Sign of others, to gain greater understanding of yourself and other people. If you do not know your Moon Sign or Rising Sign, you may consult a professional astrologer or any of a number of web sites that will calculate this information for you.

Your astrological chart is a sacred mandala that shows you the way to manifest your destiny.

DEFINITIONS

ASTROLOGICAL SIGNS

♈ Aries (March 21–April 19)
Visionary, individualistic, initiating, entrepreneurial, impulsive, assertive, pioneering

♉ Taurus (April 20–May 20)
Sensual, artistic, strong, patient, tenacious, affectionate, simple, direct

♊ Gemini (May 21–June 21)
Communicative, verbal, mentally versatile, conceptual thinking, witty, bright, clever, multi-faceted

♋ Cancer (June 22–July 22)
Sentimental, feeling, nostalgic, family-oriented, domestic, nurturing, resourceful

♌ Leo (July 23–August 22)
Dramatic, expressive, generous, gregarious, warm, strong, managerial, confident, willful

♍ Virgo (August 23–September 22)
Precise, analytical, detail-oriented, perfectionist, perceptive, healing, serviceful, unselfish

♎ *Libra (September 23–October 23)*
Balanced, peaceful, harmonious, compromising, fair, egalitarian, humanitarian, loving

♏ *Scorpio (October 24–November 21)*
Profound, intense, psychologically-aware, determined, extreme, transformational, emotional, mysterious

♐ *Sagittarius (November 22–December 21)*
Philosophical, studious, optimistic, adventurous, lucky, humorous

♑ *Capricorn (December 22–January 19)*
Industrious, hard-working, disciplined, focused, organized, serious, professional

♒ *Aquarius (January 20–February 18)*
Idealistic, altruistic, philanthropic, objective, friendly, tolerant, accepting, non-attached, supportive

♓ *Pisces (February 19–March 20)*
Spiritual, sympathetic, compassionate, imaginative, self-sacrificing, sensitive

PLANETS

Sun

The Sun expresses masculine energy. In your astrological chart, it represents the way you take action, what is important to you, how your conscious mind works, how you relate to your father, how you express fathering or protective energy (even if you are a woman), and how you relate to masculine energy. The Sun represents your conscious goals in this incarnation.

Moon

The Moon expresses feminine energy. In your astrological chart, the Moon represents feelings, your relationship to your mother, your mothering or nurturing style (even if you are a man), and how you relate to feminine energy. The Moon represents talents you carry from past lives and the energy of your soul.

Mercury

Mercury is the planet of communications, commerce, and travel. Mercury is the messenger god in Roman myth, known as Hermes in Greek myth. Mercury also is associated with Castor & Pollux, the twins of ancient Greece—one mortal, the other divine—an explanation for the dual nature of Mercury-ruled Gemini.

Mercury Retrograde

When Mercury retrogrades, the planet of communications appears to move backward from the perspective of Earth. Mercury is not actually moving backward during Mercury Retrograde, but it appears to travel in reverse when it orbits the Sun more slowly than does the Earth, due to its elliptical path. This sacred celestial phenomenon represents the continual expansion and contraction of the universe. When the communications planet is "retrograde," commerce and communication slow. When the communications planet is "direct," commerce and communication resume a brisk cadence. Mercury retrogrades three to four times a year for three weeks at a time.

Venus

Venus mediates the energy of love, affection, and aesthetics from heavenly spheres to earthly affairs. Venus is the goddess of love and beauty in Roman myth, known as Aphrodite in Greek myth.

Mars

Mars brings raw energy, power, physical dexterity, ambition, and assertiveness to the earth plane. Mars is the god of war in Roman myth, known as Ares in Greek myth.

Jupiter

Jupiter mediates the energy of luck, spiritual protection, religious and spiritual study and practice, philosophy, travel, contemplation, and positive thinking. Jupiter revolves around your astrological chart once every 12 years, bringing good luck and fresh energy to the same area of life every 12th year. Jupiter is the god of the heavens in Roman myth, known as Zeus, ruler of Mount Olympus, in Greek myth.

Saturn

Saturn mediates the energy of karma, discipline, hard work, accomplishment, professional achievement, and the overcoming of obstacles. Saturn appears to present difficulties early in your life. As you learn to surmount obstacles designed by your soul and mediated by the energy of Saturn, the karmic planet reverses itself and provides protection, structure, and efficiency. Saturn gradually reverses its effect after its first revolution through your astrological chart, which takes 29 1/2 years. This life transition occurs between the ages of 29 and 30, and is called the "Saturn return." The Saturn return enables you to pursue your life's true work. A second Saturn return occurs at the age of 59, which enables you to teach others lessons you have learned. A third Saturn return occurs at the age of 88, when you have acquired a lifetime of wisdom under the auspices of the cosmic teacher. Saturn is associated with the Roman god Saturn, known as Cronos in Greek mythology, god of time.

Uranus

Uranus mediates the energy of innovation, creativity, radical or revolutionary ideas, and *kundalini* awakening. Uranus typically exerts its greatest influence during the "mid-life crisis," which occurs from the late 30s to the late 40s, depending upon the year of your birth. Uranus returns to its natal position when you reach age 84, which brings enlightenment about the meaning of your life. Uranus travels through one of the 12 astrological signs every seven years. This cycle, combined with Saturn's quarter-revolution through the Zodiac every seven years, is responsible for the seven-year cycle of change, known as the "seven-year itch." On a physical level, Uranus is associated with lightening, earthquakes and sudden volcanoes or eruptions (along with Pluto), and sudden events. Uranus is associated with the sky god Uranus in Roman myth, known as Ouranos in Greek myth.

Neptune

Neptune mediates the energy of dreams, spirituality, subtle realms of consciousness, and the soul. Neptune provides spiritual clarity, but may be elusive or deceptive in influencing your perception of earthly affairs. Neptune enhances intuitive and psychic abilities because its oceanic power erodes the veil between earthly, astral, and causal planes of consciousness. On a physical level, Neptune is associated with floods, leaks, and accumulations of water in the physical body or in physical structures. Neptune is the god of the oceans in Roman myth, known as Poseidon in Greek Myth.

Pluto

Pluto mediates the energy of deep psychological experience, the subconscious, sex, death, transformation, and alchemy. Pluto brings buried energy and information to the surface. While Pluto may be experienced as disruptive, it actually raises truth to the surface so it may be integrated. Pluto is responsible for radical transformation due to deep revelation. On a physical level, Pluto is associated with earthquakes, and volcanoes or sudden eruptions (along with Uranus), and deep, mysterious revelations of hidden information or physical phenomena. Pluto is the god of the underworld in Roman myth, known as Hades in Greek myth.

PLANETARY ANGLES

Square

A square angle between two planets creates action, energy, and confrontation. When handled positively, integration and higher consciousness ensue. Improperly handled, a square brings crisis and confrontation. A square angle is considered stressful but full of opportunity.

Opposition

An opposition requires the integration of two opposing energies. Oppositions work through the medium of relationship, and can be stressful or beneficial depending upon the energies in opposition to each other. Venus and Mars, for example, are a more cooperative male-female pair than are the Sun and Mars, which create a competitive dynamic between male energies. An opposition between the Moon and Venus is considered beneficial if female energies are blended in a harmonious way. The opposition of Mars and Saturn is considered stressful because it creates delays, although it leads to scientific achievement and technological discovery. The opposition of Mars and Jupiter, on the other hand, creates enthusiasm and athletic achievement.

Trine

A trine is considered positive in that it easily combines compatible or incompatible energies to produce harmonious expression.

HIGHLIGHTS

♈ ARIES (March 21–April 19)
Best Food: Hot Peppers
Best Investment: Insurance
Favorite Activity: Risk-taking
Best Partners: Leo, Sagittarius
Lucky Number: 9
Color: Bright Red
Flower Essences: Impatiens promotes patience, Larkspur enhances leadership, Tiger Lily brings moderation, Vine helps put others' needs first

♉ TAURUS (April 20–May 20)
Best Food: Cake, Cookies
Best Investment: Certificates of Deposit
Favorite Activity: Gardening
Best Partners: Virgo, Capricorn
Lucky Number: 6
Color: Earth Tones
Flower Essences: Nicotiana harmonizes body and feelings, Rabbitbrush helps process multiple situations, Quaking Grass opens multiple perspectives, Willow helps accept and forgive, Oak enhances recognition of limits, Rock Water releases self-judgment

♊ GEMINI (May 21–June 21)
Best Food: Popcorn
Best Investment: Education
Favorite Activity: Learning

Best Partners: Libra, Aquarius
Lucky Number: 5
Color: All Shades of Blue
Flower Essences: White Chestnut calms an overactive mind, Calla Lily balances male and female energy, Manzanita enhances your relationship to your body

♋ CANCER (June 22–July 22)
Best Food: Dairy Products
Best Investment: Home
Favorite Activity: Staying Home, Cooking
Best Partners: Scorpio, Pisces
Lucky Number: 2
Color: Blue-Green
Flower Essences: Aloe Vera balances your energy, Honeysuckle releases memories, Evening Primrose heals feminine energy, Baby Blue Eyes heals masculine energy, Pink Monkeyflower overcomes fear, Sage develops detachment and enhances soul perception

♌ LEO (July 23–August 22)
Best Food: Strawberries
Best Investment: Clothing
Favorite Activity: Performing
Best Partners: Aries, Sagittarius
Lucky Number: 1
Color: Orange-Red, Gold
Flower Essences: Morning Glory heals your heart, Canyon Dudleya calms overexcitement, Indian Paintbrush helps express creative energy

♍ VIRGO (August 23–September 22)
Best Food: Rice
Best Investment: Personal Assistant
Favorite Activity: Analyzing
Best Partners: Taurus, Capricorn
Lucky Number: 5
Color: All Shades of Blue
Flower Essences: Lavender calms your mind, Canyon Dudleya soothes emotions, Larch overcomes fear of imperfection, Rock Water releases obsessive thoughts, Sage widens perspective

♎ LIBRA (September 23–October 23)
Best Food: Hors d'oeuvres
Best Investment: Art
Favorite Activity: Relationships
Best Partners: Gemini, Aquarius
Lucky Number: 6
Color: White
Flower Essences: Nicotiana balances physical and emotional energy, Lotus opens the body to spiritual energy, Calla Lily balances male and female energy

♏ SCORPIO (October 24–November 21)
Best Food: Root Vegetables
Best Investment: Psychotherapy
Favorite Activity: Can't be mentioned
Best Partners: Cancer, Pisces
Lucky Number: 9
Color: Black

Flower Essences: Lavender soothes your nerves, Nicotiana helps express feelings, White Chestnut calms inner turbulence, Agrimony releases inner conflict

♐ **SAGITTARIUS (November 22–December 21)**
Best Food: Tomatoes
Best Investment: Backpack
Favorite Activity: Travel
Best Partners: Aries, Leo
Lucky Number: 3
Color: Indigo/Purple-blue
Flower Essences: Dill soothes your mind, California Poppy brings focus, Sweet Pea calms restlessness

♑ **CAPRICORN (December 22–January 19)**
Best Food: Goat's Milk, Goat Cheese
Best Investment: Office Furniture
Favorite Activity: Planning
Best Partners: Taurus, Virgo
Lucky Number: 8
Color: Dark Blue
Flower Essences: Baby Blue Eyes counteracts pessimism, Blackberry overcomes inertia, Angelica helps perceive angelic assistance

♒ **AQUARIUS (January 20–February 18)**
Best Food: Fast Food
Best Investment: Computer
Favorite Activity: Sharing New Ideas
Best Partners: Gemini, Libra
Lucky Number: 4
Color: Silver

Flower Essences: Cosmos slows chaotic thoughts,
Aspen promotes healthy spirituality, Lady's Slipper harmonizes
spirituality with body rhythms

♓ PISCES (February 19–March 20)
Best Food: Fish
Best Investment: Swimming Pool, Jacuzzi
Favorite Activity: Daydreaming, Watching Movies, Swimming
Best Partner: Scorpio, Cancer
Lucky Number: 7
Color: Violet, Light Blue
Flower Essences: Yarrow strengthens your aura,
Golden Yarrow centers you, Goldenrod enhances your
individuality, Willow gives self-confidence

INTRODUCTION

Your astrological chart provides a snapshot of the position of the planets at the moment of your first breath of life. Your first breath brings an energetic vibration into your body that imprints itself upon your cells. This vibratory pattern resonates with every subsequent breath, attracting you to or repelling you from people, places, and situations that will provide the lessons you have chosen as a soul to learn in this lifetime.

The first moment of every endeavor is important—because it launches a new energy pattern that is always present in the life of a person or venture. The electromagnetic field generated by the birth of a person or venture continues to resonate long after the original act of creation. Thus, it is important to understand the original intention behind any act of creativity or procreativity—because it will continue to resonate for many years or even millennia after the initial spark of thought. Astrology can be extremely helpful in identifying your original intention as a soul in your desire to incarnate. And astrology can help you identify your purpose and decisions you are likely to make to fulfill your goals.

The Accuracy of Astrology

You may ask, "how do the positions of the planets so accurately reflect my decisions and life on earth?" The solar system is a large atom that mirrors the smaller atoms in your body. Due to the law of resonance, the planets in the solar system reflect on a macrocosmic level the atoms in your body at every passing moment. So, if the shape of the big atom changes, so too will the atoms in your body. Then, due to the same law of physics, changes at the atomic level result in electromagnetic changes in your aura and your chakras, which affect your thoughts, emotions, and physical health. These electromagnetic changes magnetize people and events that reflect the conditions of your thoughts, feelings, sensations, and the chakras that compose the auric field around your body.

The Planets & Your Chakras

Your chakras are highly sensitive spinning vortices of energy that emanate from your spinal column. Chakras also are shaped like an atom, with a defined center circled by multidimensional rings of energy. Each chakra emanates a layer of the energy field around your body, which creates your aura. Each chakra—and therefore every layer of your aura—also has an energetic connection to one of the vertebrae in your spine, which transmit celestial energy to your glands and nervous system via the spinal column.

The Sun influences your solar plexus, the Moon influences your heart, Mercury influences your throat, Venus influences your navel, Mars influences the base of your spine, Jupiter influences your brow or third eye center, Saturn influences your crown along with outer planets Uranus, Neptune, and Pluto. After celestial energy enters your chakras, it reverberates through your body. Therefore, each change in the solar system has a profound impact upon your health, feelings, thoughts, actions, attitudes, motivations, perceptions, and sense of well being.

Finally, consider that the solar system of which you are a part is an element of another larger atom that orbits a galactic center. Presumably, this galaxy joins numerous other galaxies rotating around another center, which orbits another center, until finally we reach the center of the universe, also known as God.

Free Will

God has given each individual free will, so you may potentially manifest the energies emitted from the heavenly spheres on *any* level you choose. That is where free will enters in. The planets do not *force* you to do things. The planets do not make things happen any more than a clock changes time. The planets simply reflect larger energetic patterns emanating from God, of which you are a part, to which you are sensitive, and to which you may react in any way you choose. Still, the energy you bring at the moment of your birth is always present, guiding your decisions, lessons, and the paths you follow.

Your Sun, Moon & Rising Sign

Your chart represents a special signature, one you signed at birth. Your Sun Sign is your ego. It is your male energy. Your Sun Sign describes where your will is strong, where you shine, and what you like to do. Your Moon Sign describes how you feel. It is your female energy. Your Moon Sign reflects qualities and talents cultivated in past lives. Your Sun Sign guides your actions. Your Moon Sign regulates your reactions. Your actions and reactions guide and influence each other. Your Ascendant or Rising Sign is the constellation rising over the eastern horizon at the moment of your birth. Your Rising Sign reflects your outer personality or mask, also known as your *persona*. Your Rising Sign intimately affects the way you express your feelings (your Moon Sign) and your will (your Sun Sign). So, for a complete picture of yourself, you may read the astrological chapter corresponding to your Sun Sign, Moon Sign, and your Rising Sign.

Please note that this book is based upon Western Astrology, in which the "sign," or constellation, you are born under is determined by the seasonal relationship of the Sun and the Earth. Vedic astrology, on the other hand, is based upon the fixed stars that ring the ecliptic of the Earth. Vedic means related to the Vedas, ancient Hindu scriptures. The ecliptic is the Sun's apparent path among the stars. The constellations that compose the signs of the Zodiac are located along the ecliptic. Your astrological "sign" in Western astrology is farther along in the Zodiac than the sign position ascribed by Vedic astrology due to the precession of the equinox.

Your astrological chart is the personal lens through which you view the world. No two lenses are the same. Even twins have different charts because they are physically born in different spaces and times. You will bring yourself greater happiness by synthesizing the different aspects of your nature so they work together in perfect harmony.

Why Astrology is Affecting You Now

The planetary patterns are affecting you more strongly now than at any time in recent history for a number of compelling reasons.

- First, the planets are lined up in a potent configuration from 1998 to 2012 that last occurred at the Renaissance, and during the life of Jesus Christ and the crucifixion.

- Second, numerous sunspots, solar storms, and solar flares have intensified the electromagnetic energy emitted by the Sun, the giver of life on Planet Earth. This intensified solar energy has activated latent soul issues for all beings on the planet, and has even activated latent issues and intelligence stored in Mother Earth. These intensified energies are energizing aspects of your personality, and your astrological chart, that otherwise might have lain dormant or remained in your unconscious.

- Third, global warming, and the depletion of the ozone layer and other naturally existing barriers between the Sun and the Earth have been accelerated by man-made inventions and pollution. This erosion of the protective layer around the Earth has lessened the cushion between earthly life and solar light, illuminating areas that had been difficult to see, and giving them energy.

- Forth, as part of the celebration of the advent of the new millennium, a physical capstone was reinstalled at the top of the Great Pyramid in Egypt at midnight on January 1, 2000. A capstone amplifies and enhances the impact of the pyramid structure. Pyramids resonate and harmonize with each other through the law of resonance. Therefore, at the beginning of the new millennium, the pyramid-like structure in your pineal gland, connected to your third eye chakra, was activated by the Great Pyramid in Egypt. The high vibration pyramidal energy reawakened your awareness of latent wisdom, healing abilities, and the power to project your thoughts and prayers. In the days of Ancient Egypt, the pineal gland, which etherically stores ancient wisdom, was said to be the size of a golf ball. Today, the pineal gland of most people is the size of a shriveled raisin. By opening to the light of your soul, by meditating and experiencing the celestial energies inundating the planet, you can expand the size of your pineal gland to the size of a large grape and commensurately expand your perceptions and awareness.

The aforementioned factors are some of the many influences that are accelerating evolution at this critical time in human consciousness—and awakening your sensitivity to energetic influences, such as those emitted by the planets. This awakening will bring positive perceptions and insights. But as in every period of accelerated growth, those qualities that have been repressed or hidden will rise to the surface as you unearth latent talents. Ultimately, this experience will raise your level of awareness of yourself and of the greater universe of which you are a part.

This time of accelerated growth was foreseen many thousands of years ago by ancient seers called *rishis* in India. These ancient wise men saw that the Earth and the entire universe go through continual cycles of expansion and contraction, imitating the in- and out-breath of God. These cycles are mirrored on Earth as periods of progression or regression of consciousness. The New Millennium signals the beginning of a 12,000-year period of rapidly expanding consciousness that was foreseen thousands of years ago by the *rishis*. *(Please note that the world expands and contracts in 24,000-year periods, so that this particular 12,000-year period of positive growth follows 12,000 years of decline in human consciousness. Once human awareness reaches its apex in nearly 12,000 years from now, consciousness will decline again for another 12,000 years approximately, as part of the continual expansion and contraction of the universe. The expansion and contraction correspond with human awareness expanding to encompass perception of God and contracting to encompass only awareness of visible, material creation.)*

The changes in planetary patterns, increased solar activity, and even the decision to replace the capstone on the Great Pyramid, are simply external, visual manifestations of divine patterns already set in motion by the Creator aeons ago.

♈ ARIES (March 21–April 19)

♈ ARIES (March 21–April 19)

PERSONALITY PROFILE

Aries is a cardinal, fire sign symbolized by the ram.
Your key motivations are achievement, assertiveness, leadership, initiating new ideas, and moving quickly.
Your outstanding attributes are an ability to assert authority, to rely on your instincts, and be guided by your vision.
Your karmic challenge involves learning proper use of authority and interpreting instincts and intuitions so you implement right action rather than habitual or impulsive responses.
Aries rules the head.
Mars rules the constellation of Aries.
Aries is associated with Ares in Greek myth and Mars in Roman myth.
Aries is associated with the color red, the root chakra, and the adrenal glands.
Best Day: Tuesday
Best Number: 9
Healing Gemstone: Red Coral

Aries is the first sign on the Zodiac wheel. You were born within hours, days, or weeks of the spring equinox, when the light of day begins to overtake the dark of night. The enthusiasm and feeling of a fresh start that accompanies the advent of spring commensurately fills your spirit. Aries is visionary, aggressive, pioneering, entrepreneurial, and individualistic. You are a leader with enthusiasm, drive, and energy. You need continual outlets for your exuberant energy, and you need a band of followers to help you to implement the many ideas that inspire you. It is your nature to blaze the trail before you. You have a strong will that helps you succeed in all endeavors you undertake.

You bring a burst of energy to everything you touch, as if you are solely responsible for making the zodiacal wheel spin. Aries carries the seed of a belief from prior incarnations that says, "If I don't get things started, nothing will happen." It is no wonder that many Aries get up before sunrise, or very close to the time when the first rays of the Sun peak above the eastern horizon. Aries prefers to face east or to be on the eastern side of any physical location. This is true if you are born under an Aries Sun or Moon, or if you have Aries Rising. The Sign of the Ram initiates the cycle of the seasons and is dedicated to being the first spark to light the way for others to follow.

You are a born leader who is polishing his or her leadership skills in this lifetime. In a prior life, you were a military leader, or you wielded authority in an organization or among a group of people. You resonate with hierarchical structures. Yet, chances are good that you incarnated in a family where your father, the head of the household, or male figures, did not express authority in positive ways. The female authority figures in your home may not have appropriately handled power either. The result, whether you are a man or a woman, is that you are searching for a positive way to assert your authority. As you grow older, you find your own voice and develop a personal leadership style.

Here are some pointers:

Leadership Skills

1) Understand the strengths, weaknesses, feelings, and viewpoints of the members of the group or organization you are leading.
2) Take the strengths, weaknesses, feelings, and viewpoints of group members into consideration when devising a strategy and assigning roles.
3) Make sure you plan realistically to reflect the talents of the group.
4) Communicate your plan—and the reasons for your plan—to members of the group.
5) Be willing to make compromises if others have alternatives or objections.
6) Be flexible.
7) Continually assess the feelings and viewpoints of members of the group.
8) Listen.
9) Continually assess the progress of members of the group to ensure everyone understands the goal, and that the goal is being reached. Gently make positive suggestions.
10) Praise group members for positive contributions.

As you master the above leadership skills, you will find you are easily able to accomplish goals in a group. You will experience leadership as similar to any relationship, which requires negotiation and understanding rather than absolute decrees, as you may have grown up with, or subliminally remember from prior incarnations.

Negotiation involves listening, flexibility, surrender to others, and confidence in your own position, so you know when to yield and when to stand firm. You may see the world in terms of black and white. Negotiation will force you to see shades of gray.

It is a law of nature that everything seeks to unite with its opposite. Libra, the sign of relationships, is the sign opposite yours on the Zodiac wheel. When Aries is single-minded and definitive, Libra is multidimensional and equivocal. When Aries is bold and direct, Libra is diplomatic. When Aries sees situations from his or her point of view, Libra sees situations from the other person's point of view, or from all participants' points of view. Aries and Libra can learn a lot from each other, as you learn to balance with your opposite. If you know a Libra, observe the way the native of the Sign of the Scales weighs, balances, and measures a situation before speaking or taking action. Observe the way Libra takes everyone's viewpoint into consideration before producing a compromise that satisfies everyone. Observe how willing Libra is to compromise to create harmony. Observe how much harmony surrounds Libra. Feel the peace. Is this an experience you would like to create in your life? What can you do to create peace and harmony?

Chances are good that you will benefit by slowing down. You will develop your ability to accurately judge situations, to assess risk, to anticipate consequences, and design a plan of action that best fits your nature, the situation, and the natures of the people following you. Aries natives often have a prominent forehead, a jutting brow, or thick eyebrows that may even be connected in the middle, representing your headstrong nature. This is a wonderful quality in a crisis, when immediate instinctive action is required. Aries are strongly represented among the ranks of policemen, firemen, security guards, and lifeguards. You are good at protecting others in a crisis. You have quick reflexes and strong instincts, which propel you forward in heated moments. Trouble begins, however, when there is no crisis. When a sudden response is required, there is no one faster than Aries. When a slow, considered response is required, there still is no one faster. The solution is to slow down to consider alternatives. If you cannot slow down, ask any other sign to present a range of options you may not be able to see. Every other sign moves more slowly than you, simply because, unlike you, they are not at the front of the line.

As a soul, you incarnated with a very definite purpose. You may have chosen to incarnate in a family where difficulties prevailed to help you build your strength. The heavier the weight, the stronger you become. This is the theory behind many Aries decisions. You set up challenging situations to stretch your limits. You may have overcome difficult childhood circumstances. Consequently, you have developed a strong sense of purpose. Depending upon the time of day you were born, your purpose may involve starting a family, a business, a political or religious movement, a health craze, an athletic record, or a communal project. Whatever you are committed to, you are highly committed to starting *something*. Your soul's purpose may not be clear in early life. So, you may do things quite purposefully without knowing the exact purpose for your resolute attitude. If this happens, apply your enormous energies to endeavors you consider constructive. Even if you do not know where you are going, you eventually will see a pattern in your actions. This knowledge will define the most appropriate direction.

It is the job of Aries to get things started. Even if you do not stay with projects for long, give yourself credit for the many ideas you have initiated or inspired. In the primary position, you are learning that your soul's path to enlightenment comes through leading others, while continuously turning back to unify the people who follow you. When you initiate new ideas, and gracefully lead others along the path you have blazed, you will have fulfilled the mission for which you were born.

PERSONAL GROWTH

The objective of your life is to create balance between wisdom and impulse. You are a wise person. And you have strong instincts and impulses. Sometimes, you move so quickly, you are unable to implement storehouses of wisdom inside yourself. When you move quickly, you are not always sure what is behind your motion. Is it inertia or altruistic goals? You feel a force continually driving you, as if there is a motor running in your lower energy centers. This power can promote athletic achievement, enable you to rescue an accident victim, stop a crime, or save someone's life. But, you can just as easily get into an accident, or risk your life with the same uncontainable energy.

The solution is to move the strong and fiery energy that burns in your lower chakras to your higher centers of wisdom in your heart, throat and third eye. You can do this by any form of exercise that allows your energy to circulate freely. Your energy has a natural intelligence that innately balances lower and higher centers when they become imbalanced. If you simply allow energy to circulate, it will go where it is needed. And, through perspiration and breath, you will release excess fire, heat, and stagnant energy.

You also may experiment with color to balance your energy. Red is a prominent color in your aura. The color blue balances red. You may wear blue clothing or carry a blue crystal in your pocket or wear a blue gemstone around your neck. Healing blue gemstones and crystals include sapphire, lapis lazuli, sodalite, kyanite, rubelite, celestite, or aquamarine. Or, you may visualize blue and imagine a cascade of blue light flowing from the heavens into the crown of your head. Or, imagine yourself stepping into a soothing bath of blue light. Or, feel a fountain of blue light rising from the earth, running from the base of your spine to the crown of your head. Take a deep breath, and imagine the blue light bringing stillness, peace, and harmony. You may also consider scheduling time to sit quietly and breathe. You will feel your body releasing heat and agitation. Periodically, schedule time to do nothing. You are so busy doing so many things that *nothing* is *something*!

RELATIONSHIPS

As a soul, you incarnated with a definite purpose, or at the least, you have the feeling that you have a strong reason for being. You are a magnetic soul. You draw many relationships to yourself. But how do you balance the purpose driving your life with the needs of a partner? This is where the graceful balancing skills of Libra, the sign opposite Aries on the Zodiac wheel, could be quite useful to you. Relationships may come to you at a price, the price being infringement upon your ability to manifest an important goal driving you from the depths of your soul. If you do not have a goal, you are compatible with more people than the typical Aries. But if you are aware of the reason for which you have incarnated, you will be goal oriented. So, you may ask yourself whether a relationship will enable you to simultaneously meet the demands of your soul.

As a result of the strong energy that drives you, you may attract, or be attracted to, people who follow rather than lead. If you reach an agreement in a relationship to consciously pursue this pattern, you will create a healthy, functional working relationship. Or, if you attract another strong-minded soul, you may agree to grant freedom to each other to pursue divergent goals. Or, if you are an Aries who is not pursuing a special goal, you may consider supporting another soul with your fiery, enthusiastic energy. You will grow most in a relationship in which neither partner dominates or controls, and both equally contribute to making decisions.

Aries and Aries

Two Aries in a relationship resemble two athletes trying out for the same team. Both athletes *want* to support the other. But how can they? They have devoted their hearts, bodies, minds, and souls to *winning*, not to nurturing a potential competitor. You are oriented to reaching the goal ahead of you, not to caring for the people along the way. You are narrowly focused on your path so you perceive nearly everything as peripheral. You do best in a relationship where your partner is focused on you. Or, conversely, where you are focused on your partner. If both of you are focused on an external goal, you may find you are co-existing rather than relating. You may think about a method to coordinate your lives when you are moving in divergent directions. You may work together well when you are on the same team. But if your lives move independently, the relationship may not be as permanent as you thought.

Aries and Taurus

You are attracted to the stable, grounded nature of the fixed, earth Sign of the Bull. Taurus appreciates your intensity and passion. You both appreciate the strength of the other, and accomplish much if you have a mutual goal. Taurus sits down, anticipates details, and plans. You catch a few pieces of information as you rush out the door to take action on the idea. You and Taurus produce daring results in a business relationship. In an intimate partnership, however, you and Taurus may feel impatient with each other. You feel impatient with Taurus' slow and methodical ways, and preference for tradition. Taurus feels impatient with your constant need for spontaneous change and pursuit of risky undertakings. This is a relationship that works best as a friendship. Nevertheless, you will learn a lot from this connection for the period in which it endures.

Aries and Gemini

If you choose to team up with mutable, air sign, Gemini, you will find a person with a perfect temperament to balance your intense fire. You are fascinated by the lively mind and imaginative conversational style of the Sign of the Twins. Geminis are captivated by your entrepreneurial, resourceful spirit. Geminis have a sense of perspective that enables them to step back and maintain objectivity and poise. Gemini is agile, mentally versatile, and able to keep pace with your movement-oriented life. You and Gemini are youthful, animated people with boundless enthusiasm. Life suddenly seems like an adventure with limitless potential when you come together. Please inject an element of realism as your imaginations conjure infinite possibilities for this relationship. Even if you do not understand the reason for being realistic, your Gemini partner is always ready with a justification. One thing you will not have to justify will be your feelings for each other. You love your partner without question. And if your feelings change, chances are your partner will have changed too, and both will understand.

Aries and Cancer

You are fascinated by the domestic flair and loyalty to family and traditional values of cardinal, water sign Cancer. Cancer is awestruck by your capacity for change. You marvel at Cancer's ability to maintain a stable home and routine for what seems like an eternity. Cancer marvels at the number of businesses you have started, people you have met, friends you have made, and places you have visited. Cancer loves to cook, decorate, make a family, and set down roots. You abhor the concept of roots because they limit your ability to change at a moment's notice. You are less concerned than Cancer with fine cuisine or cozy decorations, although you like the idea of family. You love to play with children, take care of cars, and work outside of the house, but if you want a stable home, you better rely on Cancer to do the work inside of the house. You have very different natures—Cancer is an introvert who is emotional and sensitive, and you are an extrovert who is less aware of feelings and more focused on external achievement. You think about your next step while Cancer thinks about the last step. If you and Cancer do not mind a partner who lives independently, you may create a stable relationship where Cancer cares for the home, and you tend to worldly business. You may have little in common, but you make a good team if you recognize your complementary skills and allow them to work together.

Aries and Leo

Aries and Leo are attracted to each other like two sparks drawn together to form a flame. Aries is a cardinal, fire sign who enjoys getting things started. Leo is a fixed, fire sign who enjoys bringing stability and strength to that which has been created. You and Leo are a dynamic couple who continually seek an outlet for your fiery energy and enthusiasm. Neither Aries nor Leo enjoy sitting still, so chances are good that you will surround yourself with much activity if you are in partnership with a Leo, or with someone with a Leo Moon, or Leo Rising. Your dynamic rhythms are compatible and elicit mutual respect due to the strength each one perceives in the other. You have much in common, and enjoy many adventures. Your mutual fire creates a warm light for all to enjoy.

Aries and Virgo

You may initially be in awe of the eye for detail and Puritanical ways of the mutable, earth sign Virgo. Virgo is initially shocked by your brash boldness and impulsivity. But as you get to know each other, you will come to appreciate Virgo's methodical plans, and Virgo will appreciate your entrepreneurial, industrious spirit. Together, you may experience many successes in business as Virgo plans and you implement the plans, or, as you conjure up a vision, and Virgo dutifully tends to the details to uphold the vision. You plant the seeds, and Virgo waters the plants and weeds the garden. This is a relationship that may lack deep intimacy and longevity, but if you agree on mutual goals, you may support each other to accomplish many things during the time you are traveling together.

Aries and Libra

You are passionately drawn to the elegance and grace of cardinal, air sign Libra. Libra is deeply moved by your passion and definite goals. You see Libra as a peaceful, refined, harmonious soul who can balance your sometimes-uncontainable energy. You and Libra are polar opposites on the Zodiac wheel. The Sign of the Ram knows how to light the fire that initiates the relationship, and the Sign of the Scales knows how to create balance, peace, and harmony as the relationship unfolds. In nature, Aries is the sign that initiates planting at the spring equinox, and Libra is the sign that initiates the harvest at the fall equinox. You both were born in the moments, days, or weeks after the light of day and night were equal. The light was growing under Aries, and diminishing under Libra. Together, you feel a kind of synthesis that transcends mortal form, and connects you to a greater cycle. While Aries may have a short attention span, this is a relationship that will hold your attention for life.

Aries and Scorpio

You are magnetically attracted to fixed, water sign Scorpio for the quiet magnetic power Scorpio exudes. It is as if your fire, combined with the watery depths of Scorpio, creates steam that is too alluring to resist. Your Scorpio partner also is enthusiastic about fanning the flames of this steamy relationship. According to traditional astrology, Aries and Scorpio are incompatible. But a surprising number of Aries team up with Scorpios, perhaps for the repartee the tense combination creates. Scorpio and Aries enjoy jousting with a partner the way two puppies enjoy a little tussle now and then. A steady diet of harmony bores you both, and this partnership offers a competent opponent for you. Emotional depth is achieved through fighting in this relationship. Closeness is created through discord rather than harmony. But if you ask the Aries or Scorpio, they will tell you they honestly love each other. This relationship is not a model of conventional love. But for Aries and Scorpio, this is true love.

Aries and Sagittarius

You enjoy the company of fellow fire sign Sagittarius because the Sign of the Archer is not afraid to speak the truth, strike out alone, or overturn the status quo. These qualities enormously appeal to you. You also enjoy the sense of humor of people with a Sagittarius Sun, Sagittarius Moon, or Sagittarius Rising. You learn a lot from Sagittarius about seeing the big picture and about thinking strategically to create positive results. The optimism of Sagittarius sparks positive energy in you that is intoxicating. Together, you have a dynamic relationship in which both can support the vision of the other.

Aries and Capricorn

You are attracted to the drive and ambition of cardinal, earth sign Capricorn. Capricorn admires your entrepreneurial spirit and your ability to get up before dawn and accomplish as much in the first hour of the day as Capricorn accomplishes in the whole day. You were born just after the spring equinox and exude the fiery enthusiasm of the growing light of the Sun. Capricorn was born just after the winter solstice, when the light of the Sun is diminished. Consequently, Capricorn energetically exudes the feeling of someone who is slowly building warmth. But once the Capricorn's temperature is raised, Capricorn's energy is among the most enduring of the Zodiac. Your ability to initiate a project, and Capricorn's ability to follow through, make you a dynamic business team. In the realm of the heart, you may seek spontaneity when Capricorn seeks predictability. Capricorn wants a partner who will support his or her upward climb. Meanwhile, Aries wants to be independent, and free to pursue his or her dreams spontaneously. This is a dynamic combination if you have similar goals, but you may go separate ways when your dreams differ.

Aries and Aquarius

You will experience a new way of looking at the world in a relationship with fixed, air sign Aquarius. Aquarius is an innovative thinker who is ahead of his or her time. You are a visionary and an entrepreneur who is entertained by risk. Aquarius will help you take your ideas from the formative stages to a highly evolved form that expands your vision and brings an altruistic angle to your astute perceptions. Aquarius' enhanced perspective reduces the risk factor in your exuberant ideas, enabling you to better manage your project at a later date. You get the ball rolling, and Aquarius keeps the ball in play, while you take off to cultivate another new idea. Aquarius appreciates your youthful enthusiasm. And you cannot help but admire the mature sagacity that enables Aquarius to bring your heady ideas to fruition, while he or she maintains a broad perspective that keeps this relationship moving endlessly forward. Even if you do not understand yourself or your relationship, Aquarius has a big-picture view that helps you enlarge your perspective and perceive the meaning of your life.

Aries and Pisces

Traditionally, water signs such as Pisces do not harmonize with fire signs such as Aries, because water puts out fire—and fire creates steam when it interacts with water. Yet, the ethereal quality of Pisces enables this evolved mutable, water sign to harmonize with the feelings of any sign, even the fieriest of fire signs such as yourself. A disproportionate number of Pisces pair up with Aries due to a sense of completeness created by the partnership. Aries initiates action while Pisces brings the action to completion. Pisces enjoys the impulsive nature of Aries. And Aries appreciates the flowing, adaptable quality of Pisces. Pisces and Aries see the world from opposite perspectives. Aries and Pisces create harmony by balancing opposites. Pisces lets go of the Self to unite with others as a way of uniting with the Divine. Aries separates from the Divine as a way of asserting the Self to unite with its own individuality. If Aries and Pisces understand their innate differences, they may create a balance between heaven and earth, a creation others admire.

Aries, no matter whom you choose as your relationship partner, make sure you and your mate understand that you have an internal rhythm playing in your head. This rhythm is your soul, and it cannot be ignored. Your partner may or may not have the same rhythm playing in his or her head. If your partner is comfortable pursuing an independent lifestyle, you will manifest the vision for which you were born, and have a happy relationship too.

SPIRITUALITY

Spirituality is a difficult subject for you because Aries develops a naturally strong sense of Self as the first sign of the Zodiac. You are headstrong, a visionary, and a leader. Spirituality involves a natural surrender to a power greater than the Self. This does not mean that one does not exercise his or her natural intelligence, judgment, and discrimination on a spiritual path. But it does mean surrendering to a partnership with a Divine intelligence. A relationship with an invisible, omniscient force may be quixotic to you.

Many religions or spiritual paths also require sitting still for a length of time for religious study or practice. This is antithetical to your movement-oriented nature. You may wonder how you will make spiritual progress if you cannot sit still long enough to partake of spiritual practice. There is a solution. Become the leader of the spiritual or religious organization that interests you. Then, your Aries temperament will shine. If you have a spiritual inclination, approach a spiritual practice with the goal of leading others. You are more comfortable blazing a trail than you are following the trail others have blazed. Keep in mind that as soon as you master the principles of your path, you are able to lead others. You are more enchanted by being a leader than a congregant.

To deepen your spiritual knowledge, try initiating a short but formal period of study of spiritual scriptures. The potential to study spiritual scriptures is endless, and if you delve into this facet of spirituality, you may find an endless supply of new experiences. You may resist sitting to study, but you will have more chances of success reading on your own than you will if you listen to a human interpreter of spiritual wisdom. You generally find lectures boring, and the people delivering the lectures are rarely as fiery and attention-grabbing as you, at least in your estimation. Therefore, go to the source. You are more likely to find spiritual sustenance that way.

Also consider a spiritual practice that combines movement and breathing as part of an overall spiritual program. This could be yoga or walking meditation. Sitting meditations are good too. It takes 20 minutes to raise one's vibration from mundane consciousness to a higher state of consciousness. Try sitting for 20 minutes when you begin. Be aware of your breath. Keep your attention at the center of awareness between your eyebrows. After 20 minutes, you will have entered an expanded state of awareness. This simple practice for 20 minutes will transform your entire day and give you patience, forbearance, and efficiency. The practice of calming yourself, even for a brief period, will transform your body, and change your sleep patterns to give you more restful sleep and lucid dreams. This alone will enhance the quality of the coming day. Combined with meditation or contemplation, you will achieve the balance you seek.

A law of nature states that everything seeks to unite with its opposite. Consider Libra, the sign opposite your own. Think about Libra's qualities of balance, poise, and composure as you try to blend these qualities with your nature. Spiritual practice may be the bridge between your present state of consciousness and the desirable state of peace and harmony that will help you feel complete.

HEALTH

You are a fire sign who thrives on anything red—red clothes, red walls, red cars, and red foods. You tend to have a fiery, red color in your skin, and you easily become hot. Red is the color of the root chakra at the base of the spine, which rules the Sign of the Ram. Your health issues often arise from an excess of fiery energy in your body. As you channel your abundant energy into productive endeavors, your positive energy will multiply, and excess energy will dissipate. Typically, you begin the day with an enormous amount of energy. You reach a crescendo, and swiftly lose energy, usually after sunset. Respect your rhythm. Practice moderation. You may feel as if there is no end to your boundless energy. Yet, sooner or later, every Aries experiences burn-out—either at the end of the day, or at the end of life. The way to avoid running out of energy is moderation, moderation, and moderation, along with self-control, self-discipline, and self-restraint.

Visualizations & Food

You also may cool the fire that energetically burns within you by drinking plenty of water, by eating a balance of stimulating red-colored foods and soothing blue- and white-colored foods, and by periodically immersing yourself in water of any temperature to calm your nerves and temper the heat in your system. You also may visualize a fountain of blue water flowing from the crown of your head, bathing you in healing, calm energy.

Flower Essences

Flower essences, which are distillations of the high vibrations in flowers, also may help you. Impatiens moderates impatience or domineering qualities. Larskspur develops positive leadership qualities. Tiger Lily curbs over-assertiveness. Vervain moderates intensity and passion so these emotions do not deplete the nervous system. Vine helps one place the wishes of others ahead of one's own.

FINANCES

You are not one to worry about money, and you always find ways to conjure up cash if you have a sudden financial need. You have plenty of friends, contacts, and clever ideas. You rarely accumulate large sums of money in a savings account because you believe money is called "currency" because it works best when it is moving. You have an excellent sense of timing, and an ability to navigate financial markets and make decisions with speed, accuracy, and luck. You have naturally good intuition with gambling and financial risk. Experience has taught you to trust your instincts, which nearly always take you to your goal. I said "nearly always" for a significant reason. Your intuition usually comes quickly, from where you cannot say. And your intuition is usually right on target. But every once in a while, you reach an incorrect conclusion. It is as if God periodically throws a curve ball to temper your enthusiasm.

Trust your intuition, but rely on a back-up system to confirm your impressions. Do you get a secondary feeling in your stomach, a pressure in your head, neck, or eyes (these are the sensitive areas in your body that may receive intuitive perceptions), or are people warning you about your perceptions? Listen to your body. If you cannot interpret the warning signals delivered by your body, then listen to other people. Their perspectives may complement yours in a positive way.

As for a budget, you are not one to keep track of expenditures, so it is likely you do not know the exact amount of money you have at any one time. This gives a "seat-of-the-pants" quality to your financial situation, but also opens you to trust that everything will be taken care of. Generally, it will. But you may check your balance every once in a while to make sure your sense of proportion is commensurate with reality.

You also have a sixth sense when it comes to selling things, from what to sell, to who needs it, how much they will pay, and when they will buy it. Use this natural talent, along with your natural advertising and marketing skills, to supplement your regular income, and you will never experience poverty.

CAREER

You are a natural entrepreneur, and you may be involved with more than one start-up venture in your life. You get a thrill from embarking upon new ventures, and you apply this drive to any career or business. The excitement of meeting a new person, finding a new product, trying a new marketing strategy, making a sale, building a home, or starting a business fuels your constant quest to create. This is the natural rhythm of your life. You bring the first breath of spring, and then move forward to recreate magic in new places. You rarely stay around to wait for things to become stale. You love the challenge, and quickly tire when routine sets in.

You are best at pursuing careers that require a short burst of energy, a short but concentrated span of attention, little focus on details, and plenty of stamina. An early start to the day also helps, because you thrive on getting a head start, hate the feeling of missing anything, and certainly would not think of getting up later than the Sun, much less start work when it was dark! You are happiest in careers that involve leadership, management, entrepreneurial skills, marketing, advertising, athletic activity, driving, or moving quickly. You like to make quick decisions, meet deadlines, and get quick results. You also enjoy sales in the financial markets because it combines many of your natural talents, moving quickly, getting to know people quickly, talking quickly, getting a yes- or no-answer quickly, and seeing immediate, quantifiable results—hopefully quickly. Sometimes, you do not care whether an answer is "yes" or "no," or whether the venture was a failure or a success. You simply want to know that you can move on to the next thing because as far as you are concerned, the next is always better than the last. Your life is driven by your enthusiasm, building on the promise of experiencing something new. Sculpt your life so it accommodates your need to explore new things. As long as you feel you are placing your feet in places where you have yet to tread, you feel as if you are fulfilling the purpose for which you were born. Movement—even if it is displeasing—is positive, because you place a high value on change.

As a result of your penchant for change, you may consider building an escape clause into the natural rhythm of any endeavor you undertake. It is not like you to stay with projects after you initiate them, after they enter the maintenance phase. Magical energy comes through you when you put a structure in place. When the rhythm and routine become predictable, your power recedes. You are better off leaving for the next enterprise. Few people truly understand your rhythm. They may try to hold you back, thinking it will be good for you—or them—if you stay beyond the initiation phase. Yet, you have less to offer an ongoing routine than you do a start-up venture. You are the one who plants the seeds. You sense when the plant's shoots are ready to sprout through the earth. You do not have to wait until the plant produces fruit. Others want to see the plant above the ground before they feel a venture has been a success. Like the spring season initiated under the constellation of Aries, you are confident beyond measure that once the seeds are planted, Mother Nature will take care of the rest.

♉ TAURUS (April 20–May 20)

☉ TAURUS (April 20–May 20)

PERSONALITY PROFILE

Taurus is a fixed, earth sign symbolized by the bull.
Your key motivations are material security, stability, sensual comfort, artistic and creative pursuits, simplicity, and predictability. Your outstanding attributes are practicality, loyalty, tenacity, manual dexterity, earthiness, creativity, flair with color, love of culinary arts, gardening, business savvy, and financial acumen.
Your karmic challenge involves balancing your fixity with flexibility, and your endurance with knowing when to stop.
Taurus rules the throat, neck, and cervical spine.
Venus rules the constellation of Taurus.
Taurus is associated with the Minotaur, the bull of Greek myth.
Taurus is associated with the color orange, the navel/sacral chakra, and the reproductive glands.
Best Day: Friday
Best Number: 6
Healing Gemstones: Orange Calcite, Carnelian

You are a strong individual in body, mind, and soul. You are the second sign of the Zodiac, following the fire sign Aries. Aries initiates the cycle of the seasons with a burst of high-speed, fiery energy and growing light in the spring. Next comes Taurus, a slow-moving earth sign responsible for mediating the heat and light of Aries with a calm slowness that reassures earthlings that spring is here to stay. You bring this calm, stabilizing energy to everything you touch. Others perceive your calm, cool, capable demeanor, and seek comfort in your secure presence.

You have a deep yearning for peace and harmony that you bring to every endeavor. Your patience, steadfastness, loyalty, and sympathy enable you to calmly evaluate situations to find the best solution. You exude a sense of solidity that others find reassuring. Your predictable, repetitive cadence creates peace and harmony under circumstances where chaos might otherwise reign.

You are a methodical, conventional, straightforward person. You do best when you know in advance where you are going and what you are going to encounter. This is why you adhere to repetitive routine and ritual. For you, a routine is a routine is a routine … is a routine. It is easier to repeat patterns than it is to change.

Your steadfast, tenacious personality can be your greatest asset or liability. There is no one more secure, reliable, and loyal than a Taurus soul, especially when he or she has made a commitment. Yet, there also is no one more stubborn, intransigent, and truculent in resisting change. This is when Taurus the Bull digs in its heels, or its hooves, as the case may be, and refuses to budge. This unchangeable quality may be as vexing to you as it may be to others. Sometimes you really, honestly, want to change. But it feels as if you are in shackles, and a constant rhythm drumming in your head is forcing you to do the same thing, over and over and over again. You fear that if you change even one small thing, you will lose your rhythm and your grip on *everything*. You secretly imagine the disorientation would bring devastation, so you create circumstances that lock you into fixed patterns, prisons from which you may feel powerless to emerge.

You resonate with the Minotaur, the mythological bull trapped in a labyrinth. Healing of this inimical relationship with change comes from doing exactly the thing you fear—change. Experiment with doing things differently—just a small bit differently from the past. You will notice devastation did not befall you, and you actually reaped benefit from the change. This experience will help you become more flexible, adaptable, and ultimately stronger, rather than weaker, as you feared. Strength comes through an ability to negotiate circumstances that are favorable to all rather than steadfastly holding your ground, especially when the ground is crumbling beneath you.

If you find yourself becoming rigid, know you are resisting change. The change will be good for you, although your reaction may be contrary, as if your life is about to be threatened. Open yourself to the creative possibilities coming to you from the outside and emerging from within. This acceptance of fluidity will help you accomplish the Divine purpose for which you incarnated.

As a soul, you incarnated in the tenacious Sign of the Bull to achieve a definite purpose on Planet Earth. This inner knowledge is one of the reasons you can be so unswerving—because inside of yourself, you know you have something to do. Yet, swerving in the service of pursuing unfamiliar yet creative new directions may be precisely the experience you need to fulfill the mission prearranged by your soul.

The presence of Taurus in your chart indicates a drive to attain the sensual comforts of earthly existence. It is likely that one of the missions your soul is the fulfillment of a material goal. This goal could involve manifesting an artistic creation, a beautiful home, a family, a piece of writing or music, a business venture, material or financial success, an athletic achievement, or it could involve creating circumstances that allow you to abundantly experience the sensual comfort of food, nature, or your physical body. While these are all worthy outer goals, another goal is to balance outer activity with the development of equally worthy qualities inside yourself.

An active practice of flexibility and faith, spirituality and surrender, and meditation and contemplation, will help you accomplish quite a lot in a balanced way, and at times, more than if you steadfastly keep your eye on one target (the bull's eye). Ultimately, it is your destiny to experience change. Very small changes will seem monumental to you, and these small experiences will contribute to a trust in life and in yourself that you never imagined.

Every soul's energy flows into physical form according to a particular pattern. If you incarnated as a Taurus, your energy enters your body in a fixed pattern that is similar to a regular, rhythmic beat of a drum. Rather than flowing, it would be more accurate to say that your energy marches slowly and decisively. The antidote to the drumbeat quality in your mind is music, meditation, movement, and exposure to the unpredictable but rhythmic waves of the ocean, or the flow of a river or stream, or the lapping sound of a lake.

You have a deep affinity with nature because of your deep resonance with the cadence of earth, tied to your incarnation as the first of the three earth signs of the Zodiac, the other two being Virgo and Capricorn. You hold in high regard the physical accoutrements of the earth, everything from trees, rivers, forests, and plants, to your physical body and physical possessions. Your resonance with the physical elements of God's creation make you an artist with everything you touch—be it food, gardening, interior design, or paint. You have a love of color, physical harmony and beauty, form and shape. You are a master of the three-dimensional world, and as such, may be quite adept at everything from fixing broken appliances to moving furniture, to sewing clothing to molding clay, or painting on canvas to painting on walls. You have a natural gift with creating shape and form with your hands. And you have a natural appreciation for the comfort these creations engender.

On a psychological level, you also have a deep appreciation for anything that creates the feeling of security. This could be secure locks on the doors, ironclad commitments from your family, friends, and colleagues, and if possible, a readily available bank account. One way or another, you are determined to create security for yourself. Often, because of your affinity and resonance with the physical world, you seek security through physical objects or external situations rather than through your inner world. One question you may ask yourself is whether you derive your security from accomplishments in the material world or from the experience of inner peace, harmony, and tranquility. A balance of attention to your inner and outer worlds will give you the true security you are seeking, and will come through material efforts as well as introspection, meditation, psychological discovery, self-confrontation, and experiencing your Self. Finally, the practice of gratitude to the Divine for all good that comes your way will do more to generate material and emotional abundance and security than any physical effort you may make.

Part of your evolution also comes through experiencing and communicating with those things you cannot see, including your intuition and your connection to the Divine. Even though something is not physically visible does not mean it is not operating in your life. Just because you cannot see the wind does not mean it is not rustling the leaves on the trees, making the chimes ring, or causing the hurricane that completely transforms the landscape. As you develop a more active relationship with forces you cannot see, you will begin to trust your intuition, your soul, and ultimately the Divine. Your intuition is the link between your soul and your conscious mind. As you follow the unseen power of your intuition, you will find it easier to go with the flow and trust the circumstances evolving around you. You will see that your intuition is leading you to the highest good, as guided by your soul and its innate connection to the Divine. Your life will run infinitely more smoothly than it did when your conscious mind was exclusively in control. As you allow your intuition and conscious mind to work in partnership, you will open a gateway to your soul and the Divine. As your mind becomes more fluid and flexible, you will experience serenity you never thought possible. Count your blessings. Notice that what you have is perfect for you. Take a deep breath, and let go …

PERSONAL GROWTH

You are a definite person who has a black and white view of the world. You see many aspects of life in absolute terms, and may have difficulty seeing shades of gray. Consider the idea that the world is a spectrum that encompasses many colors and dimensions rather than a unidimensional world polarized between good and bad, your way and their way, and us and them. There may be a war going on inside of you over absolute rights and wrongs. It is difficult for you to accept the possibility of more than one way being right, or of more than one way being right under different circumstances, or at different times. Consequently, you may fight with yourself over rigid strictures of right and wrong without stopping to discern subtle details. Or worse, you may create outer conflict that did not previously exist by rigid adherence to what you thought was right, without considering the correct application of the principle igniting the torch you are carrying, which creates circumstances that oppose your natural craving for peace and harmony. Try to stop and think about the principle or concept you are fighting for. How attached are you? Are there nuances to consider? Can you be more flexible in reaching a reasonable conclusion? Or a compromise? Can you negotiate with another person rather than make a unilateral decision?

Much of your personal growth will come through inclusion of other people, other principles, and new factors in your thinking and decision-making. Rather than going it alone, relying on rules, or looking at an issue from one point of view, try to include other people and points of view in the process. Try to see situations not only from your point of view and the point of view of the other person or people involved, but try to see the situation from the point of view of a disinterested, objective third party. Try to imagine the consequences of your decision in the future. Try to let go of rules or repetitive patterns. The object of the game, dear Taurus, is multidimensional rather than unidimensional thinking. Try to apply this principle in as many ways as you can. You will discover solutions you previously had not considered. And guess what? You will reap rewards that previously passed you by.

RELATIONSHIPS

Relationship may be one of the most significant areas of your life. This is because sense pleasures are so significant to you, and you firmly believe that objects of the five senses (sight, hearing, touch, smell, and taste) are meant to be shared. Therefore, Venus-ruled Taurus is most compatible with fellow earth signs Virgo and Capricorn, and with Moon-ruled Cancer.

Taurus and Taurus

If you are a particularly security-oriented Taurus, you will get along famously with other members of the Sign of the Bull due to the mutual goal of security and satisfaction of physical and bodily needs. Your Taurus partner understands your need for sameness and routine. A shared interest in food absorbs much attention in this partnership. You both appreciate sense pleasures, and understand the needs of the other. You each do your part to make this a stable, enduring, lifelong partnership.

Taurus and Gemini

A relationship with the mutable, air sign of Gemini energizes your intellectual side and opens your mind to new ways of thinking and seeing the world. You appreciate the clever mind of your Gemini partner, and enjoy listening to what may be an endless monologue from your peripatetic partner. Unless you have a Gemini Moon or Gemini Rising, Gemini's kinetic energy may be a bit unsettling to you if you live in close quarters. Although you are a loyal and possessive partner, you may consider loosening the bonds of a commitment you may be contemplating with this clever soul. Your Gemini partner will relish the freedom provided by a lack of commitment. And you will relish the peace and tranquility you feel when you bond with a more energetically sedate sign.

Taurus and Cancer

Cancer is a particularly comforting mate because of your mutual love of security. You crave material security while cardinal, water sign Cancer craves emotional security. Together, you create the secure environment you desire. Taurus and Cancer also are lovers of culinary and sense pleasures. You both enjoy candlelight dinners, trips to favorite restaurants, and taking turns cooking for each other. Both Taurus and Cancer are wedded to tradition and preserving the status quo. Both signs relish stability, and neither sign enjoys change. Together you create the solid relationship (as long as neither wants to change the other) you dreamed possible.

Taurus and Leo

Relationships between earthy Taurus and fixed, fire sign Leo are not recommended in traditional astrology, but the combination manifests with marked regularity. Taurus is magnetically drawn to the fiery excitement of Leo just as Leo is drawn to the earthy stability of Taurus. This combination appeals to many souls who seek a partner who is strong and stable. The strength and stability abundantly possessed by Leo and Taurus suggests a relationship that moves forward very little. But it also suggests a relationship that can withstand the test of time. Many Leo and Taurus couples find they communicate very little in a deep way. But Taurus and Leo are loyal souls who value the commitments they make, and both will go to the end of the earth to uphold the union, even if it is not the most communicative in the world.

Taurus and Virgo

You are eternally attracted to the simplicity, purity, and elegance of mutable, earth sign Virgo. Virgo is eternally attracted to your stability and predictability. You are a grounded soul who excels at gardening, artwork, handicrafts, and working with objects in the material world. Virgo is a mentally versatile, detail-oriented soul who wants to help in any way that is needed. You appreciate the sensitive sign of Virgo for its delicate sense perceptions and ability to spot details you may have missed. Your Virgo partner will give you logistical support and as much advice as you desire. You will loyally offer yourself as a lifelong mate to the pristine Sign of the Virgin. Virgo will relish the opportunity to be your partner for life. You feel supported by the presence of the Virgo in your life, and the Virgo feels content to be with you.

Taurus and Libra

You appreciate the fine, aesthetic sensibilities of cardinal, air sign Libra. Libra appreciates your artistic flair and culinary skills. According to traditional astrology, earthy Taurus does not easily harmonize with airy Libra, but many Libra and Taurus souls are drawn together by a mutual love of peace, harmony, and beauty. You relish stability and predictability in your physical environment while Librans cherish peace and harmony in their relationships. If each partner prevails in the domain in which he or she specializes, this is a relationship that will bring much happiness to the partners, and all who share in their lives.

Taurus and Scorpio

The sign exactly opposite Taurus on the Zodiac wheel is fixed, water sign Scorpio. Opposites attract. Yet, opposites are opposite. Scorpios are intense, profound souls who want to penetrate deeply below the surface of matter. In contrast, you feel as if the surface is the entire story. You and Scorpio transform each other in an intimate partnership. Scorpio helps you acknowledge significant factors lying below the surface, and you help Scorpio surface from deep-sea diving to enjoy life on dry land with you. Neither sign will permanently inhabit the realm of the other, but exposure to Scorpio's watery realms of mystery and emotion brings you a world of new perspectives, just as a respite on simple, dry land does Scorpio a world of good.

Taurus and Sagittarius

You appreciate the fun-loving, pleasure-seeking nature of the mutable, fire sign Sagittarius. Sagittarius appreciates your down-to-earth common sense and stability. You are both creative souls. Taureans are artists who create with their hands. Sagittarians are philosophers who create with their minds. You appreciate the gifts of the other. But a steady diet of each other may jangle the nerves of both the earthy Taurus and fiery Sagittarius, the way fire burns the earth in its path. Sagittarius may feel encumbered by the slow, deliberate, methodical Taurus. And Taurus may feel jangled by the spontaneous, non-detailed, non-linear, enthusiastic Sagittarian. This combination may create a long-lasting friendship, but it also may create a lot of wear and tear in an intimate relationship.

Taurus and Capricorn

The ambitious Capricorn encourages you to express your resourceful and tenacious nature. You appreciate the initiative and originality of Capricorn, a cardinal, earth sign, and no one will be a more loyal fan than you. Your warm sensuality appeals to Capricorn's tactile, sensitive, sensation-oriented nature. Capricorn's committed and security-driven side helps you feel the security you crave. Capricorn shares your love of material security, schedules, routines, and physical comfort. Capricorn appreciates your accomplishments in the world, and has a few practical suggestions to lighten your load. You appreciate Capricorn's sensible approach to life. You and Capricorn will establish a stable foundation upon which both souls may build a stable life together.

Taurus and Aquarius

Aquarians may be a bit aloof for your taste, but you each understand the strength of the other, and a mutual respect will inevitably flower in this *laissez-faire* relationship. You respect the high-minded ideals of your Aquarius partner. Aquarius respects your practical skills, and is impressed with your manual dexterity. You provide logistical support to your Aquarius partner, and Aquarius furnishes you with an alternative perspective. After all is said and done, however, you prefer to do things your way, and Aquarius prefers to do things his or her way. You may find you have little in common. In an intimate partnership, Aquarius finds security in freedom and movement. You find security in routine and stability. Ultimately, you may not be able to provide what the other is looking for. But you will learn a lot during the time you hold this relationship together.

Taurus and Pisces

Pisces is a spiritual, emotional, compassionate soul whose flowing, spontaneous, non-linear ways confound your methodical, logical mind. Taurus plans where mutable, water sign Pisces flows. The focus of the bull's eye can be extremely narrow whereas the vision of the celestial and terrestrial fish is extraordinarily expansive. Taurus thinks about what's for lunch while Pisces contemplates the fate of the universe, and forgets to eat. Taurus and Pisces make a quaint couple if Pisces does not feel tied down by the earthbound Taurus, and if Taurus does not feel destabilized by the unpredictable Pisces. This relationship may cause you to confront routines that are not serving you. Pisces could be a good balance to your linear, planned way of viewing the world. As long as both partners are conscious of their differing natures and both are willing to accommodate the other, this could be a comfortable and satisfying relationship. You could offer Pisces stability, and Pisces could help you learn to dance with the spontaneous flow of life.

Taurus and Aries

You are attracted to the intensity and passion of cardinal, fire sign Aries. Aries is attracted to your stable, grounded demeanor. You both appreciate the strength of the other, and accomplish much if you have a mutual goal. Yet, in an intimate partnership, you may feel impatient with each other. Aries feels impatient with your methodical ways and your preference for tradition rather than something new. You feel impatient with Aries' constant need for change, spontaneous pursuit of what-you-consider illusive or risky undertakings, and lack of planning. This is a relationship that works best as a friendship. No matter how you define the parameters, you will learn a lot from this partnership for the period in which it endures.

Taurus, you seek a relationship that provides security and stability. Choose your mate carefully, because once you commit, you intend to remain partnered for life. Even in the most adverse circumstances, a Taurus is usually unwilling to change partners. Therefore, consider your mate as thoroughly as you would any important purchase that can never be returned.

SPIRITUALITY

Your greatest challenge on the path to the Divine is belief that there is such a path at all. Belief in things you cannot physically see does not come easily. Divine guidance, non-corporeal beings, angels, avatars, ascended masters, all of these manifestations of divinity are not necessarily see-able with the physical eyes. It is difficult for you to imagine Spirit if you cannot physically see it. Yet, faith in the ineffable leads to an innate knowing of the truth of the existence of Spirit, which is an integral part of experiencing the presence of God on the spiritual path. You may become easily disenchanted with spiritual life because you feel you cannot trust the unseen hand of the Divine. Yet, it is precisely the development of the ability to perceive non-physical reality that opens your vistas so you may experience joy in the ineffable, including your own soul.

Consider a daily practice of meditation and a weekly period of self-imposed silence and contemplation as methods to promote spiritual advancement. It is easy for you to sit, and it would only be a matter of setting an intention to direct this energy to a higher spiritual goal. Feel your breath coming in and going out. Experience the peace that naturally surrounds you. This peace is always there. You simply need to stop to breathe it in. This simple, quiet moment focused on the Infinite—and your connection with the Infinite Source around you—will give you a sense of harmony you have always longed for.

HEALTH

You are resilient and strong and can withstand tremendous stress without losing an ounce of vital life force. Your center of body energy is in your powerful neck. Many Taurus natives have necks that are long, thick, or otherwise noteworthy. That is because when a bull hits its head into the object of its attention, it needs a strong neck to act as a shock absorber. The same holds true for you. You can withstand a tremendous amount of stress as you plunge head first into any obstacle that gets in your way. Your powerful neck usually absorbs the impact for you. But occasionally, you need a rest, which may feel frustrating because you like to keep going once you build your momentum.

If you forget to take a respite from an ongoing activity, the stress tends to express through your neck, in the form of a sore throat, laryngitis, swollen glands, stiff neck muscles, or eventual thyroid problems that can slow your metabolism. The important thing for you is to be aware when you need to slow down if you are exerting too much force over a long period of time. It is useful to know when you are pushing too hard and need to replenish your life energy, or when you need to start moving to enable your life force to shake off its lethargy and circulate through your body once again. You have plenty of power. But one way to maintain robust health is to find your middle gear, and vigilantly monitor yourself so you experience the same degree of harmonious balance in your body as you would like to maintain in your life.

Health & Foods

You tend to be willing to partake of gustatory pleasure, and you have a natural sense of what is best for your body at any given time. Pay attention to your body's rhythms and cycles. Notice what time of day, month, or year your body needs various foods. Eat in harmony with the seasons so you eat cooling foods in warm weather and warming foods in cold weather. Eat foods that grow close to the earth, and close to the area where you live. Your body is intimately connected with the rhythms of the earth, and you will feel most satisfied when you eat in harmony with the earth around you. Finally, once you have decided what to eat, decide how much of it you want to eat. As a Taurus, you have a strong appetite. While it is not always comfortable to practice impulse control, a little portion control will do a lot to give your generally robust but active digestive system a well-deserved rest.

Flower Essences

Flower essences, which are distillations of the high vibrations in flowers, also may help you. The flower essence Nicotiana harmonizes the physical strength in your body with emotions and inner life of your soul. Rabbitbrush helps you assimilate several simultaneous events while you maintain multifaceted awareness. Willow helps you accept and forgive yourself and others while you let go of resentment. Oak helps you recognize limits and know when to let go of a struggle. Quaking Grass helps you perceive and assimilate all sides of an issue. Rock Water helps you let go of overly strict self-imposed standards.

FINANCES

One of the reasons you have incarnated was to experience a form of financial security. You may have a lucrative business or career. You may have incarnated into a wealthy family. You may have made a soul agreement with an individual who has financial resources and has agreed to share them with you. Or you may have planned a situation where money would either be available to you, or where you would live in circumstances where you would not be dependent upon financial resources. Such circumstances could include living in a monastery, convent, ashram, or electing as a soul to incarnate with a handicap that would ensure that it would be considered appropriate to financially depend upon others.

If you incarnated under the Sign of the Bull, financial resources are an important aspect of your life. You may have financial resources, or you may not have them. Either way, financial resources are not a neutral topic for you. If you are a Taurus with few financial means, consider that as a soul, you designed a life that would require you to let go of attachment to financial security as a spiritual lesson. Or, if you are a wealthy Taurus, consider that your soul may have set up circumstances that would teach you to balance gratitude, generosity and possessiveness with material abundance. Or, you may be learning to let go of attachment to financial status by realizing its limited role in your ultimate happiness.

No matter what your financial situation, the greatest wisdom for Taurus comes when you let go. Allow the Divine to flow abundantly into the financial sphere of your life so you may receive all that is karmically due to you. You may also consider the biblical concept of tithing, which involves giving 10 percent of everything you earn to uphold a worthy cause. The universe is committed to giving back everything you give—times 10. You probably already do this, but there are other forms of tithing that you may consider. You may tithe by giving time, energy, love, or a listening ear. Even if no one knows about it, it will come back to you. This is the immutable law of prosperity. At every opportunity, give, give, give, and then give some more, of course, without expectation of anything in return. The lack of expectation will open a channel for the universe to give, give, give, and give some more—to you!

CAREER

You are naturally gifted with your hands, and you appreciate the fine aspects of life. These qualities make you an excellent sculptor, potter, painter, gardener, gemologist, chef, massage therapist, or healer. You also have a strong desire for material security that could lead you to the business world as a business owner, merchant, corporate executive, real estate investor, builder, contractor, stock broker, trader, or financial consultant. You appreciate the simple side of life, and may avoid cerebral avocations such as writing, computers, engineering, psychotherapy, or medicine. Yet, if you do approach one of the more technical spheres of labor, there is no one more talented. You focus deeply on the object of your interest, and you instill in your achievements a sense of pride and excellence.

You believe in quality. And you are loyal in your devotion to the object of your attention. Therefore, a commitment to any career will lead to success by sheer virtue of your unswerving determination and commitment! Finally, detach from the rewards for the work you do by performing your work with dedication to the process of the work rather than the end result. By remaining unattached to the fruits of your labor, you will gain many delicious karmic fruits from sources you did not expect.

♊ GEMINI (May 21–June 21)

♊ GEMINI (May 21–June 21)

PERSONALITY PROFILE

Gemini is a mutable, air sign symbolized by the twins.
Your key motivations are mental stimulation, verbal expression, connecting with people, travel, movement, and exploration.
Your outstanding attributes are communication skills, cleverness, conceptual thinking, mental versatility, mental adaptability, flexibility, and physical agility.
Your karmic challenge involves uniting opposing polarities in your personality to discover a middle ground between extremes of thoughts, feelings and actions.
Gemini rules the lungs, shoulders and hands.
Gemini is associated with Hermes in Greek myth, Mercury in Roman myth, and Castor & Pollux, the twins of ancient Greece.
The planet Mercury rules the constellation of Gemini.
Gemini is associated with the color blue, the throat chakra, and the thyroid gland.
Best Day: Wednesday
Best Number: 5
Healing Gemstone: Aquamarine, Turquoise, Malachite, Chrysocolla

You are a mentally versatile soul who is a master of the spoken and written word. You are clever, energetic, changeable, malleable, and restless. You gain energy like a stone rolling down hill gains momentum, by moving from place to place in your mind, or in your physical body. Your restless nature prevents you from stopping, as if you fear that slowing down will cause you to run out of energy, and prevent you from ever starting again.

On a soul level, you decided to incarnate to integrate many disparate aspects of your soul's nature. This is true if you were born with a Gemini Sun, Gemini Moon, or Gemini Rising. You developed diverse coping mechanisms and styles in previous incarnations, which correlate with varied expressions of your personality in this life. Your soul elected to experience the myriad personalities you developed in prior incarnations with the goal of uniting these personalities into one integrated whole, through which you channel your abundant spiritual energy.

As a result of the facility with which you express many facets of your personality, you possess a unique, quicksilver quality. You adapt quickly to situations. You say things with total sincerity in the moment to enable circumstances to unfold smoothly. You instantaneously shape your personality to your environment. This is a rare talent that makes you a skilled salesman, multifaceted commentator or writer, comedian, teacher, travel agent, journalist, detective, spy, or politician. You also are physically agile, which makes you an outstanding athlete, runner, biker, messenger, traveling salesman, flight attendant, pilot, driver, or guide.

If a human being could have wings, you would have them. Yet, when you stop flapping your capable wings at the end of every day, you must be with your Self. When you come to rest, the most important work you can do is love and accept yourself, and the personality or subpersonalities within you. (Subpersonalities, or significantly disparate character traits within one overall personality, are a normal psychological phenomenon. Yet, this normal psychological phenomenon may be emphasized in the Gemini personality.) Your greatest challenge is to come to peace within yourself by getting to know these diverse aspects of your personality. Subpersonalities are normal expressions of qualities developed in this life, and prior lives. These qualities are called subpersonalities because they do not completely coordinate with the principle personality, or they may be "ego-dystonic," meaning they are not supporting the ego, in psychological jargon. As subpersonalities are acknowledged, they become neutralized and integrated into the main personality. Love and accept these creative expressions of Self. Allow them to co-exist and work together, with each other, and with the main body of your personality.

Slow down, breathe, and experience the diverse qualities within you. Many Geminis identify with the parts of themselves they like. They dis-identify with the parts of themselves that they do not like, saying, "Oh, that's my evil twin," or "That person made me do it." The truth is that *everyone* possesses light and dark qualities. If they did not, they would not need to incarnate in physical form to work out discrepancies. It so happens that some people with a Gemini Sun, Gemini Moon, or Gemini Rising, may possess more diverse parts than the average person, but Geminis also possess the mental versatility to quickly traverse more psychological territory than any other sign. Thus, you may have more places to travel within yourself, but you are equipped to make the journey.

The "soul-ution" to mental challenges is to acknowledge and accept the many facets of your Self. They all are valid, even if you do not like them equally. Begin a dialogue between each component of yourself. You are a born communicator. Begin the process by having the "good" side communicate with the "bad" side. You may find out the "bad" is not so "bad," and the "good" is not so "good." There may be a middle ground you had not considered. Let your female qualities talk to your male qualities. Let your traditional side talk to your unconventional side. Let your cooperative subpersonality talk to your rebellious subpersonality, for example. Let your quick side talk to your slow side. And let your practical side talk to the not-so-sensible side. Love and accept all aspects of yourself by bringing them together rather than pushing them apart. It is tempting to push aside unworkable or unlikable qualities. It is far more productive to unite all diverse aspects of your personality into one coherent Self. As you would do with any large group of people, get them to communicate. If members of the United Nations, who speak different languages, and come from different circumstances, can find a way to bridge their differences and communicate, you can do the same. You will find abundant happiness when you honor, understand, accept, and love the voices within. You will put your endless creativity to its highest use as you blend your internal voices to speak with one unified voice!

Ultimately, you will discover that all people are united as sparks of God. The same applies to aspects of yourself, which are sparks of God expressing through you. Aspects of your personality could not exist unless these characteristics had roots in your soul. It is a law of nature that opposites turn into each other. In your case, a common thread unites you—your soul.

If you believe that souls create personalities, then you created your Self in accordance with your thoughts. Your thoughts are powerful tools for creating your reality. Each thought creates a strong electromagnetic field that engenders conditions and attracts circumstances. If you experience unity within yourself, you attract people and circumstances that enable you to experience greater unity. As you think, so it shall be.

Non-dominant Hand Writing

Practice non-dominant hand writing to become more familiar with the thoughts and feelings living inside of you. If you are left-handed, put your pen in your right hand. If you are right-handed, put your pen in your left hand. Ask yourself questions, such as, "How may I be of greatest service to the greatest number of people?" "How do I feel?" "What do I want?" Write the answer with your non-dominant hand, which is neurologically connected to your nonjudgmental, subconscious mind. You will receive an answer that is closer to your truth than nearly any method of introspection. Due to your diversity, you may choose to introspect about the answers you receive from yourself so that you may determine that the answer reflects the highest part of yourself. As you deeply penetrate your subconscious mind, you touch your superconscious, spiritual mind, where the qualities in your soul are more accessible to you.

Visualization

You may consider working with visualizations to create coherence within yourself and in the circumstances around you. By pre-visualizing and planning ahead, you create an electromagnetic field that precedes you. This electromagnetic field enables all circumstances and people to align in ways that support your progress. Without prior contemplation of consequences and the consequent realignment of energies in your favor, you may find that the energy of accelerated evolution in the world around you overwhelms your ability to spontaneously rectify situations. Think ahead, plan, and visualize so you may manage the flow of circumstances.

Focus

Stay focused as you go through the process of self-integration amidst the sometimes-chaotic circumstances you may naturally attract to yourself—or be attracted to. You are perpetually curious and always seek excitement. This is a particularly volatile combination in what is truly a more chaotic world, due to intensified electromagnetic energies inundating the Earth, multiple electronic devices, and a growing chorus of voices using these electronic mediums. The solution for you is to do one thing at a time. Bring each project to completion if possible before you pursue a new venture. You will feel more satisfied, settled and comfortable if you do one … thing … at … a … time

Anticipate unforeseen circumstances in yourself and the outside world. Visualize a strong anchor at the base of your spine. No matter what anyone says to you—or no matter what one part of you says to the other part, return to your center, the anchor at the base of your spine. Your true home is within your Self—the gateway to your soul, the ultimate goal of the journey you are on.

PERSONAL GROWTH

As always, keep your eye on the ball ... one ball at a time, that is, not the six balls you have been juggling for most of your life! Let yourself express the cleverness, mental agility, and verbal versatility you have always cultivated. But streamline if you are overcommitted, overextended, and overtaxed. Choose a cause or endeavor that is meaningful to you and connect with a group of like-minded others who can help you refine your focus, solidify ideas, and manifest your dreams. Your true evolution will come when you stay with one direction for a long period of time rather than pursuing many avenues at once.

Your goals are clarity, focus, perseverance, and faith. You have the tools. The trick is to cultivate one garden at a time rather than many at once, as you establish a rhythm in your mind that enables you to move to higher states of consciousness. This will help ground your sometimes-scattered energies and help you make meaningful progress in an area you choose. Even though you feel a constant push to explore the new, discipline yourself to stop, take a deep breath, and fully appreciate the moment you are in, and the direction you are pursuing.

RELATIONSHIPS

Your work in the relationship department may be more with yourself than others. As you bring the many sides of your nature into alignment, you will find what you are looking for in one person too. The trick here is not to believe that if you blend Person A with Person B, you will have the perfect partner. The trick is to realize that if you integrate the sides of your own nature (such as practical vs. whimsical, and freedom-loving vs. security-oriented), you will become the perfect partner and attract the same to yourself, and you will find wholesome, integrated, and healthy relationships.

Imagine blue light enveloping your body. Breathe in soothing blue light, breathe out dark purple light filled with patterns you want to release. Breathe in new. Breathe out old. Continue this practice until you feel coherence. You now are ready to take this feeling into your relationships, whether the person is intimate or unfamiliar, friend or family, professional or romantic.

Gemini and Gemini

You are attracted to the twinkle in the eye of a fellow Gemini and to the prospect of exploring innovative ideas together. You bring new meaning to the expression "Two heads are better than one," as your curious minds lead you in new directions. It is likely you will explore all forms of communication, from verbal to written to electronic to non-verbal and intuitive. This is a highly exciting relationship, and you gain much knowledge from the connection. But, you may choose to be mindful to build a bridge between the electrifying ideas in your minds and material reality. Your mutual project may be to support each other to bring your clever ideas to fruition. With your peripatetic minds, you are at no risk of running out of creative solutions to any dilemmas you may face.

Gemini and Cancer

Your Cancer partner is sensitive, vulnerable, and loves to create a comfortable home for you. You are curious, clever, talkative, and intellectual. Cancer, a cardinal, water sign, moves slowly and deliberately. You move quickly and capriciously. Your Cancer partner thinks things over too many times before acting incrementally. You think things over too few times before acting dramtically. This relationship is not an easy meeting of the hearts and minds. But with consciousness, you may learn worlds about each other and yourselves. With understanding and care, you may reach compromises that enable this relationship to flow smoothly long into the future. While you may not share the Cancer's love of home, you may enjoy knowing you may freely circulate and return to a stable home. Your Cancer mate also knows you will come back with plenty of stories, even if you forget to pick up the groceries on your way home. Provided this arrangement is agreeable to both, you may create an unconventional relationship in which each party reigns over his or her individual domain—you over your affairs in the world, and Cancer over hearth and home.

Gemini and Leo

You admire the grace, determination, and strength of fixed, fire sign Leo. Leo admires your intellect, adaptability, and energy. The theatrical nature of the Sign of the Lion holds your interest and gives you something to ponder as you circulate through life. Your verbal wit keeps Leo spellbound. You are a curious soul who loves to explore the world around you. Leo is a gregarious soul who eagerly engages in social repartee to explore reactions of others. You may share many adventures, and create a life geared to exploration—you of your relationship to your environment, and Leos of themselves and the people around them. Your mutual love of extroverted activity brings you contentment in your relationship as you both experience a life of continual change.

Gemini and Virgo

You and mutable, earth sign Virgo are ruled by the communications planet Mercury. Gemini is a mentally versatile, verbally adept, conceptual thinker. Virgo is an analytical, detail-oriented, concrete thinker. You each complement the other, and help each other gain greater perspective. You each have much to learn from this dynamic partnership. But if you are thinking of being more than friends, you may simply be thinking. Gemini and Virgo synchronize famously as friends. But your competing styles may clash if you try to share a life and living space together. Virgo is organized and orderly, preferring plans to surprises. You thrive in random and disorderly circumstances because your neural circuits fire more rapidly under the pressure of chaotic surroundings. Virgo's nerves become jangled if even one paper is out of alphabetical order. The two of you may think twice before signing a deed on a home or a lease on an apartment. But never stop being the best of friends.

Gemini and Libra

You see your Libra partner as a pinnacle of balance, harmony, and elegance. You are attracted to the demure demeanor of cardinal, air sign Libra, and it is likely you feel you have found your soul mate. Libra is expert at creating harmonious relationships, and you are expert at gathering information. This enables the Libra to perceive a fuller picture of the world. With Libra, you feel complete as Libra teaches you about domestic harmony and brings perspective and stability to organize and settle your restless nature. Your far-reaching intellect provides Libra with the information he or she needs to perceive a more complete picture so he or she may arrive at more balanced judgments and precise conclusions. You appreciate Libra's fine-tuned mind and ability to see circumstances from many points of view. Like you, Libra adapts to the needs of others, and is highly considerate. If you are looking for a relationship that will give you a center around which to revolve, a Libra partner is the solution for you.

Gemini and Scorpio

A relationship between Gemini and Scorpio may be intellectually and emotionally intense as Scorpio tries to elicit emotional reactions from Gemini, and Gemini tries to elicit rational intellectualizations from Scorpio. Both parties may be successful in eliciting what they are looking for in the other, but at what price? It may be uncomfortable for both of you to be authentic in this relationship as both parties try to elicit something unnatural from the other. You may agree to establish a harmonious home life, and you may be successful at that. Yet, there may be little in the way of compatible communication between you two.

Gemini and Sagittarius

You are fascinated by Sagittarius, the mutable, fire sign opposite Gemini on the Zodiac wheel. Opposites attract, and a relationship between Gemini and Sagittarius is no exception. Gemini is a master of knowledge and Sagittarius is a master of wisdom. Gemini gathers bits of information, for reasons it does not always know. And Sagittarius steps back to look at the big picture to discover patterns and meaning in seemingly chaotic bits of trivia. You provide information and Sagittarius provides context. Together, you have more knowledge than a library, and an endless stream of theories and ideas to fill your days as you travel the path of life.

Gemini and Capricorn

A relationship between spontaneous Gemini and systematic Capricorn may initially seem awkward, and may resemble a friendship more than a romance—at first. Yet the greatest love springs from the garden of friendship, and with mutual goals, Gemini and Capricorn may find they are willing to compromise to accommodate each other. At first, however, Capricorn's rigidity and discipline may make Gemini uneasy. And Gemini's lack of planning may seem incomprehensible to Capricorn. But gradually, the two of you will learn to see the wisdom of the other, and what at first seemed foreign may eventually seem endearing. While this is a relationship that requires compromises to accommodate the diverse styles of the partners, neither partner will interrupt the rhythm of the other, and both will offer sincere logistical support to help the other realize his or her dreams.

Gemini and Aquarius

A union between intellectually curious Gemini and forward-thinking Aquarius will generate new ideas that are ahead of their time. The superb mental faculties of mutable, air sign Gemini and fixed, air sign Aquarius create a partnership that will be focused on mental exploration, supplanting emotional sharing as the primary form of communication. You are two cerebral souls who cherish the chance to share your mental meanderings with a kindred spirit. This is an exciting meeting of the minds. You understand each other, and provide abundant support to accomplish important goals as a couple and as independent individuals. You may find this relationship works better as a romance than as a marriage, not because you are not compatible, but because a loose association better fits the restless natures of Gemini and Aquarius.

Gemini and Pisces

A Gemini-Pisces relationship may initially seem quite attractive as both parties try to accommodate the other. You both are expert at adapting to other people, and this relationship is no exception. You both must be aware of how easily your basic identities may slip away in a long-term relationship, however. Both Pisces and Gemini are malleable, meaning that each personality changes to adapt to circumstances. Two people of this mutable nature who come together may create a situation in which there is no stable center around which to revolve. This is okay if the partners are willing to stagnate or to individually spin in their own orbits. But if you are looking for a dance partner who can dance to your rhythm while remaining true to him- or herself, this may not be the relationship you are seeking.

Gemini and Aries

You are captivated by the entrepreneurial, creative, resourceful spirit of cardinal, fire sign Aries. Aries is fascinated by your lively mind and imaginative conversational style. Life suddenly seems like an adventure with limitless potential when you come together. Please inject an element of realism as your imaginations conjure infinite possibilities for this earth plane relationship. You both possess a youthful spirit and boundless enthusiasm. Your can-do energy helps you achieve many things. But make sure your expectations of each other and the relationship are aligned with realistic possibilities so you always feel satisfied rather than disappointed when you "hitch your wagon to each other's star."

Gemini and Taurus

Taurus is fascinated by your agile body and your versatile mind. You feel comforted by the stable solidity of the Taurus body and mind. A relationship between Gemini and fixed, earth sign Taurus produces a curious combination of comfort and uneasiness. Gemini energizes the Taurus mind, and Taurus soothes the Gemini nervous system. But each sign may provide too much of a good thing. Gemini's changeable nature may unnerve the most placid Taurus. And Taurus' complacent nature may curb the spur-of-the-moment spontaneity of Gemini. Unless Gemini has a Taurus Moon or Taurus Rising, the Taurus partner may create too many plans and routines for your fluctuating energy. And unless Taurus has a Gemini Moon or Gemini Rising, Gemini's kinetic energy may be a bit unsettling to Taurus if you live in close quarters. Gemini wants an interesting partner who can live with unpredictability. Taurus wants a loyal partner who can live with predictability. Taurus can learn a lot from Gemini about being more spontaneous. Gemini can learn a lot from Taurus about being more committal. Without mutual goals and interests, however, it is unlikely that two people with such different internal rhythms will be in sync with each other for long.

Gemini, when you settle on one partner, you will experience your heart opening as widely as your mind. This opening will smooth the way for loving and accepting the diverse aspects of your nature so you feel integrated and whole, fulfilling the purpose for which you incarnated.

SPIRITUALITY

You are a spiritual soul who thinks spirituality is a collection of ideas rather than a collection of experiences. Experiment with a spiritual experience every now and then. Turn off your mental motor. Feel your breath coming in and going out of your body. Go into your heart. What do you feel? Try not to judge the sensations that arise. Next, feel the base of your spine. How does it feel to be perfectly still and rooted in Mother Earth? Imagine that all of your energy is settled in the base of your spine. How does it feel to have all of your parts collected in one place? If this is an unaccustomed feeling, practice it for only a few moments, and then return to the feeling at another time if you wish.

For you, the essence of spirituality is feeling your Self, feeling the essence of God within you. You are naturally focused on the outer world, toward gathering knowledge and experience "out there." Try gathering your outgoing energy at the base of your spine. Rest your consciousness for a moment. Practice the advice of the Psalmists and "Be Still and Know that I Am God." This is a simple yet complex statement that may bear contemplation. In order to grow up, you must first grow down. In other words, the taller the plant, the deeper the roots. Feel yourself becoming grounded in your root chakra at the base of your spine. Now, you are ready to grow!

HEALTH

The sign of Gemini rules those things in the body that come in pairs, most notably the lungs, shoulders, and hands. These body parts are associated with Gemini because they support breath, communications, and creativity, activities for which you are so well known.

As an air sign, you have a highly mental, restless nature and a sensitive nervous system. You are sensitive to the air around you, especially cool winds, sudden temperature changes, and extremes of heat and cold. On the rare occasion when you are talked-out or otherwise depleted, you will feel the effects in your upper respiratory system.

Your best defense is a period of stillness and solitude once a week so you may calm your breath, still your mind, and rejuvenate your lungs. It also is a good idea to rest your voice and the soles of your feet. After all, Gemini is associated with Hermes, the wing-footed messenger in Greek myth. Rest your feet every seventh day, along with all body parts responsible for the circulation and modulation of air, including your lungs, diaphragm, esophagus, nasal passages, vocal chords, and lips.

Exercise & Food

You also will benefit from any pursuit that calms your nervous system, including meditation, yoga, massage, or quiet walks in nature. Medicinally, Vitamin B restores damaged nerve tissue. Calming foods for the Gemini system include oatmeal, warm milk, and eggs. Chamomile, passionflower, valerian root, hops, spearmint, and skullcap, are herbs to relax your nervous system before sleep. Lavender, geranium and jasmine are essences that soothe your nervous system. Or, place a drop of coconut oil on your forehead to relieve irritability or stress. Colors also affect you. Blue and pink promote relaxation, and red and yellow excite your sensitive system.

Flower Essences

Flower essences, which are distillations of the high vibrations in flowers, also may help you become centered. White Chestnut quiets an overactive mind. Calla Lilly balances male and female energy. Manzanita helps you feel more comfortable in your physical body.

FINANCES

You are not one to need a lot of money to acquire possessions. You prefer to have as few encumbrances as possible so you can change direction and take off at a moment's notice. Yet, despite your proclivity to travel light, you may have acquired more clutter than any other sign of the Zodiac. Part of the reason for your accumulation of material goods is your curiosity and desire to explore many avenues of experience. This includes the possession of anything that will support your interests, including books, gadgets, tools, electronics, appliances, even clothes. Add to that a touch of absentmindedness. You may not always remember where you put the first set, or if you purchased a first set at all, so you buy a second. Over a period of years, or when the moving van comes, Geminis often discover they have a minimum of two or three of everything!

You don't need a lot of money because you have few material attachments. You only need enough financial resources to facilitate your experiences. But if you cannot remember where you put what you have, you may spend more money than you anticipate. The solution is to slow down and contemplate expenditures before you make them—and then remember the purchases you have made. By waiting to make a purchase, you may change your mind, or you may attract a similar or better object by projecting your thoughts. Your clever mind is likely to come up with a plethora of ways to fulfill the need through someone you know, someone you don't know, or through another vehicle of verbal, written, or electronic communication. You are more interested in investing your energy in life than in physical wares. Focus on the experience rather than the physical accoutrements that accompany the experience. You may find your needs are satisfied with few expenditures. This will bring greater consciousness to financial expenditures.

You also may think about how you would like to accumulate financial resources. You have more talents than the juggler, clown, and lion tamer in a circus—put together. There is no shortage of jobs you are qualified to perform. The challenge you face is feeling committed! You are interested today, not interested tomorrow, re-interested the following day. Your attention span may be shorter than you would like. So, acknowledge the natural flow of your energy, and accommodate your natural pattern. You may make a lot of money one day, week or year, and little or none the next. Thus, you have to think about saving for the proverbial "rainy day." This means you may save money when it is coming in so you will have something to spend when money is not flowing to you. Not only can you not predict what tomorrow will bring, you cannot predict how you will feel or what you will do. So, know thyself ... and protect thyself.

It is a good strategy to save money in a place where you can touch it only in an emergency. Try to establish more than one source of income to appeal to your peripatetic nature, but still do *one* thing at a time. Plan ahead, restrain impulsivity, and anticipate consequences to bring a healthy state of financial peace of mind. Finally, try to contemplate consequences before every action, whether it is a purchase or a commitment.

CAREER

You thrive on change and variety as a plant thrives on light and water. Routine and sameness makes you feel stagnant and as if your creativity is drying up. Consequently, you may feel happiest when you are changing jobs, job locations, job descriptions, or even careers. It is not unreasonable for you to have more than one job at a time. You may accomplish far more when you are pandering to a plethora of interests than if you stubbornly try to fit yourself into a conventional mold. Yet, when you are doing one of a variety of things you are good at, concentrate to your fullest, and accomplish as much as you can with single-minded focus. Then switch to another activity. The neural pathways in your brain are sparked in a positive way by change. Know this about yourself, and accommodate this pattern in your personal and professional life. But also balance the need for change with a need for concentrated focus on the important object of your attention during the period of time in which you are responsible for the outcome.

Look for a job or create work that enables you to change and create as part of the job so you do not want to walk away from something at which you are talented and making a positive contribution. While you would be good at a job in accounting, for example, you might simultaneously be overcome with boredom unless you intersperse this linear, rules-oriented work with a spontaneous job, hobby, or pursuit. Or, you could make yourself happy if there was an aspect of this work that continuously changed, such as numerous short-term projects, clients, or various settings from which you could do your job, or multiple approaches to the same work that would keep it interesting to you.

You are happiest in jobs that involve communications, advertising, journalism, writing, art, sales or travel. You also are proficient at electronics, computers, visual and audio technology, public relations, marketing, radio or television, talk shows, entertainment, comedy, movies, or theater. You even might enjoy being a bike messenger, telephone repair person, or mail carrier. Your imagination is excited by anything that moves, or involves delivering information, goods, or services. And if you cannot move information, goods, or services, you will be just as happy moving your body from one place to another, hopefully creating positive results from the movement. Anything that creates movement pleases you—and is useful to the general public as this energy is applied in a productive direction. So, find something positive you like to do, focus yourself, and keep moving!

♋ CANCER (June 22–July 22)

♋ CANCER (June 22–July 22)

PERSONALITY PROFILE

Cancer is a cardinal, water sign symbolized by the crab. Your key motivations are emotional security, nurturing contact with women, family, comforting domestic environments, soothing taste sensations, and creating a parent-child dynamic in relationships. Your outstanding attributes are resourcefulness in domestic affairs, financial acumen, loyalty to family, need to protect loved ones, adherence to tradition, and your ability to preserve the past.
Your karmic challenge involves knowing how to use past experience to direct the future, and when to let go of the past to perceive the present.
Cancer rules the chest and stomach.
The Moon rules the constellation of Cancer.
Cancer is associated with Zeus' wife Hera, Greek goddess of hearth & home. Hera is Juno in Roman myth, wife of Jupiter.
Cancer is associated with the color green, the heart chakra, and the thymus gland.
Best Day: Monday
Best Number: 2
Healing Gemstone: Moonstone, Rose Quartz, Pearl

Cancers are sensitive, nurturing, emotional people who love tradition, motherhood, sentimentality, nostalgia, home, and home-cooked food. Cancer is the first water sign on the Zodiac wheel, and represents the first step of the individual to express the wisdom of feelings. Cancer is the astrological sign of the United States, whose birth is July 4, 1776. Cancer is intimately connected with patriotism and love of homeland because of the strong affiliation between Cancer, the home, and maternal roots. Many of the home-loving, security-oriented, and self-referential qualities of the United States are reflections of the energy of Cancer. It is no wonder that American symbols such as Mom, home & apple pie, also are associated with Cancer. Other prominent U.S. characteristics—love of freedom, tolerance, and independence—come from the nation's Aquarius Moon, and its Sagittarius Ascendant, calculated for the time of the signing of the Declaration of Independence.

On an emotional level, Cancer represents the primal aspect of feeling connected with protecting what it perceives as its own—its feelings, possessions, home, and family. Cancer does not experiment easily with alternative lifestyles. Cancer can be considered the keeper of tradition of the Zodiac, as a prelude to the creativity and daring of the next sign, Leo.

The Moon rules the constellation of Cancer. Cancer natives often have an open, moon-like face, and moods that change as often as the phases of the Moon. Many Cancers feel an affinity with the Moon and can be seen casting a wistful look toward the lunar body. The reason Cancers are so sensitive to the Moon is that the water in their bodies changes with the cycles of the Moon, and they feel these changes as turbulent shocks to their emotional systems. Cancers react not only to the waxing and waning of the light of the Moon, but they also react to the constellation through which the Moon is passing, which affects the vibration of the moonlight, and its relationship to their natal energies. As you can surmise, emotional reactions are complex for a Cancer soul.

Relationships also can be complicated for Cancers because relationships work best when the partners are more or less predictable. A Cancer's moods are unpredictable, even to him- or herself, and therefore Cancer is unpredictable. A relationship partner may feel as if he or she is having a relationship with many people due to the changes in mood and behavior, and the partner must be extremely stable him- or herself to weather the ups and downs of the Cancer's temperament. Many people find the sweet, loving, nurturing nature of Cancer so endearing that they are willing to roll with the waves of their partner's feelings. Or, the partner may be unemotional, and not react to the emotional changes of Cancer. Or, the partner may be vicariously experiencing his or her own unexpressed emotions through the Cancer partner. Of course, it is best for each individual to process his or her own feelings him- or herself, but a blending of feelingss between two people is a natural by-product of an intimate relationship. Cancers are often best able to relate to other Cancers, or other emotional souls, who sympathize or empathize with the Cancer's waves of feeling highs and lows, enabling the two to harmonize.

Relationships for a Cancer can be complex for another reason. Cancers see the world as a series of opportunities to create parent-child relationships, both in personal affairs and in business, government, and organizations. This means that Cancers want to take care of others, or be taken care of, depending upon the situation and the Cancer's maturity. Even as managers of companies, Cancers try to take care of their employees. And as employees, Cancers often expect to be taken care of. It may be difficult for Cancers to find a middle gear and relate as equals. The idea that two people can be independent, separate, and healthy, can be anathema to Cancerian consciousness.

Herein lies the core of the Cancer's struggle to individuate on the earth plane. Cancers innately believe that a lesser power (the child) follows the greater power (the parent, the company, the organization, the government), in exchange for being taken care of. Cancers believe that someone outside of themselves must fulfill their needs—as is the case of a mother and child, rather than believing individuals make decisions and meet their own needs—as mature adults. Cancers' relationship model has a somewhat divine quality in that it assumes that a greater power cares for a lesser power. Yet, this dynamic does not work among adult humans. In order to truly individuate and embark upon an independent endeavor, one has to be willing to separate from the human parent and surrender to the Divine. The transition from a human to a divine parent can represent a most difficult stage of evolution in Cancerian consciousness. Yet, this is the very step Cancers must take to achieve the security they desperately seek.

Cancers often feel insecure in the multi-faceted, fast-paced world. Yet Cancers carry a natural protection—the hard shell they wear on their backs. Why the contradiction? Many Cancers have a tough shell of bravado into which they withdraw when they feel threatened. Due to emotional sensitivities caused by lunar light, represented by the crab's soft underbelly, Cancers simply perceive threats that others do not, or that may not exist to the extent that has been perceived. The hard shell is an important defensive tool—but against what? Cancers often mount their greatest defense against their own feelings. But this defense mechanism raises more questions that every Cancer must answer on his or her path to maturity, and individuation. "What is the nature of a threat?" "How can I feel my own feelings, or the feelings of another person, without feeling threatened?" "How can I feel secure despite my natural feeling that I am insecure?" "Are the threats I perceive simply people or circumstances that make me feel my feelings?" "How can I best confront a person or thing in the course of protecting myself from a feeling without inflicting harm, creating a conflict, or hurting the feelings of another?" Every Cancer is trying to answer these questions.

Your path to enlightenment involves learning to feel your feelings while simultaneously allowing others to have their feelings too. Many Cancers struggle with a natural proclivity to block feelings with defensiveness, bravado, a retreat into their shell, blaming others for their feelings, or even, taking the offensive to stamp out the source of the feeling. The solution is to accept your highly emotional nature as the truth of who you are. Try to find as many healthy ways to express your feelings, your sensitivities, insecurities, and moods as possible. Most of this can be accomplished by being honest with your Self. You may decide to discuss your feelings with one other person, but you do not have to broadcast your feelings. Second, to deal with many fears you feel about life, consider that your fears may be exaggerated and that you are safe and protected as you are. How can this be? Thinking you are safe attracts safe circumstances to you. Believing you are unsafe attracts unsafe circumstances due to the law of resonance.

Why did you incarnate as a Cancer? In prior incarnations, you experienced a threatening situation that is ingrained in your soul. You decided in this life that you were going to create more secure circumstances so that this particular threat could never visit you again. Of course, there are no 100% secure circumstances, and you may create more problems for yourself by trying to erect a tower of defense around your life. You also naturally feel as a Cancer Sun, or if you have a Cancer Moon or Cancer Rising, that strong family bonds and a secure physical home serve as protection. This is why you are so attached to a physical home, food, your parents, particularly your mother, or to a parental substitute. It is as if a strong family will serve as a fortress against the world. You similarly armor your physical body with defensive patterns (either rigid movements or tight muscles) or armor your emotional system with defensive patterns that involve rationalizing or blocking out unwanted information. The result is a kind of inflexibility that makes it difficult to adapt to changes in your environment or to changes that are part of maturing. Your challenge is to develop a sense of confidence in yourself and the world so you may see who you truly are and be who you truly are, based on what is really going on rather than based on what you feel you need to do to protect yourself from unseen and unknown potential enemies, either in yourself or in the world.

Finally, consider directly confronting the adversaries you sense—either within yourself or others. It is the nature of the crab to walk sideways. So, Cancer is challenged to confront hesitations or uneasiness as directly as possible. Try to say exactly what you mean, to whom you would like to say it (even to yourself), as quickly as possible after you feel it. Avoid talking to others about your complaints, but go directly to the source. If your eating habits change, you are probably reacting to feelings you are not expressing. Try to make independent decision, experiment with breaking from tradition or the crowd, or assert yourself in a situation in which you feel you may alienate a supporter (even though this may not happen). Stand on your own. Protect another if you can. If the situation that needs to be confronted has originated inside of you, take an honest look at your role. Think about the steps you need to take to ameliorate the situation, and take them!

The greatest gift a Cancer native can give to him- or herself is to change to ameliorate an unworkable situation. Change is difficult for you because it raises fears that the future will be worse than the past. Yet this is rarely the case because you are more mature now than when you initially made the decision that led you to your present predicament. Thus, it is worth the price you pay to readjust and continue on a higher plane. This is the higher path all Cancers may navigate. Loosen the bonds of the tough shell that surrounds you so you may expand to fully express your loving and precious soul.

PERSONAL GROWTH

Your greatest challenge comes from healing the fear of letting go of your tough shell to expose your soft underbelly, the symbol of your sensitive emotional nature protected by armoring in your body or psyche. You were born with the sense that the world is dangerous, and that it is up to you to protect yourself and others from unseen dangers. You have a constant sense that danger is lurking. You will go to great measures to protect your personal physical, emotional, and financial safety from these imagined threats. Even knowledge that these threats do not exist or will not hurt you does not assuage the deep-seated fear of danger. This feeling comes from a history of incarnations where you perceived a threat to your security. You were not able to let go of the perception that threats would endanger you, and you incarnated in this life with the persistent perception that threats exist. You are correct. There are threats. But your perception of the threat—and the idea that the threat may actually harm you—may be exaggerated. And by focusing on the perceived threat, you may attract to yourself the very thing you are trying to avoid!

By letting go of fears and fantasies, particularly about events that may occur in the future, you liberate yourself from a form of psychological stress that leads to constraints on your life that you accept as normal, but many people would not imagine living under. You may not go certain places, engage in certain relationships, talk about certain subjects, or look at certain aspects of your personality, due to fear of perceived threats that may or may not exist. Certainly any threat is possible, but few are likely. You are neither a gambler nor a risk-taker. But you may consider taking greater risks, either going to new places, engaging in different kinds of relationships, or experimenting with different behavior patterns, as ways of testing your mettle, and learning that the world may not be as threatening as you subconsciously think. You no longer need to sidestep confrontation with yourself or others for fear of consequences. You are learning about your flexibility, adaptability, strength, and resourcefulness. These are qualities that are naturally gifted to you when you peel away the tough shell to open to your true Self.

RELATIONSHIPS

Cancers need relationships as much as the Moon needs the Sun to illumine its form. Yet, like the Moon that grows and diminishes in light, you similarly vacillate between wanting a relationship and wanting solitude. Having a relationship can be tricky, because you may crave activity and an extroverted partner when the light of the Moon is bright, and crave solitude and an introverted partner when the light of the Moon is diminished. You do best in relationships with people who are as sensitive as you, so both understand each other's waxing and waning feelings. Or, you do well in business relationships, where personal feelings are distant from the goal of the relationship.

Cancer and Cancer

You appreciate each other's moods, and respect each other's sensitivities. You understand the value of culinary pleasures, a comfortable home, a warm family, financial security, and a predictable life. You are home-loving souls who prefer the routines of a stable home rather than travel and adventure. You are creatures of habit who favor familiarity over surprise. You love sameness, and a relationship with someone who is similar to you feels safer than a relationship with someone who is of a different nature. Your emotional sensitivities enable you to harmonize with your Cancer mate, creating a loyal, nurturing, enduring bond. But please consider one additional point: Water signs such as yourselves think you *need* a relationship the way a plant needs water. But once you get into a deep, intense, emotional relationship, you may want to get out of the relationship as much as a plant needs sunshine. Plan to discuss this point with your Cancer mate before you commit to marriage and sign on the dotted line.

Cancer and Leo

Traditional astrology says Cancer does not harmonize with fixed, fire sign Leo. Yet a surprisingly large number of Leos pair up with emotional Cancers, perhaps assuming non-traditional roles in this unconventional relationship. Sensitive, domestic Cancer provides a comfortable home and a stable support structure to the ebullient, theatrical Leo who has a home-loving side. The Sun rules Leo and the Moon rules Cancer. The inextricably-linked celestial pair is reflected with remarkable frequency among loving couples, perhaps as a mirror of the eternally-linked couple in the heavens.

Cancer and Virgo

If you have intellectual curiosity brewing in your psyche, Virgo's peripatetic mind is endlessly fascinating to you. You appreciate mutable, earth sign Virgo's practical approach to life and stable emotional disposition. The earthy, grounded quality of Virgo balances your watery, emotional disposition. Virgo is attracted to your natural mothering qualities and your emotional sensitivity. You are attracted to Virgo's cool efficiency and analytical eye. You share a love of nurturing others, but you have diverse styles. Virgo helps others through logistical support and advice. Cancer nurtures through feelings and food. In the realm of food, one of your most compelling avenues of enjoyment, you and Virgo have a healthy repartee. While Virgo does not share your passion for culinary pleasures, Virgo is conscientious about health, diet, and nutrition. If you don't mind having a few alfalfa sprouts sprinkled over your delicious dish of pasta and fresh tomato and basil sauce, you and Virgo are a winning combination. Also note that you are highly emotionally sensitive—to a degree that may boggle a Virgo's logical mind. Virgo's emotions are held in check by the rational mind, and rarely do feelings get in the way of other responsibilities. Yet, you feel your feelings are your main responsibility. These differing natures may cause consternation in a relationship, but there is plenty of common ground to establish a working partnership.

Cancer and Libra

You appreciate the demure elegance of cardinal, air sign Libra. Libra admires your domestic flair, and love of home and family. You each are considerate of the sensitivities of the other. You respect Libra's need for a peaceful, harmonious relationship, and an aesthetically pleasing environment. Libra respects your need for security and predictability. You share similar values. But you may be worlds away in the realm of feelings. You react to every feeling and sensation, and give abundant attention to this level of perception. Libra transcends feelings and sensations in favor of a non-attached, mental perspective that leads to rational judgment based on objective principles. If you enjoy emotional distance in your intimate partnerships, either as a natural inclination or as a way of protecting your sensitive feelings, Libra's calm, cerebral nature could appease your emotional soul. You may receive less emotional contact or sharing of gustatory delights than you crave, but you will receive intellectual stimulation, good conversation, and plenty of space, which can be quite nurturing to you. If you are seeking a high degree of independence and freedom, a relationship with Libra could be an answer to your prayers. If you are seeking an emotional mating dance, a dating relationship with Libra is probably more appropriate.

Cancer and Scorpio

A relationship with fixed, water sign Scorpio creates a healing matrix for you to express your feelings. Scorpio is an intense, emotional, sensitive soul who seeks emotional communion, depth, and transformation. Cancer is a nurturing, sensitive, feeling soul who seeks emotional understanding and solace. You are two emotional souls who feel vulnerable unless you are with someone who is as sensitive as you. This relationship will soothe your insecurities. The emotional understanding you receive will assuage painful feelings you thought were yours for life. You feel you have finally found someone who understands you. While other signs may flee from your emotional self-involvement, Scorpio is fascinated by you. Scorpio will ask questions, listen, and offer solutions. You feel overexposed in the harsh light of the world, and seek refuge in the womb-like ambiance this relationship creates. Provided you each remain sympathetic and emotionally supportive, this is a relationship that could last a lifetime. Practice moderation, even in emotional sharing, so you may create a relationship balanced between feeling and the practical demands of daily life.

Cancer and Sagittarius

You are spellbound by mutable, fire sign Sagittarius' sense of humor, capacity for adventure, and ability to make the best of seemingly difficult circumstances. Sagittarius appreciates your domestic flair and loyalty to family and traditional values. Sagittarius has a warm place in his or her heart for you. You are friends who are fascinated by your differences. Sagittarius marvels at your ability to maintain a stable home and routine for a seeming eternity. You marvel at Sagittarius' ability to pick up and make changes at a moment's notice. You feel nostalgic about the past while Sagittarius contemplates the future. Sagittarius is thinking about his or her next overseas journey while you are thinking about what color to paint the walls. Your orientations to life are nearly opposite. You respect each other's ability to do what the other feels he or she could never do. But Sagittarius feels constrained by limitations you perceive, which he or she does not perceive. And you may become uncomfortable because the Sagittarius personality seems so alien to yours. Your diverse paths may clash in an intimate situation.

Cancer and Capricorn

Your complementary opposite on the Zodiac wheel is cardinal, earth sign Capricorn. Capricorn appreciates your home-making abilities and your family orientation. You feel secure with Capricorn's business-like demeanor, his or her desire to take on responsibility, and sensuous but serious personality. You want a partner who is sensitive and who makes you feel secure. Capricorn is as sensitive as are you, but reacts to feelings by taking action rather than taking cover, as may be your natural reaction. Due to Capricorn's astrological position opposite Cancer, the timing of Capricorn's moods are exactly opposite yours, creating a rhythmic equilibrium. When one of you feels sad, depressed, or introverted, the other feels jovial, outgoing, and buoyant. This dynamic engenders a workable partnership as each handles the extroverted demands of the relationship when the other needs solitude. Capricorn brings the energy of a competent father to the relationship, and you bring the energy of the nurturing mother. Together, your relationship dispels the insecurity that visits the Cancer and Capricorn psyches. The safety you feel in a relationship with a capable Capricorn mate is a healing experience for you.

Cancer and Aquarius

You appreciate the friendly, easygoing nature of fixed, air sign Aquarius. Aquarius appreciates your gentle, home-loving attitude, your domestic flair, and your sensitive heart. Your Aquarius partner is unflappable in situations that frustrate you. And you are stable in impersonal situations that ignite the Aquarius social consciousness. Aquarius is a good friend who is slow to anger, and non-judgmentally accepts you exactly as you are. You are a nurturing partner who listens to your Aquarius mate preach about the latest social injustice. If you desire emotional intimacy or sympathy, the affable Aquarius is far more interested in alleviating world hunger or nuclear proliferation than in the fluctuations of your emotional barometer. Aquarius is a forward-thinking, freedom-loving, spontaneous individualist. This is a harmonious relationship if you respect your Aquarian mate's need for freedom and independence, and Aquarius supports your need for domestic routines and stability. You may make emotional compromises in this relationship, but the compromises will be ones you can tolerate.

Cancer and Pisces

You appreciate mutable, water sign Pisces' compassionate, sensitive nature. Pisces enjoys your domestic flair, and is happy to luxuriate in the warmth, peace, and comfort of the domestic situation you create. You both feel you have found a sensitive mate with whom you can be yourselves. Traveling or going out in the world may be a bit elusive, as neither has the fire to motivate the other. Yet, if both individuals are self-motivated, this is a relationship with infinite potential for emotional understanding, shared sympathy, compassion, common values, and companionship. Pisces and Cancer are especially loving, protective, nurturing parents if you desire a family. If this is the case, pray for a soul to enter your family who will appreciate the emotional warmth and nurturing you provide. A child seeking independence or adventure may feel less comfortable in your family than a sensitive, emotional child who could infinitely benefit from the love created by your union.

Cancer and Aries

Cancer is awestruck by cardinal, fire sign Aries' initiative, entrepreneurial spirit, and capacity for change. Aries is fascinated by your domestic flair and loyalty to family and tradition. Aries marvels at your ability to maintain a stable home and routine for a seeming eternity. You marvel at the number of businesses Aries has started, friends Aries has made, and places Aries has visited. You love to cook, decorate, make a family, and set down roots. Aries abhors the concept of roots because commitments hamper Aries' ability to change at a moment's notice. You and Aries have very different natures—Cancer is an introvert who is emotional and sensitive, and Aries is an extrovert who is less aware of feelings and more focused on external achievement. If you and Aries do not mind a partner who lives independently, you may create a stable relationship where you take care of the home, and Aries tends to business in the world. You may have little in common, but you make a good team if you recognize your complementary skills and allow them to work together.

Cancer and Taurus

You appreciate the stable, reliable, committal nature of fixed, earth sign Taurus. Taurus appreciates your love of home and family. This is a comforting relationship because you both desire security so much—you crave emotional security and Taurus craves material security. You are two loyal souls who create a conventional relationship till death do you part. You will enjoy candlelight dinners, trips to favorite restaurants, and taking turns cooking for each other. You will help each other preserve the status quo. Both signs relish culinary and sense pleasures, sedate family gatherings, and a traditional home. Together you create the solid relationship (as long as neither wants to change the other) you have experienced in your dreams.

Cancer and Gemini

Your Gemini partner is curious, clever, talkative, intellectual, restless, and loves to gather knowledge. You are sensitive, vulnerable, domestic, and you love to create a comfortable home. Gemini, a mutable, air sign, moves quickly and capriciously, and may think things over too few times before acting on impulse. Cancer is deliberate in thought and action. You may think things over too many times before taking action. This relationship is not an easy meeting of the hearts and minds. But with consciousness, you may learn worlds about each other and yourselves. With understanding and care, you may reach compromises that enable this relationship to flow smoothly. While Gemini may not share your love of home, you may enjoy creating a stable base for your Gemini partner to come home to. You know Gemini will come back with plenty of stories, even if he or she forgets to pick up the groceries on the way home. Provided this arrangement is agreeable to both, you may create an unconventional relationship in which each party reigns over his or her individual domain—Cancer over home and hearth, and Gemini over interchange with the world.

Cancer, you ultimately seek a reliable and predictable partner. You are willing to forego excitement for the comfort of knowing you are coming home to a stable relationship at the end of the day. You are likely to recreate family circumstances from childhood in your adult relationships. If this is acceptable to you, the experience is abundantly yours. Or, if you introspect about early family memories, you may be able to rebuild your relationship patterns so you may create romantic experiences you will cherish.

SPIRITUALITY

A spiritual path can be both easy and difficult for Cancers. The process of surrender and obedience inherent in many contemplative, spiritual traditions comes easily to some docile Cancer souls. The idea of turning your life over to a Divine parent also is quite appealing. But the process of introspection and searching self-analysis that accompanies any spiritual path may challenge you. Remember the tough shell of the crab for whom Cancer is named? The tough shell is protecting a sensitive underbelly that every Cancer must come to know. Many Cancers develop a tough shell or a sense of false bravado to protect their sensitive undersides. Yet, this armoring must be undone to attune the total personality with the will of the Divine. The sensitive underside is the very thing that leads Cancer souls to a spiritual path. But it also is the very thing that can get in the way of spiritual evolution because the armor eventually creates a block to receiving the light of the Divine.

Cancers do not practice selective armoring, but rather put up an all-or-nothing system of defenses (more often all than nothing), and they vehemently resist anything that threatens the status quo, whether or not the status quo is beneficial. Usually a Cancer's emotional status quo dates from an earlier period of life, often a preverbal period that pre-dates two years of age. Believe it or not, character structure, formed in the first few years of life, often remains in place throughout a person's life unless deconstructed through the process of psychotherapy, a nurturing relationship, a breaking of the ego through spiritual discipline, or a life-altering event. In the absence of something to shake defensive structures to allow mature patterns to flourish, a Cancer will remain mired in emotional patterns that can inhibit the full flowering of a spiritual practice. In a sense, the personality must be fully formed before it can be broken by the rigors of spiritual discipline. Deep and fearless introspection and self-analysis are important tools for opening the Self to a spiritual path.

Still, Cancer natives are highly committed to the traditions of any religious path they pursue. Cancers have a talent for upholding religious ritual and routine as a form of spiritual practice. In the absence of an emotional surrender to the Divine, which can be a scary aspect of spiritual life for Cancer, a surrender of lifestyle to the rituals leading to the Divine, to following Divine law, and to the practice of devotion to the Divine, can be extremely effective means to reach a Divine goal. Through faithful practice of ritual, obedience, and devotion, the Cancer's emotional defenses will gradually fade away, giving way to the Divine communion you are seeking.

HEALTH

You are sensitive to your feelings, and the tenor of your emotional life intimately affects your health. Many people born under a Cancer Sun or Moon, or Cancer Rising, carry their feelings in their sensitive stomachs. As a result, your stomach may be remarkable in some way, either in size, sensitivity, or in its ability to sense subtle vibrations in the environment.

The stomach is also known as the "fourth eye" because it reports intuitive information to the brain via "gut instincts." Intuition functions through the "third eye" in the form of visual images of light, or mental perceptions. Instinct works through the "fourth eye" through sensations in the stomach. The astute Cancer learns to interpret these impressions as valuable information to be listened to rather than overruled by the rational mind. Visual information received through the brow is related to *clairvoyance*, or clear seeing. Sensory information received through the stomach or other physical sensations is related to *clairsentience*, or clear sensing. Auditory information received through the subtle channel of hearing is related to *clairaudience*, or clear hearing. You possess the gift of *clairsentience* through the medium of your sensitive stomach, which gives you information about the quality of your environment, an undertaking, a person, or the future, through gastric sensations, either a tight feeling or relaxed feeling in your stomach, warmth, tingling, chills, or a cool feeling. For obvious reasons, warmth or relaxed feelings indicate a positive outcome, whereas cool or tense feelings indicate a negative outcome. Of course, you have your own system for tracking sensations. Listen to these impulses and the meaning you have learned to ascribe to them.

Cancer's *clairsentient* skills are a barometer of feelings, impressions, and perceptions, and an accurate mediator of guidance from the higher Self or the soul—if the Cancer listens. Unlistened to feelings, impressions, perceptions, or spiritual guidance are the origin of the Cancer's sometimes-weighty stomach. The stomach is so busy carrying unheard or blocked feelings that it begins to swell with stagnant energy. Over time, these blocked feelings can lead to a host of gastro-intestinal disorders, or they can lead the Cancer to overeat as a way of holding down undigested feelings. If the stomach is perpetually digesting food, the vital organ, which stores feelings, does not have a chance to energetically release pent-up feelings, fears, or memories. Cancer is robbed of a vital intuitive function performed by the stomach if the stomach is blocked or continually engaged in digestion.

The stomach is the most vulnerable organ in your body, and often is the origin of other bodily disruptions. For example, an overly active stomach produces excess acid that can result in skin conditions, stiff joints, or headaches. The condition of your stomach can even influence your mood. Heaven help the person who gets in the way of a hungry Cancer! A soothing meal similarly produces a peaceful demeanor. This is the time for you to approach a controversial topic, or for others to approach you with a difficult question.

Exercises & Foods

Cancers have a sixth sense when it comes to picking soothing foods, including foods that are warming to the system, soft, rich, or with a high dairy content—dairy products re-produce the sensation of mother's milk, a desirable state for Cancer natives. The desire to retreat to the arms of a mother, or to be a mother to reproduce the mother-child bond, is a strong motivating factor for Cancer. It is not uncommon for Cancers to feel stressed by the lack of a strong mother figure, even as adults. The solution is to provide nurturing energy to yourself, through as many emotional, environmental, and culinary means as possible. Emotional solutions include re-creating emotionally comforting situations. This may mean re-creating a satisfying parent-child relationship where you are in the role of parent or child. This relationship does not have to be created with your natural parents, and a healing parent-child relationship may be created on a more conscious level with someone who is not biological family due to lack of history. Or, you may experience emotional satisfaction through a hobby such as cooking, gardening, reading, watching movies, writing poetry, or spending time in nature, to name a few. Next, create a peaceful environment. Cancers resonate with the color blue because it reminds them of their affinity for the sea. Other calming influences include soft pillows, soft lighting or candles, gentle music, and elements that remind you of the crab's preferred proximity to the shore, such as an aquarium, fountain, or a home near a lake, river, pond, or ocean.

Try this exercise to release pent-up feelings from your stomach, an emotional storage center. Consciously relax your solar plexus and imagine waves of energy departing from your stomach. These are waves of feeling. You may also visualize the waves as bubbles or rays of light to speed the process. Every second, you create waves of thought that create waves of feeling, or waves of feeling that create waves of thought. These waves can be continually released from the body through expression or letting go. Given that Cancer is a retentive sign, you may hold onto feelings, even if you express them, and you may ruminate or review stored feelings. The exercise of releasing waves of feeling from your stomach will invigorate this area of your body and enable you to process new feelings more clearly and quickly.

Also note that your desire for oral gratification, a vestige of a habit formed earlier in life, is a barometer of your emotional health. You may receive oral gratification through talking, chewing gum, chewing foods, drinking beverages, or even smoking. Knowing that you may be susceptible to oral needs, you may choose a healthy manner to meet this urge. You may also be aware that oral gratification needs will wax and wane with your feelings, the time of day or month. As you become aware of your patterns, they will have less influence upon you.

Flower Essences

You react well to flower essences, which contain distillations of the high vibrations present in flowers. Aloe Vera moderates vital energies. Honeysuckle releases nostalgic feelings so you may accept present reality. Evening Primrose heals your relationship to your femininity or to feminine energy in others. Baby Blue Eyes releases wounding from your father and heals your masculine side or your relationship to masculinity in others. Pink Monkeyflower releases fear resulting from a sense of vulnerability. Morning Glory releases attachments. Sage develops detachment to enhance an expanded perception of your soul.

Please note that your health and moods may change dramatically with the waxing and waning Moon. You will be more successful applying a healing method if you begin under the influence of the waxing Moon, from the New Moon to Full Moon, when the Moon's light is increasing. You will be more successful letting go of attitudes, memories, possessions, or even weight, when the Moon's light is decreasing from the Full Moon to the New Moon. (You may check a calendar for dates of the New and Full Moon.)

FINANCES

Cancer should be called the Sign of the Banker because you are so concerned with preserving assets you possess. You might give thrifty a new meaning as you probably would do *anything* to save money. You are a naturally retentive sign, which means you like to hold onto what you have, and it may pain you to give things away, even if you don't need them. This tendency may even extend to old papers or magazines that would find a much better home in the recycling bin. You simply do not like to throw *anything* away! So, do not be surprised if your drawers, closets, and even counter-tops are plentifully adorned with old missives. These pieces of the past give you a sense of security.

Now, back to finances. Your mottos are "Waste not, want not. A penny saved is a penny earned. A bird in the hand is worth two in the bush ..." Chances are good that you have saved a lot of money in your life. Or, if you have not saved a lot, you have figured out ways to stretch the money you have. And you have plans on top of plans inside of plans to preserve your financial security in the event of nuclear holocaust or some such disaster. You believe in taking precautions, and your financial security is no exception.

Your frugality is a wonderful quality, except for one problem. By holding onto many of your resources, you may limit the flow of new resources into your life, thus limiting the operation of the laws of prosperity and abundance. These time-tested spiritual laws state that what you give will come back to you, times 10. These laws require that you not only give what you no longer need, but that you also give something that you potentially need, to demonstrate to the

Creator your faith in His ability to provide for your needs. When you surrender your attachment to your most prized possessions or finances, and give things you think you cannot live without to others, you witness even more abundance and prosperity flooding into your life. It's spiritual law.

Many Cancers cannot bring themselves to trust the abundance of the universe or the exacting laws of karma that say that *everything* you give will return to you, even if it does not come to you from the same person to whom you gave. Trusting this spiritual maxim, and giving whenever possible without thought of personal lack, will bring you more prosperity than you imagine. Tithing is a spiritual principle that involves giving 10 percent of everything you earn to a worthy cause, a needy person, or a spiritual endeavor. This method of giving is sure to generate the financial security you seek many times over.

CAREER

You are well suited to any career that involves nurturing of people, physical objects, or property. Your most fruitful avenues of endeavor involve health care, finance, real estate, gardening, culinary arts, accessories for the home, and construction. You take great pride in managing the physical accoutrements of this material world to create greater security for yourself and others. This is why you are highly interested in bringing financial, emotional, and physical security to the object of your attention—be it a family member, colleague, or friend. You are especially adept at working with children, the elderly, and animals, because of their inherent semi-helpless condition.

You also enjoy forming relationships that simulate the parent-child bond, which is abundantly possible in caring for others, particularly if they are ill, young, or unable to speak the language, in the case of animals. Counseling in a school, institution, or private practice also satisfies your need to nurture. A high percentage of Cancer men and women also enjoy domestic responsibilities as a career. You may opt to take care of children, elderly parents, or a spouse in lieu of working in an office setting at some point in your professional life. Or, if you do not have family obligations, you may choose caretaking as a professional responsibility.

You also enjoy managing people and their affairs. You could be a personal shopper, closet consultant, interior designer, or landscape artist. If you have financial acumen or are mathematically inclined, you may translate this proclivity toward taking care of others into financial consulting, or brokerage work, trading stocks, bonds, and commodities. You also enjoy anything associated with the home, from selling culinary devices to kitchen appliances, flooring, paint, or tile. You are an excellent contractor because of your drive to create secure housing for yourself and others. You have a good ability to manage others (as long as you allow your employees plenty of freedom and do not project your need for security onto them). You also enjoy the process of construction, again because of a deep desire to see comfortable domestic situations created.

As a Cancer, you can do almost anything you like, as long as you feel emotionally connected to the result. If you are not interested, there is no one less likely to perform. But if you feel emotionally invested in your work, there is no one who will jump out of bed earlier to perform his or her tasks. As long as the environment suits your underlying motivations, there is no one happier in performing his or her jobs and responsibilities in life.

♌ LEO (July 23–August 22)

♌ LEO (July 23–August 22)

PERSONALITY PROFILE

Leo is a fixed, fire sign symbolized by the lion.
Your key motivations are capturing the spotlight, radiating light and warmth to others, creatively expressing yourself, helping others articulate their creativity, managing others, and achieving success and recognition for all.
Your outstanding attributes are a dramatic presence, a sense of style, warmth, generosity, creativity, dynamism, a gregarious nature, a strong will, and managerial abilities.
Your karmic challenge involves balancing your needs with the needs of others, seeing situations from others' points of view, and compromising your views with the opinions of others.
Leo rules the heart and spine.
Leo is associated with Apollo, the Sun God.
The Sun rules the constellation of Leo.
Leo is associated with the color yellow, the solar plexus chakra, and the pancreas.
Best Day: Sunday
Best Number: 1
Healing Gemstone: Yellow Citrine, Calcite, Topaz

Like the Sun, which rules Leo, you are warm, generous, constant, and only intermittently out of view under adverse conditions. Like the Sun, you enjoy emanating warmth and light so others may bask in your radiance. And, like the Sun, you don't mind being the center of attention every now and then. Leo the Lion is a fixed, fire sign, and is among the most loyal and devoted signs of the Zodiac.

On a soul level, you incarnated to express the light of your soul through the love in your heart. You want to love and be loved. You want to care about others, and have others care about you. You may try to win recognition or achieve success in at least one area of your life to attract this feeling. Or, you may pursue romance as a form of expressing and receiving loving feelings. You may also help others as a way of gaining their appreciation, loyalty, admiration, and support.

Your creativity is important to you. You may express your creativity by having children, through art, music, or theater, through public speaking or business, through leadership roles, or through any avenue of creative expression that fits your personality. Your creativity—and the sense of being loved that comes with creative endeavors—solidifies your sense of self-worth.

The lesson you are mastering in your earthly sojourn is that you may experience love and creativity in many ways. This is true if you were born with a Leo Sun, Leo Moon, or Leo Rising. Once you give love, it will return to you, even if not from the person to whom you gave, or the way you expect. You may find that as you love more without expectation, more love comes to you in unexpected ways. The notion of expectations—and letting them go—is a key to your happiness and the mission of your soul. The Sun, your planetary ruler, shines no matter whether people appreciate it, express gratitude, or take it for granted. You, too, are learning the art of radiating the limitless supply of love and creativity that flow from your heart. You are learning to experience the simple joy of love flowing through you. That alone is a fulfillment of the mission for which you were born.

As you grow and mature, you will learn that the love flowing through you to others is as nourishing as love flowing back to you from others. It is all love, and it does not matter whether it is coming in or going out. The attitude or approval of others does not affect your experience of love. You are always surrounded by unconditional love. The experience of the unconditional love around you and within you will nourish a sense of self-love and self-acceptance. Eventually, you will experience all love as emanating from the Divine—and from you, who are a mirror of the Divine. You will realize that no one owns love, and when you allow it to flow freely through you, it flows back to you. There is an unlimited supply of love in the universe. Your only task is to keep your heart open to give and receive the love that is already abundantly yours.

Take a deep breath into your heart, which is governed by the constellation of Leo. Feel the vital organ relax and expand. Emanate a feeling of love into the environment around you. Notice what happens. You may notice that by giving love, your heart relaxes, and you feel a warm, loving space around you. The more love you give, the more space opens inside you to receive. The heart is the strongest organ and center of energy in the body. In fact, the heart is 5,000 times more powerful than the brain. The heart is one of the first organs to develop in the fetus, and is intimately connected with the sense of hearing, which accounts for the many stories of infants responding to music or sounds they heard in the womb. Concurrently, the development of the physical heart allows the embryo to experience the love of its mother through its physical body. This experience sets the stage for receptivity to love later in life. One may not have received love in an acceptable form while in the womb, or may not have been receptive to the love that was given. But this does not preclude the future experience of love. It simply means that one must consciously give and receive love to expand the warm and loving energy naturally existing in your heart.

Once you have firmly established your relationship with love, you may shine as brightly as the Sun that rules your sign. As you shine, you emit a powerful magnetic field that attracts attention, support, and success to you. When love is radiating from your heart, everything falls into place.

As you find your center in your heart, you will access plentiful wells of creativity to fuel any endeavor. You are a highly creative soul who can think of one million ways to frame an idea, express a concept, and stir enthusiasm in others. You have special talents in drama, theater, art, and dance. You can capture an audience with your magnetism and fiery charm. Once you add the ingredient of love, you hold the attention of any crowd. Check to be sure the message you convey is coming from your heart. When your heartfelt message is clear, the warmth you feel and the success you achieve will increase exponentially.

PERSONAL GROWTH

The quickest way to speed your personal evolution is to shift your perspective from "I" to "we." You are a gallant fire sign whose strength partially derives from your vision of the world from your position at its center. But your weakness also partially derives from an inability to shift focus and see the world from its periphery, or from the perspective of another person.

While it is important as a Leo to maintain a strong center, it also is edifying to balance with flexibility that enables you to join others at their level to form alliances. Strength may come through periodically stepping down from your unquestionably lofty position to momentarily experience what others are experiencing to round out your otherwise regal point of view. Otherwise, you risk being a shiny beacon of light standing alone. Your noble position on the Zodiac wheel makes you undoubtedly the sign designated to rule with authority over others. Yet, the greatest rulers understand the subjects over whom they rule.

Step out of your position in the Sun to experience the world through the eyes of another. This may be the greatest challenge you face. You may stubbornly hold to a position you are in, even if you are unaware of what other places are available. See if you can observe situations from as many angles as possible. See if you can develop a spherical view. You may see situations from one perspective only. Try this exercise to round out your vision. Rotate your eyes in a counter-clockwise direction, as if you are following the numbers on a clock. Hold any position where the muscles feel tight for a few seconds. Repeat several times. Return to center and rotate your eyes in clockwise direction. Hold any position where the muscles feel tight for a few seconds. Repeat several times. As you open your physical vision to a more spherical view, you also are stimulating neural pathways in your brain, which enable you to coordinate both hemispheres of your brain with ease. Coordinating hemispheres promotes greater harmony within yourself and with others. The left hemisphere processes logical, linear thought. The right hemisphere absorbs intuitive, abstract information. The left hemisphere is considered masculine. The right hemisphere is considered feminine. By integrating the two halves of your brain, you become well-rounded, and able to absorb divergent points of view. Even if you are a man, you may have a feminine, non-linear way of perceiving information. Or, you may be a woman, and have a masculine, sequential method of processing information. You are best served by simultaneously engaging in both styles so you may integrate many perspectives.

Try the following exercise to enhance brain hemisphere integration. This exercise is called "cross crawl." It imitates the crawling movement of an infant, a key to inter-hemispheric integration. You may do this movement while standing. Raise your right arm and your left knee simultaneously, as if you are marching in place, and put your right palm on your left knee. Then, lift your left arm and your right knee, and place your left palm on your right knee. Continue alternating arms and legs at a brisk pace for one minute. This exercise, also known as cross-patterning, forces both hemispheres to coordinate as both sides of the body, and upper and lower halves of the body, simultaneously work together. You may practice this exercise when you are walking, by alternately swinging each arm in tandem with the opposite leg. Note that if you are swinging the arm on the same side as the moving leg, you are not coordinating both hemispheres, but are engaging in "homo-lateral motion." This connotes a division between the hemispheres of the brain, and can be remedied by simultaneously using opposite sides of the body, one body part above the waist and the other body part below the waist. This is accomplished by touching an arm and a leg from opposite sides. Or, touch a right finger to a left toe or a left elbow to a right ankle, and then do the same thing on the opposite side.

Another way of coordinating the hemispheres of the brain is to shift your focus from yourself to the other person, and their point of view. It also is healthy for you to engage in this exercise. Not only are you learning about others in the process of listening and paying attention to them, but by comparison, you are learning more about yourself too. The expanded perspective you gain from compromising and seeing the world from multiple viewpoints will open the hemispheres of your brain, and make it easier for you to feel compassion for others and to love and accept yourself. While you often project a highly self-confident image to the people around you, you may be the last to believe the image yourself. By taking time to listen to the perceptions of others, you may gain a world of perspectives. As you learn more about yourself, you develop greater self-awareness, a greater connection to your soul, and to the wellspring of love in you.

RELATIONSHIPS

Relationships are vital to the Leo soul, but perhaps not for the reason you may think. A Leo often thinks that he or she needs a relationship to feel secure, complete, or whole. Yet, as a native of the constellation ruled by the Sun, you already are complete and whole. For you, a relationship does not represent completion as much as it represents a mirror.

Many Leo souls have incarnated in families that did not provide accurate mirroring in childhood, perhaps as a way to make the Leo aware of his or her deep need to be seen and understood, so he or she may confront and heal this deep desire. Mirroring is the act of defining a child's talents, personality, and basic drives and feelings when the child is too young to define him- or herself. This job normally falls to the parents or an older sibling. Mirroring involves explaining emotional, physical, or mental sensations to a child, such as, "You are happy, sad, angry, hot, cold, tired, hungry, excited, or bored," or qualities, such as, "You are generous, you have a good sense of humor, you are honest, you are smart, or you run fast." The lack of mirroring of a Leo's physical-emotional-mental qualities leaves a psychological deficit that gives adult Leos a nearly pathological need for others to tell them who and what they are—especially if it is positive, but even a proud Leo can withstand a little negative feedback once in a while.

The first job in the relationship department, therefore, is to know yourself. Know that you need feedback about how you look, how you are doing, how the other person feels about you, and whether they appreciate you. You may look for a partner who can satisfy this need. But if you love a person, and they cannot provide this "service," try to remember this basic principle—Love Yourself! Add to that—Know Yourself! Developing these qualities will heal the strong need to have others meet an unmet childhood need in the context of an adult relationship.

One way of fulfilling a deep longing for approval is to take your talents before a larger audience so you may receive the feedback you desire from a large group of people. That will take the pressure off your partner. A large group experience also opens you to multi-dimensional perspectives so crucial for your evolution. Eventually, as the maturing process proceeds, your need for outside recognition and feedback will diminish. The result will be relationships that are more authentic, based on genuine emotional exchange, and mutual support. The one-way, mirror-based relationships of your early life will give way to genuine sharing of feelings, hopes, desires, and dreams. You also will notice a greater ability to compromise as the overwhelming compulsion to gain acceptance, recognition, and the outcome you want, gives way to a big-hearted desire to help, please, and love others. This desire to give will no longer be based on a compulsion to receive attention in return, but will stem from a deep sense of stability, maturity, and satisfaction that you have cultivated in your soul.

Leo and Leo

Strong romantic feelings are the foundation of a union between two passionate, fiery Leos. You both have a sense of style and romantic flair. You enjoy your similarities, and share a metaphorical ability to serve as mirrors for each other. Leo also is a strong-willed, tenacious sign. Two strong-willed people may produce positive results if both move in the same direction. But two determined people can produce contradictory consequences if they pull in divergent directions. Be careful if you commit to a long-term partnership with a fellow Leo. Leos are born leaders. Make sure you and your partner understand the mutual need to lead—and to take turns being a follower of the other. Also try to develop methods within yourselves and within the relationship to make compromises that accommodate the other. And, try to understand whether you and your Leo partner are moving in the same direction at a relatively similar pace. Leos tend to assume that others are as natural at following as they are at leading. Check and re-check to insure you and your partner are in sync in direction and speed. Developing these relationship skills will enhance your partnership, and all endeavors in which you are the leader.

Leo and Virgo

Traditionally, every sign is attracted to the sign following its own, because the subsequent sign represents the qualities toward which the earlier sign is striving. The combination of Leo and Virgo is no exception. Leos are magnetically attracted to the self-contained, self-effacing, efficient qualities of the Sign of the Virgin because these qualities represent the next stage of growth toward which Leo is striving. Virgo appreciates the theatrical nature of Leo, which may complement the Virgo's demure nature. Virgo, on the other hand, is moving toward lessons of harmony and balance mastered in the subsequent sign of Libra. Thus, if each partner supports the other in developing qualities required for the next stage of evolution, this could be a magical relationship based on understanding that surpasses the quality of other zodiacal combinations.

Leo and Libra

Libra is a cardinal, air sign who brings harmony to relationships. You treasure a Libra partner as he or she is determined to accommodate *you*. Libra may pay more attention to you than nearly any other sign of the Zodiac, except perhaps the sympathetic Pisces. Pay attention to your Libra mate to learn relationship skills that will enhance many facets of your life. Observing a Libra in a relationship is like watching an artist at work. Notice how the Libra weighs and balances options, opinions, and various points of view. This measured, multidimensional approach will reinforce the considered, spherical view you too are trying to develop.

Leo and Scorpio

Strong-willed Leo and strong-willed Scorpio make an unlikely pair in traditional astrology. But this combination can be found with striking frequency among long-married couples. Leo, a fixed, fire sign, traditionally does not mix easily with the fixed, water sign of Scorpio. Yet, the strength exuded by both signs creates a magnetic attraction that Leo and Scorpio feel powerless to resist. Leo is magnanimous, generous, and magnetic in an outward way. Scorpio is intense, deep, and magnetic in an inner way. These magnetic souls create a force field that perpetually draws the two together, even if not in the most harmonious way. Despite any disharmony engendered by this magnetic duo, mutual attraction and loyalty, or possibly the potential of winning a struggle with the other, seems to magnetically draw the two together over and over again.

Leo and Sagittarius

You are drawn to the vibrant optimism and witty humor of mutable, fire sign Sagittarius. You feel like you've found your soul mate who understands your need to create and share your creations with others. Sagittarius supports your efforts to reach out and touch other people's lives. Yet, Sagittarius has a considered, philosophical bent. Your Sagittarius partner will challenge you to bring meaning to your connection with the world. Your unbridled enthusiasm is quite endearing, but you may act from a sense of passion without fully calculating consequences. A thoughtful Sagittarian could give your path meaning and direction without dampening your zeal. A Sagittarian is equally enthusiastic, but prefers to discuss the vicissitudes and consequences of an action before making a move. Sagittarians look before they leap, and this quality in a partner could be quite beneficial to you.

Leo and Capricorn

Leo is magnetically drawn to relationship with the hard working Capricorn, a cardinal, earth sign. Leo and Capricorn enjoy being the boss, but in markedly different ways. Leo likes to lead in a theatrical, fiery way. Capricorn is not concerned with being the one who appears before the crowd. Capricorn would prefer to be the mastermind who controls the situation from behind the scenes, and who appears very little before other people. Together, Capricorn and Leo may create a successful company, corporation, or thriving organization. As long as you two run your relationship and family, as a business, this is a relationship destined to endure.

Leo and Aquarius

Aquarius is an air sign opposite Leo on the Zodiac wheel, making this fixed sign your complementary opposite. The Sign of the Water Bearer expresses many qualities that balance you. Aquarians so readily think about the big picture, the future, and the welfare of the group, they often forget about themselves. The utter abandon with which Aquarians surrenders to a group is an instructive experience for any sign of the Zodiac, particularly the proud Leo who is born to create a Self and live in the moment before contemplating the future or the welfare of a group. You have a lot to teach Aquarius about developing the identity of the Self, while Aquarius has a lot to teach you about letting go of the Self for the good of the group. A balanced relationship between the two of you has much to contribute to both souls and to the world around you.

Leo and Pisces

Although fire and water combinations are not favored in traditional astrology, Leo and mutable, water sign Pisces can create a harmonious union. Pisces appreciates the Leo's radiant nature. Leo appreciates Pisces' flowing, adaptable nature. Pisces forever reflects Leo's solar radiance in its oceanic depths. And Leo forever enjoys beholding itself in the mirror Pisces provides. While Leo's blustery temperament can ruffle the waters of many other signs, Pisces is a calm soul who absorbs the shock waves and experiences Leo's energy as an endearing expression of passion. This is a relationship in which the Pisces surrounds Leo with its watery compassion and support. Leo, in return, provides Pisces with a warm, stable center around which to build his or her life.

Leo and Aries

You are drawn to Aries like two sparks drawn together to form a flame. Aries is a cardinal, fire sign who enjoys getting things started. You are a fixed, fire sign who enjoys bringing stability and strength to what has been created. You and Aries are a dynamic couple who continually seek an outlet for your ideas and enthusiasm. Neither

Aries nor Leo enjoy sitting still, so chances are good that if you are in partnership with someone who has an Aries Sun, Aries Moon, or Aries Rising, you will surround yourselves with much activity. Your dynamic rhythms are compatible and elicit mutual respect due to the strength each one perceives in the other.

Leo and Taurus

Relationships between fiery Leo and fixed, earth sign Taurus are not recommended in traditional astrology, but the combination manifests with marked regularity. Taurus is magnetically drawn to the fiery excitement of Leo just as Leo is drawn to the earthy stability of Taurus. This combination appeals to many souls who seek a partner who is strong and stable. The strength and stability abundantly possessed by Leo and Taurus suggests a relationship that moves forward very little. But it also suggests a relationship that can withstand the test of time. Many Leo and Taurus couples find they communicate very little in a deep way. But Leo and Taurus are loyal souls who value the commitments they make, and both will go to the end of the earth to uphold the union, even if it is not the most communicative in the world.

Leo and Gemini

Gemini is a mutable, air sign who relates through spoken communications. Gemini will follow your plans while providing simultaneous verbal commentary. You enjoy Gemini's wit and wisdom. You are fascinated by the speed with which this active sign moves from place to place. The airy quality of Gemini fuels your fire. Your fiery temperament warms and stabilizes Gemini's peripatetic, restless mental nature. You and Gemini may travel together, and explore many new approaches to life. It is certain your relationship will never be boring. You may even need to practice periods of silence so you may each recharge your high-powered batteries.

Leo and Cancer

Traditionally, Leo does not harmonize with cardinal, water sign Cancer. Yet a surprisingly large number of Leos pair up with emotional Cancers, perhaps assuming non-traditional roles in this unconventional relationship. Sensitive, domestic Cancer provides a comfortable home and a stable support structure to the ebullient, theatrical Leo who has a home-loving side. The Sun rules Leo and the Moon rules Cancer. The inextricably-linked celestial pair is reflected with remarkable frequency among loving couples, perhaps as a mirror of the eternally-linked couple in the heavens.

Whomever you choose as your partner, know that this contact will teach you much about yourself. You incarnated with an agenda of creating a Self. The opportunity to create and re-create yourself in the context of a relationship is an experience that will bring deeper meaning to your life.

SPIRITUALITY

Spirituality for a Leo can be a tricky proposition. A true spiritual path involves a number of qualities, including concentration, devotion, discipline, faith, love, and ... surrender. This means surrender to a higher power, a being greater than yourself, to the natural intelligence of the universe, or to God. This does not mean surrender to people. For a Leo, concentration is not a problem. Nor is devotion, faith or love. Discipline can be elusive if this quality is not natural to your disposition, or if you do not fully believe in your path. But surrender? This is one of the most difficult leaps of faith for the Leo soul.

You see, surrender means giving yourself over to a power outside of yourself. This does not mean the power of another human being. It means the power of the Creator. This is a concept whose application can confound you. Not that you do not understand and accept the concept of a Creator. You do. Yet, bowing down to a being outside of yourself can feel threatening. You may feel challenged by the concept of the power of God rather than loved by the presence of God, the purpose of tuning in to God through spiritual practice.

When you do surrender to the presence of an Omniscient Creator, obeying this presence is yet another obstacle. Obedience of others, even if the Other is God, may not your specialty. You naturally have a strong will. Doing what you are guided to do by a larger force, an invisible one at that, may not be comfortable for you. In theory, you respect the largeness and omnipotence of God. But it may be difficult for you to follow directives that emanate from outside of yourself, or from the Divine, be they The 10 Commandments of the

Judeo-Christian Bible, the Eightfold Path of Buddhism, the *Yama-Niyama* injunctions of the Hindu scriptures, or the proscribed methods of any spiritual path.

You are a creative soul who incarnated to create your own way so others could follow you. You are not built to follow others—on the earth plane, that is. However, on the spiritual path, one is often required to cultivate qualities opposite from those qualities that one naturally possesses. This means that the quality that was your strength on the earth plane is actually a deficit on the spiritual path. This means that even though a strong will, self-directedness, or tenacity, may be important survival tools in physical realms, opposite qualities of surrender and obedience are needed for spiritual evolution.

Consider meditation as a method to promote spiritual advancement. It may not be easy for an active fire sign such as yourself to sit in meditation. Try affirming to yourself that you are okay, and that everything is okay while you are meditating. Experience the peace that naturally surrounds you. This feeling may at times elude you as you busily go about managing your life. But peace is always there. Simply tune in to it, either in a moment of quiet contemplation, meditation, or silence. These simple, quiet moments will give you the sense of mastery you have always longed for. Open your big, beautiful heart, and receive the spiritual blessings all around you!

HEALTH

Leo rules the heart and spine. You were born with a big heart. Your heart is literally and metaphorically your biggest asset. It can be your Achilles' heel too. That's why you may have experienced an irregular heartbeat or palpitations at some point in your life. You are like the Sun as you radiate light and warmth in every situation. But if you hold back or are forced to hold back, you will feel like the Sun on a cloudy day—overshadowed. This is not a healthy condition for the Leo soul, and may lead to cardiac problems either in the immediate moment or later in life. It is important, therefore, to let yourself shine as part of a healthy regimen for your heart.

"Letting yourself shine" means honest self-expression. For you, saying what you really think and feel is more important to a healthy body than any vitamin. That is because you are a fire sign, and when you are happy, the heat in your body burns up negativity, such as toxins. But when you are unhappy, your body will burn any substance, even if it is healthy. Therefore, it is important to feel psychologically and emotionally balanced to preserve a healthy body.

Mental and emotional health give you a regular heartbeat, strong circulation, easy absorption of vitamins and minerals from your food, easy elimination of toxins, and a sense of wellbeing that reflects in a strong, straight spinal column. Emotional, mental, and psychological imbalances manifest in your heart and spine. If you cannot correct inner disharmony, which manifests in your spine, try to force yourself to lengthen your spine by gently stretching or by standing and sitting as straightly as possible. The physical change will cause an increasing sense of emotional, mental, or psychological harmony. For inner disharmony that manifests in your heart, concentrate on this vital organ and send it positive thoughts and healing. Like you, your heart enjoys receiving attention and feeling love. Love is the most potent prescription for any ailment.

Feeling a sense of confidence, which stems from giving and receiving love, is vital to your health. More than any other sign, you need to feel good about yourself to function in a healthy physical and psychological way. All else springs from your sense of loving and being loved. Paradoxically, when you no longer seek something—in this case, love, attention, admiration, and support—you are more likely to receive what you are looking for. The act of non-attachment to a perceived desire seems to be an essential ingredient for getting one's needs met. As you give, and consequently receive love, affection, warmth, and attention, you will feel a sense of confidence overflowing from within. This will strengthen your body, mind, and feelings.

Herbs and Foods

On a physical level, hawthorn berry, sarsaparilla, and cayenne pepper promote circulation and stimulate your heart. For injuries to your heart, the homeopathic form of digitalis helps strengthen heart muscles. When you are feeling depleted, all red foods are stimulating and nourishing to your system, including red peppers, tomatoes, beets, strawberries, and apples. When you feel anxious, frustrated, or overheated, it is best to avoid red foods, and practice calming exercises such as deep breathing. You may imagine yourself surrounded by healing purple-blue light to bring balance to your system.

Flower Essences

Flower essences, which are distillations of the high vibrations in flowers, also may help you. The flower essence Morning Glory is beneficial to balance energy around your heart. And the flower essence Canyon Dudleya calms overexcitement. The flower essence Indian Paintbrush helps unblock creative energy, which rejuvenates your spirit.

Expressing your creativity is another way of healing a heavy heart, if you ever have this experience. Experiment with painting, singing, writing, or dancing to circulate your life force, if you feel blocked, depressed, or physically out of balance. If you are feeling really down, any form of social contact, even with strangers, opens your heart and helps you reconnect with the playful child in you, which reinvigorates your sense of purpose. Even though small talk will not give deeper meaning, the social stimulation opens your heart so you may re-gather your energy.

FINANCES

You have fine tastes that run from elegant to outrageous. Whatever it is, you believe you and your loved ones deserve the best. And financial restraint does not suit your style. What do you do when your appetite exceeds your ability to pay? It is not easy for you to detach from a desired object. And it is not easy to accept second best. The solution is to purchase only the best when the item is something you truly covet. Otherwise, wait.

You will know you truly desire an item when you have thought about it for a long time, searched to identify alternatives, and finally reach a sound conclusion. Avoid impulse buying. Try not to be influenced by sales unless you truly want an object. Avoid purchasing products of inferior quality. Do not buy something just because others are buying it. Resist buying something because someone tells you it looks nice or you should have it. Think hard before spending.

Think hard about earning money too. It is a natural tendency of Leo to be a manager or a director. It is not always easy to be the one doing the hard work. This stems from past lives in which you feel you were taken advantage of. Being exploited is an experience you desperately want to avoid in this life. While it is important to avoid being taken advantage of, it also is important to make a contribution to the environment in which you live. Your contributions are significant because they improve the world around you, because your positive actions give you good karma, and because making a contribution and being needed are important components of your self-esteem.

Consider also that even if you feel you are giving more than you receive in return, you eventually will be equitably compensated. Due to the exacting laws of karma, *everything* in the universe is equitable. You may not be aware of karma that is leading you to a particular moment where you are playing a special role. You may feel as if you are giving more than you are receiving in a specific moment. You may not be aware of positive rewards that are awaiting you in the future as a result of your efforts. Or, you may not be aware of negative consequences from past actions that you are working through in the present, or of the negative karmic consequences of not performing the positive action. Since one never knows the positive effects one is creating for the future as a consequence of one's present efforts, it is always a good idea to give as much time and energy as you can, knowing that only good will return to you as a result. This attitude will richly reward you in all of your financial undertakings so you are continually tapped into the source of material and spiritual abundance flowing to you.

CAREER

Your expectation that others will follow you and work toward your goals could be quite auspicious if you have a brilliant idea and a well-structured company or organization from which to launch your idea, product, or service. But, if you are not in a strong position of power or in a situation where you can manage others, this attitude can work to your detriment. That is because you may encounter more frustration than success as you wave your magic wand to get others to respond. You may only meet with blank stares—and there is nothing worse than a non-responsive audience for the Sign of the Lion.

There are a number of components of your career happiness. The first requirement is that you have some control over your destiny, whether you are the chief of an organization, corporation, or governmental body, or the lowest person in the ranks. There is no quicker way for you to feel dispirited than if you feel you are not the master of your fate. As a result of this feeling, look for a situation in which you can make your own decisions, and possibly even make decisions for others. This could be managing a department, an organization, a publication, or an event, or running your own company. Second, you like to feel you are periodically at the center of any activity in which you participate. Many Leos choose performance careers in order to guarantee they will receive the applause they so deeply crave. And many Leos are successful performers, musicians, singers, and dancers, not only because they want the applause, but because they possess a dramatic, creative flair—and they are really good! Separate the desire to be a performer from the desire to receive accolades and praise. If you really enjoy performing, then perform. If you are performing, or doing anything simply for the reaction of others, think about whether the action is in your highest good before you undertake it.

Your greatest interests are in marketing, advertising, public relations, and performing arts. You also have a flair for fashion design, costume design, set design, interior design, screenwriting, film and stage directing, producing, and editing. Within these fields, you often are happiest if you are the one managing the group rather than an underling following a chain of command. You also are wonderful at staging events, parties, conferences, or workshops. Remember, you love to coordinate large groups of people, and you love to have a lot of people around you. If you put your heart into what you do, you can make a success of any career you choose!

♍ VIRGO (August 23–September 22)

♍ VIRGO (August 23–September 22)

PERSONALITY PROFILE

Virgo is a mutable, earth sign symbolized by the virgin. Your key motivations are selfless service to help people and organizations, orderliness in your mind and feelings, self-improvement, healing yourself and others, charitable service, achieving purity and perfection in body, mind, and feelings. Your outstanding attributes are your perceptive, refined, analytical mind, your organizational abilities, your ability to focus on details, your endless capacity for hard work, your courage in the face of life's travails, the purity of your motives, and your desire to improve upon what exists.

Your karmic challenge involves applying perspective to your highly accurate and perceptive mind so you may prioritize and balance what is important with what is not, so you see the big picture rather than small details only, and so you may calm your nervous system and accomplish even more in a shorter amount of time.

Virgo rules the small intestines.

Mercury rules the constellation of Virgo.

Virgo is associated with the Greek goddess Demeter and her daughter Persephone and the Roman goddess Ceres and her daughter Kore.

Virgo is associated with the color blue, the throat chakra, and the thyroid.

Best Day: Wednesday

Best Number: 5

Healing Gemstones: Aquamarine, Turquoise, Chysocolla, Malachite

Virgo is a sign that is loving, generous, helpful, resourceful, versatile, empathetic, and pure of heart and mind. Yours is a sign that can be misunderstood by yourself and others because your highly active mind can mire you so deeply in details that you lose touch with the beautiful spiritual and creative qualities you abundantly posses.

Your powerful mind—your most salient feature among many admirable qualities—is your strength and your weakness. This is true if you were born under the constellation of Virgo, or if you have a Virgo Moon, or Virgo Rising. You are highly perceptive and sensitive, and you have sharp and accurate insights into yourself, your environment, and other people. You use your perceptive abilities to come to the aid of others and to improve yourself. You have a healing presence because of your desire to help, to be of service, and to make things better.

You see the correct way out of a problem because your perceptions are so accurate. People listen to you because you are so often correct, but due to their own resistance, they do not always implement your sage advice. And this annoys you to the point of distraction. This is where it would be helpful to develop perspective and patience.

Perspective may be one of the most important qualities your industrious Virgo soul can cultivate in this lifetime. Perspective will help you stand back and let go of attachment to the results of your efforts. Perspective will help you see the boundary between yourself and others. Perspective will help you see that possibly, maybe, perhaps, the issue that is front and center in your mind may not be as important to the other person, or in the general scheme of life, not an important matter at all! Practice stepping back from *every* situation to see the big picture. See if you can perceive simultaneously the big picture and the details. Or, if you can only see them alternately (one at a time), switch between focus on the details and a large panorama. You will be amazed at how this puts your worries and concerns into perspective to help you let go of an over-focus on miscreant details. And finally, add a little patience to the equation to help you wait to see your actions come to fruition, possibly at a later date.

Your insightful approach to life is precious. Your perceptions are ubiquitous. The depth, breadth, and scope of your awareness, interests, and insights are virtually fathomless and omnipresent. As a result of all you know, you can easily be a genius. It is important for you to think strategically to devise ways to put all of your powerful insights to good use. Consider being a business or financial consultant, counselor, psychotherapist, advisor, spiritual teacher, or coach. Or, apply your creative mental abilities as an editor, critic, film producer, or director. Or, choose a health care profession where you are paid to diagnose problems and prescribe solutions.

Otherwise, where are your powerful insights to go? Insight and awareness without a receptive audience is an accident waiting to happen. Put another way, when you do not have an avenue to express your precious awareness, you are prone to worry. Why is it like this? How can I fix it? How did it get this way? Why is everyone so foolish? Why can't I help? Why doesn't everyone do it my way?

Where do you draw the line? And how do you draw it? The answer to these questions is to focus on improving yourself rather than others, and only give of your endless supply of logical solutions and advice if asked, or if paid to supply this information. Then, your creative perspective and endless insights will be gratefully received. Otherwise, you risk being accused of overstepping your boundaries.

Somewhere in the life of every Virgo's quest for perfection comes a moment when he or she simply gives up the quest in favor of a more workable approach to life. He or she throws up his or her hands and cries to the heavens, "Why did you make such an imperfect world???" It is then, and only then, that the Virgo soul can accept the inevitability of imperfection, and begin to accept omnipresent imperfection within him- or herself, within his or her environment, and within others. The acceptance of imperfection will help the Virgo soul perceive a higher level of perfection. He or she will see a higher order to the disorderliness, perhaps the hand of God or the workings of karma that will better explain people and situations that do not fit the rational preconceptions of the linear human mind.

The acceptance of imperfection also begins a process of self-acceptance and self-love that is a crucial step on the path of every spiritual seeker or seeker of higher consciousness. This is the ultimate motivation of every soul who has chosen to incarnate under the Sign of the Virgin. Every Virgo soul wants to explore the vicissitudes of perfection, knowing well that the end of the quest will lead to surrender to the imperfection of God's creation. This reality leads to a host of profound transformations for the Virgo soul, including mastery of the lesson of tolerance, non-judgment, surrender to the will of the Creator, love and acceptance of the Creator's imperfect creation, and finally, mastery of the all-important qualities of self-love and self-acceptance.

Yet the journey to tolerance, non-judgment, non-attachment, love and acceptance, is littered with paradoxical lessons for the Virgo soul. Virgo is a quixotic sign in that at its purest level, Virgo is seeking to selflessly serve, to give, and to love. But Virgo works to achieve the goal of selfless service through the faculties of exacting analysis, detail-orientation, judgment, criticism, and perfectionism, which can undo the good will that motivates this beautiful sign—all in the service of becoming a servant of the light!

Virgo is a sign that, paradoxically, must let go of the things that make the sign so unique—to an extent—to find balance rather than absolute perfection. That means releasing perfectionism as a route to finding perfection! When the balance is perceived, you can most perfectly manifest the pure and beautiful qualities lying abundantly within your soul. For every Virgo, the innate and inimical quest for perfection must end in total acceptance and love of imperfection! Why didn't they hand this to you in a guidebook when you were born? The dilemma of your life peacefully concludes with the acceptance of the harmonious co-existence of light and dark, good and bad, perfection and imperfection, as part of the perfect nature of God's creation.

An ancient myth from the heavenly realms helps you understand the Virgo journey. In ancient times, the constellations Virgo and Scorpio were said to be one sign. They were passionately attracted to each other while simultaneously feeling repelled. Eventually, Libra came between the two to bring peace and harmony to the warring constellations. In the separation, Virgo took its proclivity for light, and Scorpio took its penchant for dark. Ever since, Virgos are gifted with an enormous capacity for light and purity with an equally strong disdain for the dark. This has left Virgos with the karmic imperative of loving and accepting the darkness within themselves and others. Conversely, Scorpios have a nearly insatiable appetite for darkness with a commensurate revulsion to light when it becomes too bright. This leaves Scorpio with the karmic imperative of allowing in the light without feeling it will undermine their personal power or will. So, in addition to all of the other tasks you must carry out as an industrious Virgo soul, you also must transform yourself into a Scorpio and relish the dark just as a Scorpio must transform him- or herself into a Virgo and relish the light.

The Greek myth of Demeter and Persephone (known as Ceres and Kore in Roman myth) also captures another complex aspect of the Virgo personality. Demeter, goddess of the harvest, has a daughter named Persephone. Demeter represents the mothering aspect of the Virgo character and Persephone represents the independent and rebellious, yet shy and demure aspect of the Virgo personality. Demeter and her daughter Persephone were quite attached to each other. But as Persephone grew into adulthood, she craved freedom from the mother-daughter bond.

One day, the young maiden was picking flowers in a field when the earth opened up. Out came Hades, god of the underworld, on his horse-drawn chariot. Hades abducted Persephone, brought her to his secret underworld abode, sexually violated her, and kept her in his underworld abode. Demeter, Persephone's mother, was so grief-stricken at the fate of her daughter, she cried until her tears covered the earth. Eager to save the world from the flood of Demeter's tears, the gods on Mt. Olympus convened, and sent Hermes, the wing-footed messenger, to rescue Persephone. Hermes arranged for

Persephone's release from Hades, on one condition: that she not take anything with her when she left. All agreed. But on her way out, Hades offered Persephone seven pomegranate seeds. Persephone accepted, fully knowing she would have to return to the underworld as the result of her action. She took one step out of the dark realm and Hades proclaimed, "She is mine for half the year as she has accepted a gift from the Land of the Dead." As a result, Persephone spent six month of every year with Hades, as Queen of the Underworld, which is why we have six months of diminished light in autumn and winter. And she spent the other six months in the upper world with her mother, Demeter, which is why we also have six months of brighter light in spring and summer.

On a deeper level, a Demeter and Persephone live within every Virgo, man or woman. Demeter represents the mothering, nurturing quality of Virgo, and the strong attachment to the "child," which is the idea or creative endeavor of the Virgo soul. Simultaneously, Persephone represents the complex relationship to purity and darkness present in every Virgo psyche. Persephone wants to uphold the high standards of her mother, but she creates a situation (by accepting the pomegranate seeds) where she will be "forced" to live in the underworld. It is difficult for Persephone to initiate this underworld voyage, just as it is difficult for Virgo to accept the inevitability of imperfection or impurity. Yet, once entreated to enter the darker realms, Persephone is transformed into the queen of this domain, as is every Virgo who accepts his or her underworld journey by accepting the inherent imperfection of life itself.

PERSONAL GROWTH

Your greatest evolution comes through your love and acceptance of yourself and others exactly as you and they are. This is not easy, given your cosmically-ordained role as "Editor of the Zodiac." You are more exacting, discriminating, precise, and informed than any other sign on the astrological wheel. In fact, you are so sensitive to disruptions to the way things "should be," you often feel like the princess in "The Princess and the Pea." You are the one who not only perceives the pea beneath the pile of mattresses, as did the princess of the fairy tale, but you are the one who feels the ill effects too, just as the princess who woke up feeling hurt by the small pea even though it was far from her body.

How do you put all of this sensitivity and awareness to good use? First, acknowledge yourself for being perceptive enough to perceive something as subtle as a pea that few others would perceive. Second, remove the pea and go to a chiropractor to relieve your aching back. Third, don't allow the memory of the pea to haunt you. And most of all, don't let it ruin another night's sleep! This is a difficult piece of advice for the sensitive Virgo. Your fine-tuned nervous system receives many important messages through your sensitive body. You may get a stomachache or headache when you are doing something that is not aligned with your soul, or if you are with a person who is not aligned with your highest good or the good of someone with whom you are close. You may, therefore, interpret physical disruptions as messages from your soul, telling you that something is amiss. So, how do you let go of a feeling of misalignment once the sensation has invaded your physical body? The best antidote to a soul that speaks through a sensitive body is to listen, and listen as soon as possible when the symptoms set in. Don't ignore the symptoms and hope they will go away. They won't go away … until you listen. Next, practice listening to the precursors of the stomachache or the headache, or the rash, or the tight muscles, or the twisted ankle, or whatever message you regularly receive. Notice the signs that precede the injury or disruption. Are the signs a rapid heart rate, rapid breathing, insomnia, chills, blushing, or freezing? When you experience a sign, pay attention before it turns into a malady. Finally, take action on the intuition you receive. When you feel heat rising in your body, for example, what does this mean? What is going on in the present moment that is out of alignment? What should you do to correct the balance? What can you change in yourself? And how quickly can you change it? Quick reactions do more to relieve the Princess and the Pea syndrome than delayed reactions. In other words, when you feel out of alignment, take action! If you suspect there is a pea under the mattress, take it out before you go to sleep rather than wait to see what it will do, hoping it will be okay. Accept the fact that you are sensitive rather than wishing you were otherwise. You are sensitive. It is okay to be sensitive. Use to your benefit the information your senses give you, and be happy your intuition is working well!

As you develop a better relationship with your intuition, a greater ability to listen to your Self, and to be guided by your inner wisdom, your intuitive impulses will become stronger and more accurate. Your intuition could be your greatest gift, or at least the greatest asset in your quest for perspective. With intuition, insight, and perspective, you will accomplish more than you ever thought possible with your service-oriented, selfless nature. You possess beautiful qualities whose expression can create many beautiful things.

It is part of the path to enlightenment of every Virgo soul to sacrifice his or her needs for the benefit of another. Selfless service helps the Virgo discover his or her power, endurance, and capacity for love. The experience of letting oneself go in favor of another is an alchemical event that forever transforms the Virgo into the deep, compassionate, strong, stable, and loving soul you were meant to be.

RELATIONSHIPS

Virgos are compassionate, generous, understanding, loving, and forgiving in relationship. So why does the Sign of the Virgin have the highest rate of singles of any Zodiac sign? Part of the answer stems from the karmic imperative that Virgos put their work ahead of personal concerns, even relationships, and give to others before they give to themselves. This alone inhibits the freedom to enter a relationship with little concern for outside demands.

The strength that Virgos build over the course of their lives makes them versatile, resourceful, self-sufficient, and self-contained. Ultimately, Virgos often have the ability to meet many personal needs themselves. This gives Virgos the independence they cherish, which makes it less imperative to enter traditional relationships because dependency needs are so few. Virgos also possess highly critical mental faculties. These faculties can be used to discover problems and solutions, or they can be used to find fault. Typically, the Virgo's critical faculties are used in both ways. Virgos' motives are pure, and they find fault in others with the intention of helping. Yet this critical faculty can intimidate or alienate the person who is the object of the criticism, or more often, it can dissuade the Virgo from uniting with such gross imperfection. These imperfections loom large in the eyes of the Virgo, whereas they would seem small, forgivable features to nearly any other sign. Yet the discriminating Virgo eye is so trained on spotting imperfections—in the service of healing—that he or she shies away from imperfect-seeming relationships that others would perceive as simply perfect. Remember, the lesson of the Virgo soul is that there is no perfection, and this lesson resonates particularly strongly in the realm of relationships.

Another part of the relationship dilemma stems from the way Virgos relate to other people. As in the myth of Demeter and Persephone, Virgos are most comfortable in giving or in service-oriented relationships, such as mother-child, healer-client, teacher-student, or doctor-patient. Professional and parental relationships flow extremely smoothly for the Virgo soul, but a relationship of equals is not a natural path, as it is for the subsequent sign of Libra, the Sign of the Scales. Relationships function best for Virgos when there is a mutual goal outside of pure relationship, be it professional accomplishment, team sports, healing, parenting, or teaching. Virgos are social, relationship-oriented people, who enjoy interacting with the mortal members of God's creation, even in the midst of imperfection, which incidentally, most Virgos perceive most glaringly in themselves!

Virgo and Virgo

You relish a relationship with a fellow mutable, earth sign Virgo because you have found someone who understands you—and who wants to help you and please you as much as you want to help and please him or her. Your Virgo partner understands why you <u>must</u> do certain things in a certain way at a certain time. Your partner is sympathetic toward you if something that does not bother others—or does not bother your partner—bothers you. This could be a small detail, a loud noise, an obvious smell, synthetic materials or foods with preservatives, or a picture on the wall that is askew. Your partner anticipates what will disturb you. He or she notices your routines, and helps you keep them. Your partner is sensitive to your needs, and you are sensitive to the needs of your partner. This reciprocity is a welcome comfort. A relationship between two service-oriented Virgos is a healing experience that enables you and your industrious

Virgo partner to help others, and contribute something of lasting value to the world. As long as the Virgo relationship takes the high road of mutual, selfless service rather than mutual critique, this relationship is peaceful, harmonious, long enduring, and produces much happiness for all involved.

Virgo and Libra

Virgo and Libra, a cardinal, air sign, have plenty of common ground upon which to build a harmonious relationship. You and Libra are considerate, thoughtful, and polite. You both appreciate the fine sensitivities of the other. You are consistently cordial and friendly. Yet, rarely do these refined signs enter into intimate partnership. It may be that Libra and Virgo shy away from a steady diet of the other due to lack of innate understanding of the basic motivations of the other. Virgo is work-oriented and attracted to circumstances in need of repair. Libra is relationship-oriented and attracted to circumstances filled with harmony. Libra may misunderstand Virgo's penchant for details. And Virgo may despair at Libra's inability to understand that tending to details is the Virgo's way of showing love! Conversely, Virgo may not understand Libra's objective, detached perspective. And Libra may despair at Virgo's inability to understand that this is Libra's way of building a harmonious relationship. Whereas Virgo is compelled to act on subjective opinions, Libra prefers to act on objective principles. Virgo and Libra may come to the same conclusion, but Virgo forms its opinions through close, detailed analysis of fact, and Libra renders judgment through detached consideration of principles. If you and Libra understand you each have slightly different but complementary approaches, you will experience a level of peace and harmony that both will cherish.

Virgo and Scorpio

Virgo and fixed, water sign Scorpio were once eternally linked as one constellation in the heavens. To this day, Virgo and Scorpio are magnetically drawn to the mystery of the other. Virgo wants to understand Scorpio's relationship to the psychological shadow. Scorpio wants to understand Virgo's relationship to purity and perfection. Both want to become intensely close to the other, but the intensity of each sign's relationship to the quality in which it specializes, also force the two apart. Virgo may become overwhelmed with the intensity of Scorpio's fascination with psychological shadow material. And Scorpio may feel overexposed by the purity and perfectionism of Virgo's psyche. Both need to encompass the qualities of the other. Integration of the opposing polarities represented by Virgo and Scorpio may be done in the context of the relationship, or individually. But ultimately, wholeness is achieved for Virgo and Scorpio by embracing light and shadow.

Virgo and Sagittarius

You are drawn to the witty humor and brimming enthusiasm of mutable, fire sign Sagittarius. Sagittarius will broaden your vision. And you will help Sagittarius refine details he or she has overlooked. This is a highly productive business relationship. Yet, in the realm of the heart, you may find that you see the world from such different perspectives that it feels impossible to find a middle ground. Sagittarius feels that only the big picture matters, and the details will naturally fall into place. Virgo feels that only the details matter, and the big picture will build upon the orderly structuring of the small pieces. The truth is a combination of the two philosophies. A large vision is needed to determine direction. Refinement and details also are necessary to manifest the vision in physical reality. Virgo and

Sagittarius feel happiest when they blend the skills of the other. A relationship entails spontaneous reactions. There may be too much attachment to competing philosophies in this relationship for a rapid, smooth, flowing meeting of the minds on a daily basis.

Virgo and Capricorn

You are naturally compatible with cardinal, earth sign Capricorn. Although the Sign of the Goat may be more conventional than your peripatetic mind may have dreamed, you and Capricorn consistently support each other and your goals. A natural sympathy and understanding flows between both earth sign natives, which creates a mutual sense of loyalty and desire to please the other. You each understand the importance of earth plane constraints, such as financial security, organized paperwork, being on time, and keeping your word. Whereas other signs may not understand your mutual attachment to the orderly cadence of your lives, you and Capricorn naturally harmonize in your daily routines. Make sure you take a moment from your industrious projects to enjoy emotional communion in this relationship. Chances are good that you will responsibly undertake many endeavors together. Success is bound to come from this harmonious union.

Virgo and Aquarius

You are fascinated by the lightening-quick mind of Aquarius, a fixed, air sign. You are mentally versatile too. But you focus on concrete details where Aquarius focuses on universal concepts. You appreciate Aquarius' high-minded commitment to friendship. Aquarius' idealism appeals to your logical, orderly mind. If you are interested in refining the ideas of your Aquarius mate, and of helping him or her to put his big ideas into practice, you may have a perfect partnership. While many

Virgos and Aquarians are highly compatible, they often prefer to remain friends rather than enter an intimate partnership. The Aquarius may be erratic while the Virgo may prefer cleanliness and order. These divergent qualities may create stress in an intimate relationship. While the Aquarian may accept the Virgo's lifestyle, it is possible the Virgo's nerves may be jangled by the Aquarian's easy-going but unpredictable temperament.

Virgo and Pisces

Pisces is a mutable, water sign, located opposite Virgo on the Zodiac wheel. Opposites attract, and the sign opposite your own traditionally brings balance and harmony to your life. Virgo is hard-working, industrious, and service-oriented. Pisces is flowing, feeling, sensitive, and dedicated to harmonizing spiritual and human realms. While Pisces and Virgo are oriented to helping others, their methods are quite different. Virgo gives service through compassionate action. Pisces gives service through compassionate feeling. Virgo and Pisces may be so opposite in their earthly versus watery ways that the two signs struggle to understand each other. A conscious effort to understand each other yields luscious fruit of mutual compassion and service to the relationship and to others. Without awareness of the natural difference between the organized, methodical, down-to-earth systems of the Sign of the Virgin, and the flowing depths of the Sign of the Fish, the two signs may each feel as if they have encountered a being from another planet! Again, understanding brings awareness that mutually transforms both partners, and brings out the hidden flow in Virgo, and the hidden organization in Pisces.

Virgo and Aries

You may initially be shocked by Aries' brash boldness, but as you get to know this cardinal, fire sign, you may come to appreciate the entrepreneurial, industrious nature of the Sign of the Ram. You are a stickler for details, and the Aries simply plants the seeds—metaphorically new ideas—before embarking upon new endeavors, without poring overe details. If you and Aries agree to work together as a team, you will find many paths to explore. Aries will initiate the new ideas, and you will take responsibility for upholding the details of the vision. This is a relationship that may at times lack deep emotional intimacy, but if you agree on mutual goals, you will support each other to accomplish many things during the time you are traveling the same path together.

Virgo and Taurus

Taurus, a fixed, earth sign, is eternally attracted to the Sign of the Virgin. Taurus appreciates the simplicity, purity, and elegance of fellow earth sign Virgo. While you may periodically enter complex realms of your own psyche, Taurus will never ask questions, and will loyally offer him- or herself as a lifelong mate. You appreciate Taurus' stability and ability to make you feel secure. You also marvel at the physical endurance and strength of the Sign of the Bull, as you tend to feel a more tenuous relationship to your physical body. Similarly, Taurus marvels at your versatile mind, as Virgo cultivates a strong relationship to its mental faculties. Taurus is a grounded soul who excels at gardening, artwork, handicrafts, and working with objects in the material world. You feel supported by the presence of Taurus in your life, and Taurus feels content to be with you. This is an enduring partnership.

Virgo and Gemini

You and Gemini are ruled by the communications planet Mercury. Gemini, a mutable, air sign, is a mentally versatile, verbally adept soul who will fascinate you with his or her wit and charm. You both are curious souls with peripatetic minds. You will never tire of going to museums, movies, exhibits, conferences, and going on trips. Life will feel like one big carnival to Gemini and Virgo, and it will seem as if one or the other of you is always winning a prize. This is a heady relationship that will expand the horizons of both partners. As long as Virgo does not try to create structure in the Gemini's life, and the Gemini does not disrupt the Virgo's order and routine, this is a beneficial partnership that will bring greater knowledge to both partners.

Virgo and Cancer

You are attracted to the natural mothering qualities of the Sign of the Crab. You also share a love of nurturing others, but you have diverse styles. You nurture through logistical support and advice. Cancer, a cardinal, water sign, nurtures through feelings and food. If you and Cancer make an effort to understand your differences, your grounded, earthy qualities will balance the watery, emotional disposition of your Cancer mate. In the realm of food, one of the compelling avenues of expression for Cancer, you will create a most interesting balance. While you do not share Cancer's passion for culinary pleasures, you are highly conscientious about health, diet, and nutrition. You will patiently watch Cancer concoct a culinary work of art while you calculate the vitamins, minerals, and calories you are about to take in. As long as your Cancer mate does not realize (or care) that you are looking at the technical rather than sensual aspects of the meal, you will be on your way to a harmonious union. Also note that Cancers are highly emotionally sensitive—to a degree that may boggle your logical mind. Your emotions are held in check by your rational mind, and rarely do feelings get in the way of other responsibilities. This is not the case for Cancers, who feel their feelings are their main responsibility. These differing natures may cause consternation in a relationship, but there is plenty of common ground to establish a working partnership.

Virgo and Leo

Traditionally, every sign is attracted to the sign following its own, because the subsequent sign represents the qualities toward which the earlier sign is striving. The combination of Virgo with the fixed, fire sign Leo, is no exception. Leos are magnetically attracted to the self-contained, self-effacing, efficient qualities of the Sign of the Virgin because they represent the next stage of growth toward which Leo is striving. Virgo appreciates the theatrical nature of the Leo soul, which may complement the Virgo's demure nature. Virgo, on the other hand, is moving toward the lessons of harmony and balance mastered in the subsequent sign of Libra. Thus, if both support the other in developing qualities required for the next stage of evolution, this could be a magical relationship based on understanding that surpasses the quality of other zodiacal combinations.

SPIRITUALITY

Virgo is a highly spiritual sign, with a strong determination to serve the Creator through selfless service. The path to Virgo perfection often leads through a maze of experiences that include hard work, self-sacrifice, selfless service, unrecognized contributions, and potential consternation at the seeming injustice of it all. Every Zodiac sign has a challenge to face. And for Virgo, the challenge is the imperative of being self-effacing, self-sacrificing, hard-working, and often facing life's challenges alone, in order to access the true strength that resides within you—to fulfill the karmic purpose you have undertaken as a soul when you decided to incarnate.

As a soul, Virgo committed to do an extraordinary amount of work as a symbol of devotion to the Divine. Prior to one's incarnation, it is theorized that one plans the circumstances one will encounter during an earthly sojourn. You determined that you would gain strength and steadfastness through service. By necessity, you had developed a capacity for hard work and the ability to surmount adversity in prior incarnations. So, the intelligence of your soul chose to continue its evolution through service to others. You have a natural sense that your hard work is best devoted to spiritual causes, charitable organizations, and upliftment of the downtrodden.

Use your intuition to guide you to the best ways to follow your spiritual path. Your intuition may guide you to work with one person at a time, with a group, in an organization, or in a combination of the above. Selfless service to a cause you believe in will do more to help you feel spiritually fulfilled and aligned with your soul's purpose than any other activity or event.

You also are a natural renunciant in that you require little in the way of material comfort to feel happy. As long as you are surrounded by peaceful people, places, and vibrations, and the elements surrounding you are clean and orderly, you have the potential to feel quite content. To you, this is a spiritual experience! Feel gratitude for the positive things in your life because that opens a channel for the universe to provide more of what you appreciate. For you, the practice of gratitude and appreciation may be the essence of spiritual experience!

You may augment your spiritual inclination toward service, peace, harmony, and cleanliness, with a practice of contemplation or meditation. You may feel as if you naturally spend your entire life in contemplation because you have such an active mind. Precisely for this reason, it is important for you to develop a spiritual practice that teaches you to *clear* your mind to give it a much-needed rest from ceaseless mental activity. Begin your contemplation practice by choosing one thought or object, and focus only on that thought or object, without allowing your mind to wander. This rhythmic pattern in your mind will have a soothing effect on your nerves. Or, engage in a meditation practice by sitting, and observing the rhythmic pattern of your breath. Watch it go in, and watch it go out. That is all. For a few moments, you do not have to solve all of the world's problems! Enjoy the peace of these rhythmic activities.

Finally, try to love and accept yourself exactly as you are. Even if you find a flaw, love it and accept it. This is the easiest way to let it go. In fact, this is the solution to all dilemmas you may face. Love the problem, watch it dissolve in the light of your love, and let it go. Also consider a daily or weekly period of self-imposed silence as a method to promote your spiritual advancement. It is not easy for you to sit without doing "anything." Try affirming to yourself when you are sitting that everything is okay, that you are accomplishing much by the practice of silence, and that by systematically quieting your mind and outward expression, you actually will gather more energy, wisdom, and awareness to better live in your periods of activity. You will be amazed at how much more you accomplish when you intersperse periods of intense activity with periods of rest and quiet and what looks like "emptiness." The emptiness actually will fill you with the essence of your soul that you may bring with you into all activities.

HEALTH

Your natural ability to heal, your innate knowledge of healing, and conversely, your susceptibility to disruptions to your own physical health, have made you a jack-of-all-trades in the health department. You probably have experienced a health issue during your life, or you have been close to or cared for someone who has had a health problem. Consequently, you have developed a set of skills to heal yourself and others, which derives from many prior incarnations as a healer, doctor, or nurse.

As a Virgo, you have chosen a life situation that makes use of your enormous storehouse of healing knowledge and energy. You either will choose to enter a health care field, you will informally care for others, or you may work out issues of health through your own body. Virgo is the sign of the doctor and the patient, and it is likely that you have been either one in different chapters of your life. It is highly likely that you have elected to work out some of your karma through your physical body in this lifetime.

A soul can work out karma through the physical body, emotional experience, or through mental faculties. As souls, Virgos choose to bear at least some of their karma in their physical bodies. This may be karmically necessary due to an unresolved health situation in a prior life, or it may stem from a decision to learn life lessons or work out prior karma through your body rather than through your mind or your feelings. You generally take pride in the efficiency of your mind and your well-functioning feelings, talents developed in prior incarnations. Thus, your body may be more vulnerable than your mind and heart, given that no one can be perfect in everything!

Consequently, many Virgos draw on innate healing abilities or acquire knowledge about medicine or natural healing to cope with physical challenges.

Every constellation resonates with a particular part of the human body. The constellation of Virgo rules the small intestines, the part of the body that discriminates between what should be absorbed and what should be eliminated. In addition to a highly discriminating mind, you also are highly sensitive to those things that are out of order, or simply do not make sense. The small intestines are a hidden component of the gastro-intestinal tract. They are the bridge between the stomach that prepares food for digestion, and the large intestines, which eliminate waste. Virgos often feel like the hidden bridge between people, and you are excellent at networking. Virgo souls also work tirelessly behind the scenes, just as the small intestines work virtually constantly with little acknowledgement by the human being whose body they inhabit.

As a result of Virgo's association with the small intestines, you may have a sensitive gastro-intestinal tract, food allergies, or food sensitivities. Typically, Virgos play host to a variety of low-level ailments until they utilize their natural healing abilities to overcome the physical disharmony. Your healing abilities may be latent, but sooner or later, every Virgo learns to tap into this limitless resource within him- or herself. Overcoming a vulnerability naturally leads to development of strength in that area.

Just as the small intestines sort the usable from the non-usable in the body, Virgos' active minds are continually sorting out experiences, feelings, memories, and impressions. Properly deployed, the Virgo mind will solve problems, implement solutions, and let go. Improperly used, the Virgo mind may ruminate and review. At best, this will engender nervous energy and anxiety. At worst, it will degenerate into health issues from indigestion to tight muscles to headaches to rashes. Anything that is related to a nervous disorder can potentially visit a Virgo physique.

Emotionally, you are strong, poised, and self-possessed. You can uphold your responsibilities, manifesting a calm, coherent outward appearance, even if a turbulent emotional storm is raging within you. But this level of responsibility can take its toll on you. Along with the nervous mental energy, unacknowledged or repressed emotional energy may manifest in your body as disruptions to your health.

Given the efficiency with which you manage yourself, you should have no trouble managing your active mind and feelings so they work to your benefit. When your mind or heart start to race, and you review the same issue over and over, stop, relax, take a deep breath, and count to 10. Remove yourself from the source of discomfort and gain perspective. Deep breathing, meditation, and visualizing yourself in a calm state will quell the turbulent storms that may periodically beset the Virgo psyche.

Exercises, Herbs, and Foods

Yoga and gentle stretching are extremely helpful to your physical well being. They also calm your mind and your sensitive feelings. You do best with foods that are calming to the nervous system. Virgo's association with the goddess of the harvest also means that grain is especially nourishing. While it is important to periodically include raw foods in your diet, cooked foods agree with you due to the sensitivity of your gastro-intestinal tract. The earth sign of Virgo also tends to be cool more often than warm. Therefore, assimilating foods that have been warmed or that have warming properties is beneficial to you. Conversely, foods that are too spicy or hot will disrupt your sensitive equilibrium, and ultimately you feel best with foods that are in the middle of the temperature range. All foods in moderation serve you better than a strict diet of any one food, or large quantities of any one food. Helpful herbal remedies that calm the nervous system include valerian root, hops, skullcap, passion flower, and chamomile. Vitamin B and calcium also soothe your nerves.

Flower Essences

Flower essences, which are distillations of the high vibrations in flowers, also assist you. The flower essence Lavender calms an overactive mind. Canyon Dudleya soothes aggravated emotions. Larch help you overcome obstacles due to fear of being imperfect. Rock Water releases obsessive thoughts and feelings. Sage widens your perspective so you may express the abundant wisdom you have gained in your life.

FINANCES

You are more interested in what you do for work than in how much money you make in the course of performing your job. You are highly idealistic, and believe it is better to do what you believe in than to sell your efforts to a person or a cause you do not support. Your strong principles guide you to right action in every endeavor you undertake. Over the course of a lifetime, you will accrue much positive karma in the sphere of finances. Your generosity will return to you many times over. The law of karma is exact. And because you are a service-oriented, altruistic soul, you are bound to receive much in return for your continued and committed service.

Much of your good karma is bound to reach you in the form of financial rewards. One way or another, you are likely to be financially self-sufficient, even if not ostentatiously wealthy. In fact, it is highly unlikely you will be ostentatiously wealthy, because ostentation and show are so antithetical to your self-effacing nature. Even if you have a lot of money, no one would know it. And you may even forget about the numbers in the bank, because ultimately, it really is unimportant to you.

You also like to give as much as you can to help others. You will do this with your time, your energy, your feelings, your listening ear, your understanding, and your financial resources. The universe abundantly returns all that you give, even if not by the person to whom you gave, so you feel an invisible energy supporting you as you go through life. While it is unlikely that you will be wealthy to an extreme, most Virgos plan well, and keep their expenditures low. Money tends to come into the Virgo bank account in small portions rather than large amounts. Virgo's natural flow of energy is refined and focused on the small elements rather than on the big picture. As a result, money flows to you in the same manner. You may derive your income from a collection of sources rather than one large benefactor. This is a reflection of the careful, piece-oriented, detail-directed vision of Virgo. It is your nature to look at life as a series of components rather than as a panorama. Consequently, life presents itself to you in parts rather than as a whole. You may have noticed that you can feel overwhelmed if too much information comes to you at one time. You would prefer to receive nearly everything, be it food, guests, information, or gifts, one at a time rather than in a large quantity. The same applies to money, whose role in your life is a reflection of the way that you think.

If the flow of money through your life is not satisfactory to you, visualize abundance. Surround your image in golden light. Release your light-filled image to the universe and allow the universe to respond in the way that is in the highest good of all concerned. Try not to imagine the details. By trying to anticipate exactly how the abundance will come, you may limit the potential avenues of its arrival. Allow the universe to be infinitely creative with you. It will teach you a lot about the infinite creativity that naturally resides within you!

CAREER

Your highly efficient mind makes you well suited for virtually any career. You have strong administrative, organizational, and managerial skills. You flourish in an office setting. Your good memory and incisive mind make you a good editor or writer, secretary, mechanic or electrician, computer programmer or technician, gardener or landscape designer, forest ranger or architect, librarian or scientist, researcher or executive. Your interest in health, your intuitive healing abilities, and your natural compassion and empathy make you an excellent doctor, nurse, healer, counselor, or psychologist. You have a natural sense emanating from your soul that you should contribute to charitable causes or be of service to others. This natural instinct toward giving service should be followed in any endeavor you pursue.

Having a job or a career is an important component of the Virgo life. Part of the reason you incarnated as an earth sign is so that you would have a natural affinity for work. You have strong endurance, concentration, and ambition. You are a clear thinker. You have integrity and honesty. You care that a job is done properly, efficiently, and on time. These are all excellent qualities for success in nearly any career.

There are no challenges in the realm of work for the Virgo soul, because you genuinely *like* to work, whether at home or in an office, in a school or in a store, in a restaurant, in nature, or even in a car. You have *all* of the ingredients required for success. So, once you have an idea of what you would like to do, step back, gain perspective, decide what you need to do, make a list either mentally, electronically, or on a piece of paper … and you are ready to prosper!

♎ LIBRA (September 23–October 23)

♎ LIBRA (September 23–October 23)

PERSONALITY PROFILE

Libra is a cardinal, air sign symbolized by the scales of justice. Your key motivations are relationships, harmony, and balance. Your outstanding attributes are fairness, equanimity, loving kindness, understanding, compassion, a peace-loving nature, and an ability to mediate conflict.
Your karmic challenge involves asserting your truth even if you feel it may alienate another, experiencing the way in which honesty brings greater harmony.
Libra rules the kidneys and sacral spine.
Venus rules the constellation of Libra.
Libra is associated with Aphrodite in Greek myth and Venus in Roman myth.
Libra is associated with the color orange, the navel/sacral chakra, and the reproductive glands.
Best Day: Friday
Best Number: 6
Healing Gemstone: Opal, Carnelian, Orange Calcite

You are adept at harmonizing, balancing, and creating fairness in everything you are involved in, be it a relationship, a legal agreement, or a work of art. In fact, a relationship is a precious work of art to you. And it is meant to last a lifetime, as far as you are concerned. You would not think of doing anything to upset the balance in a relationship. Others deeply appreciate your tact, diplomacy, ability to see situations from their point of view, and your desire to preserve peace. You will even sacrifice yourself in order to preserve harmony.

So, it is difficult for you to understand why anyone would upset the delicate balance you conscientiously create—which they occasionally do. The truth is that there may be a reason why a person upset the status quo—or no reason at all. Few other signs of the Zodiac, unless they have a Libra Moon, Libra Ascendant, or a number of other planets in Libra, are able to see the importance of preserving peace and harmony as clearly as you. Or, if they understand the importance of preserving peace, they cannot see how to do it. This is why so many people marvel at your grace under pressure, your advanced skills in negotiation and compromise, and your ability to finesse an agreement without ruffling feathers.

You are so adept at harmonizing in relationships because you are able to see situations from many points of view and put another person ahead of yourself. You can imagine how another person feels. You can put your needs aside. And you can act on behalf of the other person. These are precious and rare qualities. To you, balancing with others is the meaning of life. To act selfishly or in one's own interests is contrary to your personality, and contrary to the reason for your existence. It is hard for you to understand why some people act from their own limited point of view because you see things from so many points of view. Your ability to be so all-inclusive is why everyone wants to be your friend. There is no one better with whom to be in partnership. As a result, you have developed a high degree of discrimination. While *everyone* can have a harmonious rapport with you, not everyone can have an intimate relationship with you, from your point of view.

You are happiest with fellow Librans or fellow air signs Gemini and Aquarius because they share your non-attached perspective and give you the emotional, mental, and physical space you need. Fire sign Aries, which is your complementary opposite on the Zodiac wheel, also is an obvious choice as a partner because you so naturally balance with your opposite. Fire signs Sagittarius and Leo also please your harmony-loving nature because the heat of the fiery Sagittarian and Leo balances the cool quality of your airy nature. Earth signs Taurus, Capricorn, and Virgo make excellent partners in work because of their common sense and dependability. You are less likely to feel warmed by the earthy nature of their make-up, however. The water signs Cancer, Scorpio, and Pisces bring greater emotional energy to your daily experience. You may not completely understand the emotional depths of these water signs. But your airy nature enables you to accept their feeling nature and maintain appropriate distance.

You also are fastidious about your environment, preferring cleanliness and order to disorganization and chaos. Your nervous system is highly sensitive and easily jangled by loud noise, disruptive behavior, or inappropriate intrusions into your space. You tend to favor white because of its purity and harmonizing effect upon your nervous system. You also may like white because it reflects all colors—a democratic concept quite appealing to you.

You incarnated as a Libra because of your soul's desire to harmonize in relationships, aesthetics, and art. You may have come from a past life that lacked harmony, leaving you with a strong desire to establish a peaceful environment. Or, you have had a long incarnational history of harmonious relationships and surroundings. You desired to continue that pattern.

Your challenge, therefore, is to adapt not only in the sphere of relationships and situations so that they run smoothly, but to adapt in relationships and situations when they do not run smoothly. Despite your best efforts, you may not be able to bring harmony to inharmonious situations. Witness peacemaking past President Jimmy Carter, a Libra. Try as he might, he could not negotiate peace with his staunchest foes. And sometimes his efforts to engender peace created more problems because he was seen as too changeable, adaptable, or even soft. Again, your peace-loving nature is a precious quality. But the harsh realities of the world do not always accommodate your peace-loving temperament. In fact, the harsh realities of the world may run rampant over your peace-loving nature.

The antidote to being a peace-loving soul in a war-loving world is to emanate peace into your environment through the waves of your thoughts, prayers, and affirmations. Feel the peace within you. Allow this feeling to emanate from you and harmonize with others. You will find others who agree with and support your loving motives. Like-minded others may be fewer than you would like. But when you find others who have relationship standards as high as you own, you will form precious bonds that will last a lifetime.

One of your challenges is to manage the periods of change, transition, and imbalance that inevitably visit every life. Like the in- and out-breath of God, your fortunes will naturally go up and down. Planetary influences also create inharmonious patterns that you must harmonize with. And vestiges of your own karma may attract situations to you that may polish the rough spots of your personality the way the oceans erodes stone. Even with the harmonious qualities you possess, there inevitably are rough spots that can be worn down through unbalancing situations. There is a higher reason for events that do not proceed in a harmonious fashion.

You often imagine how things should be, at least in an ideal world. And when you think you are right, you know you are right, and there can be no one more rigid. This is where the eroding and polishing quality of disruptive circumstances can be so enlivening for you. Difficult, but ultimately empowering to you because these disruptive circumstances broaden your perspective, teach you about alternatives, and erode any remaining rigidities in your personality. Unbalancing circumstances bring to the fore qualities in need of healing, which otherwise would have remained buried beneath a harmonious exterior.

Like the scales for which your sign is named, when perfect balance is achieved, even a slight gust of wind can unbalance the previously balanced scale—and that is when previously buried aspects of your personality gain freedom to surface. While this may initially feel unsettling, the moments of imbalance allow the greatest truth to surface for healing, expression, and rebalance.

You have been balanced many times, and you will be balanced once again. But in the meantime, accept that a little imbalance is inevitable due to the nature of the world. And imbalance is beneficial to bring out beautiful qualities and strengths that are hidden below your surface—in addition to bringing out the ability to accept the perpetual imbalance in the balance of it all.

PERSONAL GROWTH

You do not like to make an enemy. Sometimes this seemingly good quality prevents you from speaking your truth. You will lean one way, then the other, hoping the conflict will resolve itself before you commit to a viewpoint. Often this strategy works. But making a commitment to what you stand for is an equally important strategy. Try to balance between avoiding conflict, and actually creating greater conflict by not expressing yourself earlier in the game. You are learning that a relationship can exist even if two people do not agree. In fact, a relationship can become stronger as two diverging parties become more confident individuals and as each develops trust that the relationship will continue after the disagreement is openly aired.

It is difficult for you to tolerate conflict nonetheless, either within yourself, with another person, or among people around you. It is as if conflict represents the epitome of darkness, which ultimately it does not. Conflict may be the necessary precursor to the synthesis and balance you so crave. Allow yourself to confront conflict through the peaceful means that come so naturally to you. Embrace the shadow in yourself and others. By showering light and love on disowned aspects of yourself and others, you actually dissolve the power of the shadow elements and bring peace and harmony to yourself and your relationships.

RELATIONSHIPS

Libra, the Sign of the Scales, is located at the exact midpoint of the Zodiac wheel. The astrological year begins at the spring equinox in the sign of Aries when the light of day begins to overtake the dark of night. It is time to plant the seeds. The astrological calendar culminates six months later at the autumn equinox in the sign of Libra. It is the harvest season when the moments of dark begin to overtake the light of day. Under the influence of Libra, the products of the earth are collected, weighed, and measured before the earth rebalances itself to prepare for spring.

Libra's journey is a reflection of the finely tuned balance constantly unfolding in nature. You bring well-honed balancing skills to the art of relationship. Libra represents the point at which the psychological orientation of the entire Zodiac turns away from preoccupation with the self to preoccupation with others. This inclination begins with Libra and grows in the next five signs. Libras want to have a relationship with another human being. Scorpios want to have a relationship with the subconscious depths of the human psyche. Sagittarians want to have a relationship with a higher philosophy of life, which ultimately leads to Spirit. Capricorns want to have a relationship with accomplishments in the world. Aquarians wants to relate to a global human family. And Pisceans seek a relationship with the infinite or the Divine.

Of course, one has to have a Self in order to relate to others. Libra represents the perfect balance possible in a relationship between two fully integrated, balanced, and harmonious beings. The delicate Sign of the Scales is masterful at creating boundaries around him- or herself, so he or she may remain objective and balanced in relating to other human beings. This enables both beings to maintain their individualities without being subsumed by the other, while the two individuals function as a team. Whereas the first five signs of the Zodiac tend to see the world through their own individual lens without being able to compensate for the view of another, the last five signs lean toward seeing the world through the eyes of another, rather than their own.

Libra is a master of equal partnerships. This comes from the Libran's ability to simultaneously stand in his or her own reality while simultaneously seeing the truth of another. The ability to balance between two diverse views, represented by the Sign of the Scales, is the magic that helps so many Libras maintain relationships over time.

Yet, the challenge still remains for many Librans to maintain their sensitive balance in the face of myriad demands from another person. While you have a good sense of your own values and direction, you also can get a sore lower back because you are prone to bending to accommodate others. Assert yourself so you and your partner can recalibrate and create a true balance that is fair and equal. This is the key to ongoing contentment in your relationship life.

Libra and Libra

You and fellow cardinal, air sign Libra create a relationship that is a model of equality, balance, peace, and harmony. You have a democratic partnership where each has equal say, and you take turns accommodating the other. Each partner tries to balance with and support the other. It is more important to both of you to be fair than to have your way. It may be virtually impossible to fight in this relationship. You eternally want to please the other. This is a relationship that others admire. Yet, where there is light, there is shadow. The shadow of your relationship may be that you and your Libra partner suppress authentic aspects of yourselves to preserve what you perceive as harmony. If you are holding aspects of yourself in check, ask yourself—and your partner—if the price of peace and harmony is worth the price of suppression. Your relationship may become even more vibrant when you freely express *all* of who you are. This is a relationship you both will cherish for a very long time.

Libra and Scorpio

Libra and fixed, water sign Scorpio are the two most relationship-oriented signs of the Zodiac. Yet, you have different styles of creating intimate relationships. You approach intimate partnership with objectivity and balance. Scorpio approaches intimate partnership with intense passion and feeling. Scorpio believes a relationship is real if feelings, passions, and flaws are revealed so the relationship may exist in a raw state of authenticity that disrupts the status quo, and brings hidden feelings to the surface. Libra believes a relationship is real if feelings, passions, and flaws are transcended so the relationship may exist in an atmosphere of peace and harmony. Many Librans and Scorpios are drawn together as partners, existing in a tense balance between Libra's pristine notion of an ideal relationship of equality, fairness, peace, and harmony, and Scorpio's unvarnished notion of two bodies, minds, and souls intertwined in a deep, passionate, transformational, potentially messy, merging union. You both seek matrimonial bliss, but you must understand you have *very* different definitions of what constitutes marital harmony.

Libra and Sagittarius

You appreciate the candor, wit, and humor of mutable, fire sign Sagittarius. Sagittarius appreciates your fine taste, elegance, and calm demeanor. You rely upon the can-do spirit of your Sagittarius mate to help you overcome obstacles you prefer to avoid. Sagittarius cherishes your graceful, demure charm. Sagittarius is driven to speak the truth. You are skilled at framing your partner's truth in a diplomatic way so others can hear what he or she has to say. In a professional relationship, you accomplish positive change without ruffling feathers. In a personal relationship, you share a refined, peaceful home and many cultural and artistic activities in the outside world. Your shared sensibilities and values support each other's continual growth.

Libra and Capricorn

You appreciate the hard-working, dedicated, conscientious outlook of cardinal, earth sign Capricorn. Capricorn appreciates your poise, balance, and sense of fairness. Capricorn and Libra have a strong sense of justice and you both want to do the right thing. You are excellent business partners, and share a mutual respect for systems, hierarchy, protocol, and procedure. But where is the fun in a romantic relationship? While both Capricorn and Libra have the ability to conduct a fair and equitable relationship, neither sign possesses a naturally romantic inclination toward the other, as if the mutual respect, deference, and formality that reigns in the business aspect of the partnership precludes a relaxed, flowing affair of the heart.

Libra and Aquarius

You appreciate the forward-thinking, egalitarian values of fixed, air sign Aquarius. Aquarius understands your need for secure personal boundaries to sustain your balanced and precise objectivity. Your Aquarius partner gives you plenty of space to express yourself. You value your Aquarius partner's detached perspective, and will do anything to help Aquarius pursue his or her ideas. You have shared values, and can endlessly debate the merits of any argument—without allowing personal feelings to interfere. Aquarius may be more interested in affairs of the world, and you may be more interested in the interaction between the two of you. You both are patient, objective people who can easily stand back from your own needs to meet the needs of your partner. It is likely you will settle any disagreement with a solution that is the utmost in fairness, and take turns meeting the needs of the other. This is a model relationship.

Libra and Pisces

You appreciate mutable, water sign Pisces' compassionate, flexible, accommodating approach to relationship. You are a peace-loving soul who does not allow small problems to overwhelm an otherwise harmonious relationship. You and Pisces have a solid foundation of shared relationship values upon which to build. You both respect the right of the other to pursue a unique path to happiness, and you each do your part to support your partner's path. Yet, you have quite different ways of approaching life. You are a cerebral person who values detachment, objectivity, and perspective. Pisces has a mature perspective that enables him or her to detach, but Pisces is not a detached person. Pisceans easily empathize with others, and feel their feelings as their own. You are an emotionally dispassionate person who transcends your feelings to create harmony in your life. You may either feel overwhelmed by the emotional intensity of Pisces, or you will welcome the challenge to deepen your own relationship to your feelings. To create balance in this otherwise harmonious relationship, open yourself to experience the emotional depth of Pisces, and ask Pisces to seek alternative ways to express the feelings so innate in his or her nature if you feel overwhelmed. Despite the mismatch in emotional intensity, this is a relationship you both cherish.

Libra and Aries

You are deeply moved by the passion and definite goals of cardinal, fire sign Aries. Aries is passionately drawn to your elegance and grace. Aries sees you as a peaceful, refined, harmonious soul who can balance Aries sometimes-uncontainable energy. You and Aries are polar opposites on the Zodiac wheel. In nature, Aries is the sign that initiates planting at the spring equinox, and Libra is the sign that initiates the harvest at the fall equinox. You both were born in the moments, days, or weeks after the light of day and night were equal. The light was growing under Aries, and diminishing under Libra. Together, you feel a kind of synthesis that transcends mortal form, and connects you to a greater cycle of nature. The Sign of the Ram knows how to light the fire that initiates the relationship, and the Sign of the Scales knows how to create balance, peace, and harmony as the relationship unfolds. Your life purpose is to balance opposites, and a relationship with Aries will make you feel you have found your purpose. While Aries may have a short attention span, this is a relationship that will hold Aries' attention for life. You each have much to learn from the other, and the balance will come from learning to incorporate a few shades of the other into your own repertoire.

Libra and Taurus

You appreciate the artistic flair and culinary skills of fixed, earth sign Taurus. Taurus appreciates your fine, aesthetic sensibilities. According to traditional astrology, airy Libra does not easily harmonize with earthy Taurus, but many Libra and Taurus souls are drawn together by a mutual love of peace, harmony, and beauty. You cherish peace and harmony in your relationship and Taurus relishes stability and predictability in his or her physical environment. If each partner prevails in the domain in which he or she specializes, this is a relationship that will bring much happiness to both partners, and all who share in their lives.

Libra and Gemini

You appreciate the intelligence and verbal versatility of mutable, air sign Gemini. Gemini sees you as a pinnacle of balance, harmony, and elegance. Libra is expert at creating a harmonious relationship, and Gemini is expert at gathering information. You are attracted to each other for the scintillating conversation and constant banter this relationship produces. You never tire of each other, and you likely feel you have found your soul mate. This is a harmonious relationship in which each has much to teach the other. You settle and organize Gemini's restless nature with your mature perspective and stability, and teach Gemini the art of balance in relationship. Gemini's far-reaching intellect provides you a wealth of information about any subject you choose, giving you the data you need to arrive at balanced judgments and precise conclusions. If you are looking for a relationship that will never bore you, Gemini is the answer to your prayers.

Libra and Cancer

You admire the domestic flair, home-loving and nurturing qualities of cardinal, water sign Cancer. Cancer appreciates your demure elegance and grace. You each are considerate of the sensitivities of the other. You respect Cancer's need for security and predictability. Cancer respects your need for peace and harmony in your relationship and your aesthetically pleasing environment. You share similar values. But you may be worlds away in the realm of feelings. Cancer reacts to every feeling and sensation, and gives abundant attention to this level of perception. You transcend feelings and sensations in favor of a non-attached mental perspective that leads to rational judgment based on objective principles. You enjoy the nurturing side of Cancer, but the emotional needs of the Sign of the Crab may puzzle you. Still, your calm, cerebral nature soothes the Cancer soul, and helps Cancer maintain emotional perspective. If your Cancer partner can tolerate the emotional distance you may require, this is a relationship that could last a lifetime. If you feel overwhelmed by the emotional needs of others, you may consider a more casual repartee with a sensitive native of the Sign of the Crab.

Libra and Leo

You are captivated by the dramatic flair of fixed, fire sign Leo. Leo is impressed with your elegance and grace. You moderate Leo's fiery exuberance, and Leo awakens passion in you. You will never run out of creative ideas in this harmonious relationship. Sun-ruled Leo and Venus-ruled Libra never tire of supporting each other. You boost the ego of your Leo partner as you patiently listen to his or her endless tales of his or her life. Your feel positively regal as your Leo partner sings your praises and tells you how much you are needed for the positive role you play. The Leo's fire warms your cool, detached, airy nature, and your air settles the Leo's intense fire. Your Leo partner gives you a stable center around which to orient your life.

Libra and Virgo

Libra and Virgo, a mutable, earth sign, have plenty of common ground upon which to build a harmonious relationship. You and

Virgo are considerate, thoughtful, polite, and friendly. You appreciate the fine sensitivities of the other. Yet, rarely do your refined signs enter into intimate partnership. It may be that Libra and Virgo shy away from a steady diet of the other due to lack of innate understanding of each one's basic motivations. Virgo is work-oriented and attracted to circumstances in need of repair. Libra is relationship-oriented and attracted to circumstances filled with harmony. Libra may misunderstand Virgo's penchant for details. And Virgo may despair at Libra's inability to understand that tending to details is the Virgo's way of showing love! Conversely, Virgo may not understand Libra's objective perspective, thinking the Libra is emotionally cool. And Libra may despair at Virgo's inability to understand that this is Libra's way of building a harmonious relationship. Whereas Virgo is compelled to act on subjective opinions, Libra prefers to act on objective principles. Virgo and Libra may come to the same conclusion, but Virgo forms its opinions through close, detailed analysis of fact, and Libra renders judgment through non-attached consideration of principles. If you and Libra understand each has a slightly different but complementary approach, you will experience a level of peace and harmony that both treasure.

Libra, whomever you choose as a relationship partner, it is certain that you will create peace and harmony. Make sure when you enter a long-term partnership that you feel love for your partner in your heart rather than mentally pulled to the challenge of harmonizing and balancing with your potential partner. No doubt, you will be successful at creating peace and harmony. But first, feel your heart, and make sure your head is following your heart rather than your heart following your head. You are an attractive mate who will have no shortage of prospective partners. Carefully weigh your relationship decisions. They could be the most important decisions of your life.

SPIRITUALITY

For you, spiritual experiences will come through embracing the light—and shadow—in all situations. Shadow is not easy for you to accept because it runs counter to your pure and straightforward nature. Yet, the integration of the polar opposites of light and dark will help you make sense of your earthly sojourn, the shadow side of which has not entirely pleased you. You see disharmony, unfairness, poverty, and lack. And you cry to God, "Why do You allow such disharmony to persist?"

Why would a God who is fair and just permit such chaos? This is a complex spiritual question. It is a question for which there are many answers. And it is a question whose answer you ought to consider pursuing to enhance your spiritual evolution. One answer is that God is light that created darkness to enable seekers to see His light. The darkness is theoretically necessary to turn seekers toward light. For without the darkness, there would be no ability to perceive light. Even this answer may seem quixotic. "Still," you may think, "why do people have to suffer?" Many scriptures explain that suffering is the result of disharmonious actions performed by an individual or group in the past. Many other answers to this question lie within nearly every religion, and you will feel happy when you come to terms with some of the conclusions others have drawn.

Ultimately, you are learning to love that which seems distasteful to you. This spiritual lesson will prove to be one of the greatest challenges you surmount—and the one that will deepen your commitment to the spiritual spark that lies within you. Without this reckoning, you may find yourself feeling a bit agnostic. In other words, you may feel that either there is no God, or if there is one, He may not be someone you want to relate to. As your most important relationship may be the one you develop with your own soul, a deepening of your relationship with your Creator may also be a critical part of this process. A deeper relationship to the Divine, and to the Divine spark in you, will lead you to more meaningful and harmonious relationships with other people and with the Divine spark in them.

Given that the basic motivation of your life is to perfect relationships, the most worthwhile endeavor will be to deepen your relationship to your soul. You can access this "still small voice" within you through quiet contemplation, relaxation, creativity, writing, or meditation. Anything that helps you contact and express your natural rhythm. As a Libra, you naturally adapt to the needs and feelings of others, and you fastidiously follow the rules, which comes from the association of Libra with the Scales of Justice. As a result, you may favor conformity over creativity. The quality of free and liberal self-expression is the antidote to a soul laced by the strictures of society and the demands of other human beings ... and it may be the path to your own spirituality. Relax every once in a while, tune in to what you really want, and follow your course with *élan*!

HEALTH

Libra rules the kidneys and the lower back, and these are the most sensitive areas of your body—sensitive to any disharmony in your inner life or external environment. As you become more comfortable with the state of disharmony and chaos that necessarily precedes a period of greater order, you will more easily accept disruptions in yourself, other people, and your environment. This acceptance will lead to more vigorous physical, mental, and emotional health. In the meantime, however, there are many things you can do on a physical level to protect your lower spine.

Visualize healing light and energy circulating through your lower back. Surround the vertebrae and disks with an image of golden, pink, and blue light and a feeling of love. Imagine each vertebra lifting to the heavens, creating greater space for the vertebrae below. Imagine a cushion of pink and blue light enveloping each vertebra, protecting each one from impact and inflammation. Imagine golden light encircling your spine. Feel a soothing sensation replace stress or tightness.

Exercise & Food

You also may bring harmony to your lower back through gentle exercise and stretching. Create greater space between the vertebrae in your lower spine as you lie on the floor and pull your knees to your chest, being mindful of stretching the muscles in your lower back only to the extent comfortable. Then, try to stretch your hamstrings, the long muscles that run down the back of your legs. These muscles are intimately connected to the flexibility of your spine. You can stretch your hamstrings by extending your legs along the floor and reaching for your toes. Do not force yourself to go beyond your natural limits. You gradually will be able to stretch farther over time. You also will find if you hold a position without forcing, your muscles will naturally relax and lengthen within 60 seconds. You also may consider stretching your hamstrings by lifting one leg at time. Place the heel of the foot of your extended leg on a higher surface, either a chair, box, or bed. Reach for your toes as you gently stretch your lower back and legs. Hold this position as long as is comfortable, or until your hamstrings release. Also consider stretching the muscles that run along the inside of your legs. These muscles connect to tendons and ligaments that hold your pelvis in place. By opening the muscles around the pelvic region, you will allow this significant foundation of your spine to naturally rest in a healthy position.

Finally, consider a regular practice of yoga. This ancient system of exercise rejuvenates your body, mind, and soul. It is designed to open the energy meridians flowing through your body to allow greater spiritual energy to flow unobstructed through your nervous system, musculature, circulatory system, glands, and organs. This rhythmic, balanced system of spiritual and physical exercises will bring greater peace to your physical body, mind, and emotions.

Another important way to energize your kidneys is through diet. You can do this by balancing your sugar and salt intake. Sugar is expansive and salt is contractive. Both enhance energy levels if taken in proportion to each other. Some medical texts caution against over-imbibing in salt. However, salt is rich in minerals and trace minerals, and is essential to the body's ability to absorb minerals and vitamins from other foods. Salt also is necessary to counterbalance sugar.

Thus, on any given day, if you have one, you may want to balance by having the other. Seaweed and sea salt are excellent sources of minerals for the Libran body.

Flower Essences

Flower essences, which are distillations of the high vibrations in flowers, also will help you. The flower essence Nicotiana balances the energy of your heart with the strength in your physical body. Lotus helps to bring the energy of spirituality into your physical body. Calla Lily helps to balance male and female energies.

FINANCES

You have a multi-faceted relationship to money. You are able to balance your spending with your income. You can balance a checkbook and a budget. But do you like this? Noooooo. You have an eye for elegance and a taste for excellence. You dislike the constraints placed on you by money. You will do *anything* to avoid these limitations. I do not mean *anything* in the sense that you will break the law. But you will pray, bargain, barter, exchange, or work to attain the objects of your desire, which often are objects of beauty, art, or ways of beautifying yourself or the ones you love.

You dislike the disequilibrium poverty brings, and you will likely do everything in your power to avoid anything close to entering an impoverished state. You are a hard worker and a clear thinker. You have a pleasant personality that is easy for others to get along with. Consequently, you should have no trouble attracting people and circumstances that support your financial prosperity. Greater abundance will come, of course, if you give more to others, which you already know. You have likely put your bigheartedness into action many times. You are a highly idealistic and altruistic soul. Your have put your ideals into practice, and due to the laws of karma, whose justice is exact, you receive in return as much as you give. Thus, it is highly likely that the abundance you experience is a reflection of generosity you have expressed in the past. Continue to express your abundant magnanimity and the warmth of your heart, and more of the same will come back to you.

CAREER

Many avenues of endeavor appeal to your industrious, hard working, clear thinking nature. You are an excellent entrepreneur because it is easy for you to see how to fit your business ideas with the needs of others. You are a brilliant negotiator, mediator, and arbitrator. You build harmony through understanding, communication, and compromise. Of course, you have an innate sense of the law, justice, and impartiality. Therefore, you are naturally attracted to being a lawyer, legal professor, or judge. You also possess refined communications skills, enabling you to excel in the fields of writing, journalism, public relations, marketing, advertising, and public speaking. You have bright insights into the human character, which make you an excellent counselor, marriage and family therapist, psychologist, or healer.

You feel best when you bring harmony to disharmonious situations. This is a quality that is greatly needed in all spheres of life—from personal to professional. Nurture this precious peace-making quality in yourself. And share your gifts and insights with others. Your words of wisdom will help many people. You will receive thanks, gratitude, and appreciation from others for many years to come.

♏ SCORPIO (October 24–November 21)

♏ SCORPIO (October 24–November 21)

PERSONALITY PROFILE

Scorpio is a fixed, water sign symbolized by the phoenix, the scorpion, and the eagle.
Your key motivations are deep psychic exploration, discovery of hidden information, understanding deeper levels of yourself and others for self-protection and transformation, deep relationships, and creating a cycle of death, rebirth, and renewal in all areas of life.
Your outstanding attributes are depth, intensity, passion, perceptivity, patience, power of recuperation, and perseverance.
Your karmic challenge is to balance between extremes of silence versus zealous investigation to unearth the truth and use this information to heal yourself and others.
Scorpio rules the organs of reproduction and elimination.
Scorpio is associated with Hades in Greek myth and Pluto in Roman myth, god of the underworld.
Mars and Pluto rule the constellation of Scorpio.
Scorpio is related to the color red, the root chakra, and the adrenal glands.
Best Day: Tuesday
Best Number: 9
Healing Gemstones: Obsidian, Onyx

Ancient Hindu scriptures portray God in three roles—*Brahma*, the creator, *Vishnu*, the preserver, and *Shiva*, the destroyer. Each role is equally important in the scheme of creation. One aspect of God creates the world, another aspect preserves the world, and a third aspect of God destroys the world to usher in a higher order.

Scorpio is the *Shiva* of the Zodiac. The Sign of the Scorpion rules death, and ultimately rebirth on a higher level. Like *Shiva*, Scorpio's acts of destruction are directed at destroying physical, emotional, mental, and spiritual blocks—virtually anything that is worn-out and no longer serving a higher purpose. Under Scorpio, the prevailing order is upset to reformulate the bonds of the old in a new way. It is a law of physics that the highest order is created from the greatest disorder. Scorpio follows Libra, the Sign of the Scales, and unbalances the balance established in the previous sign. Scorpio engenders the cleansing that precedes new acts of creation, and many Scorpios feel a sense of impending emptiness and anticipation of what is to be born from the unknown.

Scorpio also is known as the Sign of the Eagle, because the scorpion transforms itself into an eagle through the alchemical process of death and rebirth. Death and rebirth are symbolic of the psychological process of self-discovery that leads to a letting go of the false Self for the progressive rebirth of the true Self—the soul. The scorpion gains the truth of eternity in the process and then soars like the eagle. Scorpio also is known as a phoenix, the mythological bird that rose to great heights from its own ashes. The ashes are the remains of the false Self or ego that must die before the spiritual aspirant can emerge in a meaningful way, ready to undertake a spiritual quest, symbolically initiated under the subsequent constellation, Sagittarius, the Sign of the Archer.

Scorpio's mythological counterpart is Hades, god of the underworld. Hades ruled his empire with an eye toward extracting gold from the souls who entered his realm, symbolically bringing the riches hidden in every individual to the fore. Everyone comes away from an encounter with Hades in changed form. This is the gift of the Scorpio soul. No one, including the Scorpio him- or herself, comes away from contact with the god of the underworld without being changed. The process of change can be painful, as many Scorpios attest. The process involves peeling away the ego to allow soul energy to emerge. The end result is beautiful, and worth the painful process of death, rebirth, and renewal so familiar to the Scorpio soul.

As a water sign, Scorpio works through the medium of feeling. Scorpio forms an energetic bridge between the conscious and subconscious minds, enabling the Scorpio to interpret the actions and reactions of itself and other people through feelings. This is why people with the Sun or Moon in Scorpio, or Scorpio Rising, make such brilliant counselors and psychotherapists. Yet, why do Scorpios have a reputation for a biting sting? The Scorpio stings when he or she is not sufficiently aware of the power of his or her own subconscious feelings, and these feelings rise up and overpower the Scorpio's conscious mind. A gentle sting without the poison of Scorpio's subconscious can prod a person to look into his or her dark side, or shadow, to heal its contents through the light of awareness. A vicious sting loaded with the poison of the subconscious mind, on the other hand, can kill an opponent when this may not have been the Scorpio's intention.

Scorpio is a mysterious sign, even to itself—and the issue of the sting can be among the most quixotic mysteries of the Scorpio psyche. The Scorpio sting accompanies a surge of passionate feelings. These emotions may be love or anger, even though a Scorpio's sting does not feel much like a gesture of love when one receives it. Even though the Scorpio native has tremendous power of self-control, he or she may not consistently be able to control actions engendered by feelings, and a Scorpio may initiate a stinging action, word, or even look, at a time when he or she may not consciously wish to emote this way. This is the greatest contradiction in the Scorpio's behavioral repertoire—the Scorpio native may deliver a sting in the course of trying to receive love, attention, reassurance to assuage insecure feelings, or an indication that he or she will not be abandoned. The power behind the Scorpio's sting builds as Scorpio's emotional needs mount. For a Scorpio, the sting may be part of the relationship, a way to test a partner's loyalty and endurance, or a way to explore a person's reactions. A Scorpio wants to make sure that his or her partner will stay in the mating game—no matter what. If the person stays after the sting, the Scorpio feels he or she will be eternally loved and never abandoned. If the person leaves, however, this proves the Scorpio's deepest underlying fear that he or she will be abandoned. In an effort to protect him- or herself from abandonment, Scorpios create the scenario they so vehemently wish to avoid. Either the Scorpio is abandoned because a partner wants to evade a future sting, or if the partner stays, the inflicted wounds may raise a host of dysfunctional future patterns, most notably sado-masochism, revenge, retribution, hurt, mistrust, and fear of betrayal.

Does the Scorpio's psychological game become so complex that it turns against the Scorpio? This is a question that every Scorpio must ask him- or herself. When does the psychological intrigue stop? When does the effort to protect oneself from hurt turn into one's undoing? When does psychological exploration turn into psychological destruction? And how can the incisive sting be used to create psychological gain rather than turmoil?

A gentle, non-emotionally fierce sting can actually help another person—or the Scorpio him- or herself—heal a psychological complex. The Scorpio may help a person realize a hidden truth or courageously face a difficult insight. Scorpio's goal is to unearth—and have others look at—buried information. A Scorpio's penetrating insight can be enormously revealing to a person in the moment, or in the future, as part of a healing process. Yet, the intensity of the Scorpio's "gentle" nudge can overwhelm a person. This is not the intention of the Scorpio soul. Scorpios simply do not know their own power. Nor do Scorpios fully comprehend how other people perceive—or do not perceive—darkness. Darkness is glaring in the eyes of the Scorpio native because he or she is so sensitive to subconscious material and so fascinated by its power (the subconscious mind is labeled as dark because it is a repository of thoughts, memories, and feelings of which a person is unaware). Other signs, however, feel rather distant from the perceptions that daily (and nightly) haunt the Scorpio's mind. Thus, the Scorpio's perception of darkness may be out of proportion with other people's perception of its size, gravity, and intensity. Not that the darkness is not there. Yet, its perceived importance is greater to a Scorpio, because as a soul, Scorpio has chosen to penetrate his or her own psychological mysteries, as well as those of other people, as part of the healing process.

Attention to the dark side is the primary role assigned to Scorpio in the natural cosmic order. God creates the world in the first seven signs just as He symbolically created the world in seven days. On the symbolic eighth day, God destroyed those aspects of His Creation that were no longer working. Scorpio is the eighth sign of the 12 signs of the Zodiac. Therefore, the job of eliminating the unworkable aspects of God's Creation falls to the Scorpio soul. The astrological cycle begins with the planting of the seeds under the constellation of Aries and culminates with the harvest under the seventh sign of Libra. Next, the earth orbits through the eighth sign of Scorpio. Under Scorpio's influence, the remnants of the harvest begin to decompose to clear the way for new growth in the spring. Scorpio initiates the clean-up that culminates at the 12th sign of Pisces, when the land lays fallow, awaiting the arrival of spring when planting begins anew. On a psychological level, Scorpio also forms the bridge between the orientation toward personal relationships in Libra and the expanded consciousness of the subsequent five constellations of the Zodiac. Libra wants to relate to the outer person whereas Scorpio wants to relate to the inner person as the last step of mastery before surrendering the ego to a quest for the Divine, which begins in the ninth sign of Sagittarius.

An ancient myth aptly illustrates the reasons for Scorpio's commitment to plumbing the depths of the psyche as a last act before moving into the light. Scorpio and Virgo were one constellation in ancient times, but they were fighting—Scorpio championed the dark while Virgo championed the light. Neither exists alone in this world of light and shadow. Each side needs the other, but Virgo and Scorpio could not agree on the need for both to co-exist harmoniously. Eventually, Libra came between the two to restore peace and harmony. In the separation, Virgo took a proclivity for light, and Scorpio took a penchant for shadow. Ever since, Virgos are gifted with an enormous capacity for purity with an equally strong disdain for shadow. This has left Virgos with the karmic imperative of loving and accepting the darkness within themselves and others. Conversely, Scorpios have a nearly insatiable appetite for awareness of hidden truths (also known as the shadow or darkness) with a commensurate fear of the power of light to expose the true Self. As if the power of light could break the power of Scorpio's strong will, a Scorpio may resist the light of awareness if his or her ego feels threatened. Scorpio's relationship to light gives the Scorpio the karmic imperative of allowing the light of awareness to illumine the true Self without feeling the light will undermine his or her power. The method involves struggling with the lower nature so it can be brought to consciousness rather than repressed in the subconscious. This can be done through self-confrontation, honesty, and embracing all sides of yourself.

The more perilous route to self-discovery, often embraced by the Scorpio in lieu of psychological confrontation, is the path of challenging, life-threatening, death-defying experiences that throw you into such a state of imbalance that repressed feelings, memories, and thoughts are forced to surface. (Not all subconscious thoughts, memories, and feelings are bad. Some may be beneficial, and may have been repressed at an earlier stage of life or time in social evolution when a talent, skill, behavior, or memory was perceived as unacceptable.) The path of challenging, or even death-defying, experiences is pursued by many Scorpio souls who want to learn about their hidden resources and simultaneously test their limits. Both methods—self-confrontation or life-challenging experiences—

lead to consciousness of repressed thoughts, feelings, and memories. Many Scorpios choose a combination of both methods, and through evolution, follow the path of wisdom (self-analysis) over the path of experience (entering life-threatening experiences either consciously or subconsciously). Thus, the powerful energy stored in the lower chakras—the *kundalini* energy coiled at the base of the spine—is transmuted and transferred to the higher chakras. The lower chakras include the base of the spine, the navel-sexual center and the solar plexus. The higher chakras include the heart, throat, brow, and crown. Part of the journey of every Scorpio soul involves becoming conscious of the powerful energies stored in the lower centers of the body, including sexual energy, anger, rage, strong appetites and desires, to transmute these energies into a higher state of consciousness more closely aligned with your soul. Symbolically, the lower centers are the scorpion, and the higher centers are the eagle. It is part of the journey of every Scorpio soul to transform from a scorpion to an eagle, over and over again.

PERSONAL GROWTH

More than any other sign, Scorpio has the ability to rise to marvelous heights or sink to the deepest depths. You have a strong will that can be used to build empires or to destroy what has been built. When you set your sights on a goal, no one is more determined, driven, focused, or concentrated. But, when your desires are thwarted or when you do not have an outlet for your enormous power, or you feel things are not going the right way, no one can be more obsessive or destroy him- or herself more quickly. Consciousness is the best, and probably only, tool to help you rise to the heights for which you were created. For you, consciousness includes developing powers of perspective, objectivity, and the willingness to let go when it is no longer possible to exert your will.

One of the greatest gifts you possess is your accurate emotional barometer. Of the three water signs, Cancer, Scorpio, and Pisces, you represent the bridge between the conscious and subconscious minds. Each sign of the Zodiac wheel represents consciousness as it evolves from the self-oriented sign of Aries to the other-oriented sign of Pisces. Similarly, the water signs undergo an evolution in feeling that begins with the self-referential feelings of Cancer. Cancer's emotional awareness is limited to feelings recorded by the conscious mind, particularly relating to physical comforts in the immediate environment. Awareness of feelings expands in Scorpio to encompass subconscious feelings and their roots. Feeling extends in Pisces from the subconscious to the superconscious. Pisceans are aware of feelings emanating from others, while sometimes remaining less aware of their own feelings. That is why Pisces may be labeled as a "cold fish." It's not that Pisceans are not feeling. In fact, Pisceans are compassionate and feel *everything*. Pisces people feel so much that they sometimes shut out the barrage of feelings they perceive, and appear cold, when they are quite the opposite. So, each of the water signs has a particular way of navigating the mysterious realms of feelings, and yours is through creating a bridge between the conscious and subconscious minds.

As a result of your expertise in linking the conscious and subconscious realms, you are highly adept at navigating the psychological depths of yourself and others. Many Scorpios are brilliant counselors, psychotherapists, psychologists, psychiatrists, shamans, or healers. Even Scorpios who do not engage in one of these professions are highly skilled in understanding deeper levels of human motivation and feeling. Do not be surprised if psychological awareness is one of your main motivations.

If you do not engage in some sort of psychological exploration or growth, you run the risk of turning your abundant supply of psychological energy on yourself or on others close to you. If not properly expressed, Scorpio's powerful drive for psychological exploration and growth may turn into psychological mind games or power struggles within yourself, with other people, with the "system," or with society itself. This is one job hazard of the Scorpio mind. It is a powerful force seeking an outlet. When the proper channel has been found, Scorpios bravely undergo the alchemical process of turning the lead of the personality into the gold of the soul. Scorpios also can brilliantly guide other souls into their own depths, so light of awareness may illumine the subconscious for healing and transformation. Improperly channeled, Scorpio's energy can degenerate into self-immolation or non-productive struggles.

Ultimately, your challenge is to find a way to express your powerful drive for self-knowledge and understanding of others so it creates a spark of light rather than a fire.

RELATIONSHIPS

Think about the behavior of the scorpion, the creature for which the Sign of Scorpio is named, to understand your relationship patterns. Scorpions engage in an elaborate mating dance as part of their regenerative cycle. Their reproduction begins when the female scorpion woos her partner with an elaborate mating dance. Once the scorpion couple mates to produce their offspring, the female emits a sticky substance that traps her partner so she can destroy him. A fight to the death ensues. Sometimes the male escapes, and sometimes he does not. At the very least, both partners are injured. All this in the act of procreation! For Scorpios, there is a thin line between life and death, creation and destruction, love and hate. If you get one, you get the other.

So goes the relationship dance of the average Scorpio. Scorpio is a sign that can manifest as the scorpion or the eagle. A conscious Scorpio is the eagle. He or she can muster all of his or her considerable strength and bring tremendous quantities of love and light to heal him- or herself and others. An unconscious Scorpio is the scorpion. He or she is equally powerful, but powerless to control the considerable forces working through his or her psyche. Thus, without conscious control, the Scorpio may channel large quantities of energy through the subconscious, which is the repository of unresolved complexes that have yet to be neutralized by the light of awareness. In theory, light is equated with self-awareness. Lack of light is equated with lack of self-awareness. Self-awareness comes with honestly confronting oneself about one's true feelings, motives, and qualities. The greatest light comes to those who are aware of the totality of who they are from many perspectives and are aware of the possibility of channeling this energy in a positive way. The determination to align with love, hope, generosity, and kindness in a relationship is crucial to creating the conscious and constructive relationship you deeply crave.

How do potential relationship partners perceive you? You appear strong, independent, alluring, magnetic, and sexual—and you are, but on the inside you are a steaming cauldron of feeling waiting to be shared. Underneath, you are vulnerable, dependent, and seeking emotional security. You desperately want a relationship in which you can share all of your deep feelings and profound insights. You deeply crave someone with whom you can penetrate the deepest reaches of your heart, psyche, and soul. You want a partner who is interesting, complex, and even contradictory. That combination is sure to give you plenty of material for exploration—and the possibility for mutual transformation through the alchemical process of relating.

Volumes could be written about Scorpio in relationship. Scorpio is a sign intimately drawn to the experience of merging two souls to become one. This is a process that is possible through the medium of relationship. Scorpio is the bridge between the everyday functional level of relationship perfected in the preceding sign of Libra and the spiritual quest initiated by the following sign of Sagittarius. Scorpio represents the level of relationship that transcends mundane ways of relating and moves closer to a relationship with the Divine, in which one loses oneself as one merges with Spirit.

A relationship with a Scorpio is bound to be extraordinary in one way or another. A conscious Scorpio relationship will alchemically transform the psychological depths of both parties. A conscious Scorpio relationship is cleansing and purifying. An unconscious Scorpio relationship is a sticky story. Remember the mating dance of our friends the scorpions? An unconscious relationship with a Scorpio can resemble the death struggle engaged in by the scorpion couple. "Why," you ask, "would two people be willing to risk a struggle to the death in the course of having a relationship?" Remember the *Shiva* energy? It has to go somewhere. If the destructive energy is consciously channeled, it will destroy the unworkable and re-create anew. If unconsciously channeled, the powerful energy wreaks havoc on the participants. It is like nuclear energy. It can power a business or community, or it can destroy, depending upon the inclination of the user. So it is with the power of Scorpio.

Also note that while psychological awareness is a key to the higher functioning eagle level of the Scorpio, a Scorpio's psychological sensitivity may interfere with the Scorpio's ability to enjoy a relationship because he or she perceives feelings so intensely. While an emotion that the Scorpio detects on his or her radar screen may be accurate, it also may be exaggerated. Herein lies one of the keys to negotiating peace in a Scorpio relationship—perspective. "Yes, you are right, but the degree to which you are perceiving this infraction is not in proportion to reality."

As a result of psychological sensitivities, Scorpio souls may carry deep psychological wounds within themselves. As souls, Scorpios possess deep healing powers to cope with inner trauma. Often healing comes through relationship because deep relationships unearth buried feelings, some of which have been held in check since childhood—or past lives. Relationships also give Scorpios the security they need to feel and express pain. The ability to feel what is already there, held in the subconscious, is an aspect of relationship that alleviates enormous pressure on the Scorpio psyche.

One of the deepest feelings nurtured in the secret depths of every Scorpio is the feeling or fear of being abandoned. The fear of abandonment and the experience of having been abandoned lead to a host of psychological complexes that lay dormant in many Scorpio psyches. The feelings range from a general sense of mistrust to a sense of betrayal, and in extreme cases, paranoia. This sense stems from a deep desire to love and be loved, eternally, endlessly, and merged as one with another individual. While the intensity and passion of this natural feeling is probably more appropriately applied to a relationship with the Divine, many Scorpios try to create this experience through the vehicle of human relationship. And it simply does not work to the degree that the Scorpio soul desires. The result can be a rallying of the destructive urges if the disappointment in human relationship is not transmuted into an equally strong drive to unite with the Divine. This struggle is the linchpin of every Scorpio psyche, the bridge that needs to be crossed to transmute the urge to merge with a human love object to merge with the love of the Divine.

Very often, Scorpios seek to fulfill a deep yearning to merge by pursuing the act of sexual union. Many Scorpios have abundantly strong sex urges and bodies that reflect this desire with a concentration of energy in the lower body. Depending upon whether the Scorpio expresses, represses, or transmutes the energy, he or she has either an extraordinarily thin and agile—or heavy and rigid—pelvic region. If this energy is accessed and transmuted to higher centers, the Scorpio native experiences high states of spiritual consciousness. If repressed, the Scorpio feels fatigued or depleted because a vital resource is not accessible. (It also takes quite a bit of energy to hold in this energy.) If expressed through sexuality, the Scorpio native finds he or she has enormous reserves of sexual energy beyond the average person. Ultimately, this sexual energy best serves the Scorpio if at least some of it is channeled to higher centers in the heart, throat, brow, and crown.

How do you channel pooled energy at the base of the spine to higher centers of awareness? Sit quietly with a straight spine and palms facing the heavens. Breathe in from the base of the spine. Imagine golden light and energy ascending up your spine to the crown of your head. Breathe out as the golden light descends down the front of your body, circling back to reconnect with the base of your spine. Your energy has natural intelligence. As you consciously breathe, you draw in magnetic currents from Mother Earth that heal and balance your energy in your lower spine. As you breathe out, you release negativity and pull highly charged energy from the heavens into your glands and nervous system. The circuit of earthly and heavenly energy circulating through your body balances the natural sexual currents stored in the base of the spine with your intense longing to merge with Spirit. Gradually, this balance translates into your relationships, giving you greater perspective and an ability to manage constructive and destructive urges naturally roaming every psyche. Constructive and destructive urges may be particularly emphasized—in both directions—in your psyche.

In relationships, you may face complex issues because you may perceive a relationship partner not as a separate individual, but as an extension of yourself. This is where relationships can be so tricky for you. Your initial intention in entering intimate relationships is pure. You want to love another person. You want to give. You want to help. You want to heal. You want companionship. You really do. But if the desire to merge with a human love object—and the ensuring fear of abandonment—enter the partnership, the result is a love-hate relationship that may manifest as a desire to control a partner (to keep the partner close or push the partner away, depending upon the level of one's fear at a given moment), a desire to manipulate (again, to achieve the desired level of intimacy), a desire to consume a partner (to imbibe all of the positive characteristics in case they leave, or insure they will not be able to leave), or a desire to destroy a partner (also to insure they will not be able to leave, and ultimately achieve the highest level of control over another). This is a possible path of the unconscious Scorpio until he or she becomes conscious of his or her true motivation—union with the Divine. When the conscious Scorpio realizes this is what he or she is truly seeking through the passionate depths of relationship, he or she will be able to unite with the Divine and bring the loving splendor of the Divine to all partners and friends. Thus, the only antidote to the Scorpio mating dance is a four-letter word: LOVE. The absence of an abundance of love in a relationship will create misery due to the psychological complexes that are easily constellated with a lack of love—power struggles, psychological manipulation, control, deception, harmful actions, and ultimately hurt feelings on both sides.

In addition to expressing unselfish love in as many ways as possible, there are several other strategies for orchestrating a fulfilling, healthy, and successful relationship. Try to be as direct as possible. Your natural tendency is to be indirect to avoid a confrontation in which you might be hurt. Direct, honest, candid statements to a partner are the best antidotes to a psyche that fears being hurt. Your honesty will not only help you feel you are safe to express who you are, but your candor will give your partner a greater sense of security that he or she knows who you really are—and that he or she can also express the truth of who he or she is. If you feel hurt, ask a question rather than make an accusation. Given your tendency to accurately perceive the truth, but potentially out of proportion to reality, check with the other person before harboring a resentful feeling. Your tendency is to either loudly point a finger of blame—or say absolutely nothing, holding in your pain about an unconfirmed perception, which embitters you. Ask questions! Begin with "Is it possible that …?" or "Did I correctly understand, or did I misinterpret?" State your case, but also have an open mind to the other person's truth. Be aware that you may be raising an issue about which your partner has no awareness because you tend to be more psychologically perceptive than many other people. Explain your perception. Try to be patient if the other person professes ignorance. They may be truly innocent. Explain that you will let go of doubt, but if the situation arises again, you would like an open line of communication to raise the subject. Secure a promise that the topic is one that you can openly discuss in the future. This will help you feel you do not have to bury feelings, and it will raise the person's awareness of what they may have been doing, of which they previously were unaware. Finally, consider accepting a relationship based upon healthy boundaries of two people operating side-by-side at a workable distance. Practice open dialogue, boundaries, distance, and perspective with another conscious person, or with a person who loves you and is willing to work toward a conscious relationship. You both will soar to heights known by the scorpion transformed into an eagle.

The best signs with whom to engage in a healthy mating dance are fellow water signs Cancer, Pisces, and fellow Scorpios because they share your emotional sensitivities. Scorpios also are strongly attracted to Taurus, the opposite sign on the Zodiac wheel. Both Scorpio and Taurus have strong passions and desires that they may express through mutual physical attraction and activities. Both share a desire for security, Scorpio for emotional security, and Taurus for material security. Together, both can establish a firm foundation for an enduring, stable relationship. Due to their emotional sensitivities and fear of being abandoned, Scorpios tend to distrust many people who move too quickly for them to clearly read. This assessment would apply to fire signs Aries, Leo, and Sagittarius. Still, many Scorpios feel a strong attraction to the forthright and aggressive manner of Aries and Leo, and Scorpios appreciate the spiritual inclination and optimism of Sagittarians. Earth signs Virgo and Capricorn make good working partners for Scorpios, and can be strong relationship partners if they share mutual goals. Although Scorpio is attracted to the sparkling wit and sharp minds of air signs Gemini, Libra, and Aquarius, air signs' emotional detachment may frustrate Scorpio's sensitive, emotional nature.

Scorpio and Scorpio

With a fellow Scorpio, you may feel as if someone finally understands you. You talk about deep, intimate feelings and your partner meets you with equally deep revelations. You present a conundrum you cannot fathom, and your introspective partner provides a searching analysis that enables you to solve the mystery. You each understand and respect the quirks of the other. And moods are not a problem. In fact, they are an opportunity for greater exploration of each other and the relationship. A relationship between two conscious Scorpios who take responsibility for expressing and understanding their feelings will positively and profoundly transform each partner. An unconscious relationship between two Scorpios can be equally as powerful, but in a less constructive way.

Scorpio and Sagittarius

You are fascinated by the optimism and spirituality of mutable, fire sign Sagittarius. Sagittarius appreciates your focused intensity, and your ability to listen and understand the subtle and not-so-subtle ramifications of his or her words. Your piercing eyes give Sagittarius a sense of being understood. Sagittarius' boundless faith and confidence enable you to relax and trust the natural flow of the universe. You may try things you never considered before in this adventurous relationship. Sagittarius has much to teach you about how to use positive intentions to create positive results. You have much to teach Sagittarius about calculating consequences to bring greater success to his or her creative endeavors.

Scorpio and Capricorn

A relationship between you and cardinal, earth sign Capricorn is bound to provide what you are looking for in the realm of relationship. You appreciate Capricorn's hard working, ambitious approach to life. Capricorn appreciates your strategic style and penetrating insight. You support each other to get ahead in ways that are mutually beneficial. You and Capricorn feel comfortably united in a partnership that could last a lifetime. You may only experience discord when you do not share a similar point of view. You are both willful individuals who like to prevail. When you disagree, your confrontations may be intense. But you feel it is a small price to pay to be with someone who understands you so well.

Scorpio and Aquarius

A relationship between Scorpio and Aquarius, a fixed, air sign, could leave you feeling a bit deprived in the emotional department. You will delight in Aquarius' *avant-garde* ideas, keen insights, and relaxed attitude. Aquarius will marvel at your depth and perceptivity. But Aquarius will not engage in deep, emotional jousting with you. This situation could lead to power struggles, in which you try to engage your Aquarius partner. It is probable the Aquarian will avoid confrontation, leading to further frustration on your part. You may not feel safe to expose your emotional depth in this relationship. You and Aquarius may share many creative, business, or intellectual ideas. But you may not satisfy many of each other's needs on an intimate level. This relationship does not ultimately create harmony, even if it appears complacent at first. Over time, the divergent needs of the two signs—Scorpio for in-depth awareness of the Self and the relationship, and Aquarius for expanded consciousness of the world—pulls you and Aquarius in two directions. A stable middle ground is difficult to maintain.

Scorpio and Pisces

You resonate with the emotional depths of mutable, water sign Pisces. Scorpio and Pisces experience intense feelings and reactions that originate from deeply subconscious levels. If both signs are aware of the role that the subconscious mind plays in relationship, this partnership could stimulate plentiful psychological growth. If the subconscious realms are ignored, and both pretend they are playing house, subterranean feelings may churn under the surface and erupt when least expected. Efforts to develop greater self-awareness will help you avoid misunderstanding. A conscious relationship between Pisces and Scorpio is romantically, sexually, and emotionally transformational.

Scorpio and Aries

You are magnetically attracted to cardinal, fire sign Aries like a tennis player in search of a partner. Your Aries partner is equally as enthusiastic about joining the game. Aries and Scorpio are not compatible according to traditional astrology. But a surprising number of Aries team up with Scorpio, perhaps for the repartee the tense combination creates. Scorpio and Aries enjoy jousting with a partner the way two puppies enjoy a little tussle now and then. A steady diet of harmony bores both the Sign of the Ram and the Sign of the Scorpion, and this partnership offers a competent opponent for each. Emotional depth is achieved through fighting in this relationship. Closeness is created through discord rather than harmony. But if you ask any Aries or Scorpio in partnership, they will tell you they honestly do love each other. This relationship does not model a conventional form of love. But for Aries and Scorpio, this is true love.

Scorpio and Taurus

The sign exactly opposite Scorpio on the Zodiac wheel is fixed, earth sign Taurus. Opposites attract. Yet, opposites are opposite. You are an intense, profound water sign who wants to penetrate deeply below the surface of a story. In contrast, Taurus thinks the surface is the entire story. Taurus and Scorpio transform each other in an intimate partnership. Scorpio helps Taurus acknowledge significant factors lying below the surface, and Taurus helps Scorpio surface from deep-sea diving to enjoy life on dry land. Neither sign will permanently inhabit the realm of the other, but exposure to Scorpio's watery realms of mystery and emotion brings a world of new perspectives to Taurus, just as a respite on simple, dry land does Scorpio a world of good.

Scorpio and Gemini

A relationship between Scorpio and Gemini may be intellectually and emotionally intense as Scorpio tries to elicit emotional reactions from mutable, air sign Gemini, and Gemini tries to elicit rational intellectualizations from Scorpio. Both parties may be successful in eliciting what they are looking for in the other, but at what price? It may be uncomfortable for both of you to be yourself in this relationship as both parties try to elicit something unnatural from the other. You may agree to establish a harmonious home life, and you may be successful at that. Yet, there may be little in the way of compatible communication between you two.

Scorpio and Cancer

A relationship with cardinal, water sign Cancer creates a healing matrix for you to express your feelings. Cancer is a nurturing, sensitive, emotional soul who seeks emotional understanding and solace. Scorpio to the rescue! You also are a sensitive, emotional soul who feels vulnerable unless you are with someone who feels more vulnerable than you do. Welcome to a successful relationship with a receptive Cancer soul. You feel you have finally found someone with whom you can share your passionate, emotional depths. Whereas other signs may flee from your emotional intensity, Cancer relishes the experience of someone who feels as much as he or she does. You both feel over-exposed in the harsh light of the world, and seek refuge in the womb-like ambiance this relationship creates. This relationship will soothe the tattered emotional nerves of Cancer and

Scorpio. Provided you remain sympathetic and emotionally supportive of each other, this is a relationship that could last a lifetime. If either of you use your emotional depths to create entanglements with the other, you may at times feel overwhelmed by too much feeling. Practice moderation, even in emotional sharing, so you may create a relationship balanced between feeling and the practical realities of functioning in the world.

Scorpio and Leo

Strong-willed Leo and strong-willed Scorpio make an unlikely pair in traditional astrology. But this combination can be found with striking frequency among long-married couples. Leo, a fixed, fire sign, traditionally does not mix easily with the fixed, water sign of Scorpio. Yet, the strength exuded by both signs creates a magnetic attraction that Leo and Scorpio feel powerless to resist. Leo is magnanimous, generous, and magnetic in an outward way. Scorpio is intense, deep, and magnetic in an inner way. These magnetic souls create a force field that perpetually draws the two together, even if not in the most harmonious manner. Despite any disharmony engendered by this magnetic duo, mutual attraction and loyalty, or possibly the potential of winning a struggle with the other, seems to magnetically draw the two together over and over again.

Scorpio and Virgo

Scorpio and mutable, earth sign Virgo were once eternally linked as one constellation in the heavens. To this day, Virgo and Scorpio are magnetically drawn to the mystery of the other. Virgo wants to understand the Scorpio's relationship to its psychological shadow. Scorpio wants to understand Virgo's relationship to purity and perfection. Both want to become intensely close to the other, but the intensity of each sign's relationship to the quality in which it specializes, also pull the two apart. Virgo may become overwhelmed with the intensity of Scorpio's fascination with psychological shadow material. And Scorpio may feel overexposed by the purity and perfectionism of Virgo's approach. Both need to encompass the qualities of the other. The integration may be done in the relationship, or on one's own. But ultimately, wholeness is achieved for Virgo and Scorpio by embracing light and shadow.

Scorpio and Libra

Scorpio and cardinal, air sign Libra are the two most relationship-oriented signs on the Zodiac wheel. Yet, you have very different styles of creating intimate relationships. Scorpio approaches intimate partnership with intense passion and feeling. Libra approaches intimate partnership with objectivity and balance. Scorpio believes a relationship is real if feelings, passions, and flaws are revealed so the relationship may exist in a raw state of authenticity that disrupts the status quo, and brings hidden feelings to the surface. Libra believes a relationship is real if feelings, passions, and flaws are transcended so the relationship may exist in an atmosphere of peace and harmony. Many Librans and Scorpios are drawn together as partners, existing in a tense balance between Libra's pristine notion of an ideal relationship of equality, fairness, peace, and harmony, minus the interruption of emotional and mental discord, and Scorpio's unvarnished notion of two bodies, minds, and souls intertwined in a deep, passionate, transformational, potentially messy, merging union. You both seek matrimonial bliss, but you must understand you have *very* different definitions of matrimonial bliss.

Scorpio craves emotional exploration so strongly that emotional contact with any sign is a potentially positive learning experience. Just make sure your partner, no matter what their sign, reads this section on relationships so he or she better understands you—and the relationship the two of you have the potential to create!

SPIRITUALITY

Spirituality is not the easiest avenue for you to pursue. Not that you are not a spiritual soul. You are. In fact, you are a highly spiritual soul. But you are so naturally inclined to psychological awareness of yourself and others, and to alchemical transformation of yourself through psychological work and emotional intimacy, how do you have time for spirituality?

Just as the Zodiac wheel turns from Scorpio to Sagittarius, stronger spiritual desires will evolve in you. Psychological exploration is a precursor to spiritual awareness, and this is a methodical progression of which you are intimately aware. How can you surrender yourself to Spirit if you do not have a Self to surrender? You are deeply committed to solving the mysteries of your own psyche and soul before you surrender to a spiritual path.

It is highly likely that you have pursued a number of intimate relationships or encountered a number of highly challenging or even life-threatening experiences. This is part of the karmic path you have chosen to learn the limits of your strength and power to regenerate yourself as a phoenix rises from its ashes. Chances are good that you have attracted at least one death-defying experience on a physical, emotional, mental, or spiritual level. If a cat has nine lives, a Scorpio has many more. After you have recovered from a sufficient number of symbolic near-death experiences, you probably will begin to seek a more predictable path—or at least one that subjects you to fewer ups and downs. When you realize you are practically powerless to alter your psychological predisposition to attract challenging experiences, you will turn to Spirit for assistance, and perhaps, stability. As you go along the spiritual path, you will turn your strong will and desires to the heavens, and due to your strong resolve, you will be as successful in discovering spiritual enlightenment as you were in surmounting material challenges you attracted to test yourself. Simply be prepared for a transition period as you surrender your strong personal will to the will of the Creator. The transition to a spiritual path will require you to release your attachment to your ideas, visions, plans, and strategies. While this is not always a smooth transition, your transformational energies will ensure the shift.

In the Tarot, this stretch of your spiritual journey correlates with the "Hanged Man," the 12th of 22 cards in the Major Arcana of the Tarot. The Hanged Man is pinned upside down on the cross of matter with his feet facing heaven and his head dangling toward earth. Symbolically, this represents the idea that your feet are rooted in Spirit, but your head is peaking down on Earth. Your conscious awareness is directed "up there." But your sense perceptions are "down here." As you relinquish your curiosity about the level of Creation around your physical body in favor of devotion to the invisible realms above, you will return to divine form as the "Hanged Man" does in the next 10 cards of the Tarot. The Tarot is a pictorial synthesis of ancient spiritual wisdom contained in diverse spiritual traditions and illustrates the fall of man and the return to the Divine.

HEALTH

You have the strongest recuperative powers of any sign of the Zodiac. But you also have the greatest ability to bring yourself down. You are a person of extremes who feels that if you do it, do it big. Your definition of big may know no boundaries, initially, as you test your strength to recover from the challenges you present yourself. You are so strong that you want to see where your strength leads you, and where your strength ends. Not one to respect boundaries, you often manifest extreme conditions in your body that give you a chance to completely regenerate—to test your mettle. It is as if you want to show others—and yourself—that you are no mere human and can perform superhuman feats. You often transcend challenges that other mere mortals succumb to. But occasionally you take on a challenge that overpowers you. This is when you step back and retreat into your emotions, lick your wounds, and regenerate your spirit in preparation for the next challenge.

The most vulnerable parts of your body are your organs of regeneration and elimination. Scorpio rules the root of the spine and all functions emanating from the base of the body. Scorpio also is associated with the sexual energy coiled at the base of the spine, known as *kundalini* in Hindu texts. *Kundalini* energy is often strong in the Scorpio native, and is progressively transmuted to higher centers. In the meantime, however, Scorpios will find that their greatest strength—and their greatest nemesis—lies at the base of the spine. You store tremendous strength and recuperative powers in this area of your body. But you also may store unresolved emotional issues, sexual issues, repressed energies, anger, or frustration in the same place. As a Scorpio, it is important to address this energy. Bring the light of consciousness to this seemingly mysterious part of the body. Become aware of the mysteries that lie within you. Release energetic or sexual blocks. Allow the precious life force pooled at the base of your spine to flow in a free, healing, and transformational way. You can do this through gentle movement of the pelvis, followed by meditation on the lower centers of the body. Imagine old energy leaving as healing golden light enters the base of your spine.

Exercises and Food

Yoga promotes the smooth flow of energy through your body. You benefit from yoga that moves energy through the lower chakras, particularly *kundalini* yoga, which combines exercises of the spinal column with breathing practices that infuse oxygen into the system. Vigorous exercise may be periodically necessary to move pent-up energy through your system.

Red-colored foods such as peppers, tomatoes, strawberries, beets, and paprika promote warmth and circulation in your body. Blue, white, or off-white foods, and whole grains such as rice or millet, or fruits such as blueberries or figs, will cool and calm you. Your system tends to run to extremes, so you may need a combination of both.

Flower Essences

Flower essences, which are distillations of the high vibrations in flowers, also will help you. Lavender soothes overstimulated nerves. Nicotiana helps you express feelings when you are projecting a false sense of calm that masks real feelings. White Chestnut helps calm ceaseless churning of the mind, and Agrimony helps release hidden inner conflict.

FINANCES

You are a strategic thinker who has excellent intuition. You are an astute investor and investment strategist, and you have a flair for making resources go farther than they appear they should. You have a sixth sense in the stock market, commodity markets, and banking. You also have a well-earned good reputation as a financial consultant and advisor. Your good eye for investments for others comes from your accurate perceptions of people's needs and your ability to devise plans to match needs with financial instruments and psychological strategies.

You also have a strong potential to inherit money from a relative, a friend, or even from people you do not expect. Scorpio's karma, whether you have a Scorpio Sun, Scorpio Moon, or Scorpio Rising, often attracts money from sources other than one's own labor. Therefore, be aware that you may work hard and earn positive karma. But money may still come to you through other people.

As a Scorpio, you may be personally rich or poor. No matter what your financial status, you are savvy, resourceful, and perceptive. You are a survivor. As a result, you can spot a strategic way out of nearly any financial situation. Despite any adversity you may face, you are like a cat with many more than nine lives—and you always land on your feet.

CAREER

You have a naturally steadfast personality that will lead to success in any endeavor you set your mind on. Your primary gifts are your incisive intuition about human emotions and thought, your ability to think strategically, your ability to probe beneath the surface to obtain otherwise inaccessible information, and your ability to deliver perceptive counsel that provides valuable insight.

The myriad skills that help you penetrate life's mysteries and reach a profound level of understanding are assets in many fields of service, including psychological research, analysis, and counseling, police and detective work, financial planning and consulting, troubleshooting in technology-based businesses, and consulting in any business that requires a profound understanding of mechanisms operating beneath the surface. It is interesting to note that more United States Presidents have been Scorpios, or have had a Scorpio Moon or Scorpio Rising than any other sign. Scorpio's strength, stamina, and stealth, enhance a person's ability to fill a prominent role and simultaneously please diverse constituencies.

Your ability to solve mysteries also qualifies you as the Sherlock Holmes of any business you enter. If there is a puzzle you will put it together. If there is a secret, you will discover it. Not one to let competitors outdo you, you are attracted to competitive businesses and sports and usually are the victor of any contest. Your penchant for strategic thinking also makes you an ace in formulating a plan for starting, reinvigorating or revamping a business, raising venture capital, fundraising, and budgeting or reallocation of resources. You can be a little shy about advertising or promoting yourself, but you have a keen eye for spotting talent in others, and you are not shy about hiring a fire sign like Leo, Aries, or Sagittarius to promote your business for you. You have no shortage of ideas, no shortage of endurance, no shortage of willpower, and no fear of the darker side of life, including sickness, crime, or death. This is an excellent combination for success in business, legal affairs, law enforcement, healing, and hospice work. You also have an excellent sense of timing and an eye for opportunity. You will be successful at implementing any strategy you embrace.

♐ SAGITTARIUS
(November 22–December 21)

♐ SAGITTARIUS (November 22–December 21)

PERSONALITY PROFILE

Sagittarius is a mutable, fire sign symbolized by the archer or centaur.
Your key motivations are exploration, travel, adventure, learning, spirituality, philosophy, seeking the truth, understanding, and unlimited possibilities.
Your outstanding attributes are warmth, generosity, honesty, and optimism.
Your karmic challenge involves balancing idealism with reality, and enthusiasm with limitations.
Sagittarius rules the thighs, liver, and gall bladder.
Sagittarius is associated with Zeus in Greek myth and Jupiter in Roman myth.
Jupiter rules the constellation of Sagittarius.
Sagittarius is associated with the color indigo, the third eye chakra, and the pineal gland.
Best Day: Thursday
Best Number: 3
Healing Gemstones: Lapis Lazuli, Sapphire, Sodalite

Sagittarius is the sign so adept at making lemonade out of lemons that potential obstacles seem like growth opportunities to your optimistic soul. This is true if you were born under the Sagittarius Sun, Sagittarius Moon, or with Sagittarius Rising. You are innately aware that the rhythm of life is perfect as it is. You see perfection even in the imperfect, and this helps you make peace with almost any situation. You are a seeker who perpetually asks, "Why?" Yet, underlying your question is the assumption that things are meant to be the way they are. Your seemingly boundless faith attracts positive circumstances to you that not only confirm your core belief that everything will be okay, but confirm that everything already is okay. You generally believe that the universe is good, and you struggle with anything that disproves this perception. You often conclude, as did Candide in the play by Voltaire, that all is for the best in the best of all possible worlds. Your accepting attitude gives you a perennial sense of contentment that attracts harmonious circumstances to you.

You assume everything will take care of itself. This attitude enables life circumstances to follow your vision. A proverbial light bulb joke aptly explains your nature—"How many Sagittarians does it take to change a light bulb?" The answer is—"None. The sun is shining, the day is young, we have our whole lives ahead of us, and you are inside worrying about a stupid light bulb? It will take care of itself!" And it usually does. This is the allure of the Sagittarian personality. The sheer strength of your belief that everything will be okay creates an electromagnetic field that attracts the positive people and circumstances you need, making you practically impervious to the ups and downs that affect others.

The optimistic archetype associated with Jupiter, your planetary ruler, explains the lucky star that shines on you. No matter how bad things get, you always find a solution. As explained above, your faith attracts positive circumstances. But where does this faith come from? Let's look at Jupiter, the planet with which Sagittarius is aligned. Jupiter is the Roman name for Zeus, who was the ruler of Mt. Olympus in Greek myth. Armed with a positive outlook, Zeus traveled the world seeking adventure. He found plenty of people and places to explore. Even in adversity, he escaped unharmed and wiser as a result of his experience. His eternal belief in the power of Spirit protected him from downfall. So it is with you. Your natural belief that the Divine is protecting you provides a shield of protection not available to others who do not hold your steadfast belief in Spirit. The accumulated experience of invincibility gives you faith in the limitless possibilities of the Divine—and the divinity in you.

Your strong belief that the Divine is in partnership with you creates a thought-based electromagnetic shield around you that gives you a sense of security few others experience. People marvel at your willingness to take risks they would not. You do so because you not only believe—you know—everything will be okay. One way or another, it always has been. Why have any doubt? You possess a natural wellspring of trust, and at the risk of being too repetitive, this is the reason the universe mirrors your positive expectations to you.

Your boundless faith may cause others to call you naïve. You may scale back your expectations to allow greater leeway for the limits of time and space. But even if your do, your faith in the power of the Infinite may help you surmount obstacles that others face, enabling you to accomplish feats others could not. This could involve moving more quickly, thinking more expansively, or receiving the right phone call at the right moment to provide exactly what you need.

You have an excellent sense of timing, and an ability to move more quickly than time—in many, but not all, circumstances. How do you know when your "magic" powers are going to work, and when they are not? This is something you may never know because your power comes from a realm beyond your control. You may open yourself to receive this power, but you may never control how quickly or strongly it will come. The rhythm of your life is partly determined by karma (cause and effect) based on actions from your past, and from your past lives. The rhythm of your life also is determined by your relationship to the Divine, which involves surrender. If you always could count on this power, you might feel the power *is* you rather than coming *through* you. If the Divine hides from you periodically, not only will you appreciate His presence when it arrives, but you will remember once again that you live in a reality proscribed by time and space. The solution is to calculate for traditional time and space—and hope for better.

You also naturally possess a strong mind. When a person's mind is strong, he or she has great power to project his or her thoughts. The universe responds by giving everyone what he or she expects. If they expect good, good they shall have. If they expect negative, well, unfortunately, that comes too. Your natural assumption that all is okay makes it so. Combine this with a powerful mind to send positive thoughts. Circumstances are bound to align in your favor, time, after time, after time.

Additionally, you have strong visual abilities. The subconscious mind easily responds to visual images, enabling a greater part of your mind to support your conscious thoughts. If you think a thought, and a subconscious visual image accompanies the thought, your conscious and subconscious minds are working together. Add your faith in divinity, which activates your spiritual superconscious mind, aligning with your subconscious and conscious minds, your soul, and Spirit. This powerful combination will force spiritual, mental, emotional, and physical energies to align with your thoughts.

Your ability to coordinate thoughts with visual images is a gift you may cultivate with increased concentration. You may already rely on this talent to create positive results. This talent is akin to prayer with the added dimension of a visual image. Try the following exercise to strengthen your natural visual abilities. Visualize what you would like to create. Surround your vision with golden light. Project this image along a beam of purple-blue light naturally emanating from your third eye, at the center of your forehead. Surrender your vision to the wisdom of the universe. Pray for its highest fulfillment. Have faith in the universal wisdom. Be patient as the universe responds. And receive the fruits of your prayer with gratitude. As you feel grateful, a universal channel opens to increase the supply of the quality for which you expressed gratitude.

As you gain greater experience manifesting your visualizations in the outer world, you also become adept at manifesting visualizations that pertain to your inner world. See if you can manifest greater calm, peace, contentment, satisfaction, and joy. These are spiritual qualities that naturally reside within you. Use your powers of visualization to re-kindle the memory of the spiritual bliss of your soul. Your sign is so highly connected to your soul and spiritual memory, you will feel positive energy every time you invoke these impressions.

The Zodiac symbol for Sagittarius says a lot about your life. The centaur is a mythological half-man, half-horse. The centaur—with the upper body of a man and the lower body of a horse—is the only sign of the Zodiac that does not have a counterpart in the physical world. The centaur is the stuff of imagination and myth. Most Sagittarians also have active imaginations, and you see your life as a mythic quest for experience, discovery, and wisdom. You love travel, exploration, and adventure. Your repeated success at venturing off the beaten path has emboldened you to seek unusual experiences. It is likely you have traveled many places or are highly educated about places that lie beyond your own back yard. And if it has been physically impossible to travel, you will travel in your mind, seeking answers through spirituality, philosophy, literature, or even a newspaper.

You also identify with the deeper symbolism of the character whose human upper body represents the dominance of the mind over the senses, represented by the lower body of the horse. You respect the equine characteristics of speed, strength, courage, and love of freedom, symbolically the lower half of your nature. Yet, you understand the need to rein in these powerful instincts with the abundant wisdom of your spiritual mind and soul.

Reawakening your divine memory while in a physical body is part of the reason you incarnated with a Sagittarius Sun, Sagittarius Moon, or Sagittarius Rising. You are seeking meaning for your physical incarnation. You are a little like Dorothy in *The Wizard of Oz* who traveled to Oz to find "there is no place like home." The answer she was seeking was in her own back yard. Similarly, your quest will show you that the divinity you are seeking has always been within you. After a period of spiritual seeking that may involve travel, adventure, exploration, reading, and study, you will discover that by sitting quietly and *listening to yourself,* you will find the answers you have been seeking in books, religion, sacred places, and sacred journeys. All of these are excellent tools to awaken Divine memory. But remember these are simply tools to help you find what has always been in you. When you sit still and take a break from what may feel like ceaseless seeking, you will discover the "still small voice" within. This is your Divine birthright waiting to be recovered.

PERSONAL GROWTH

There is no one more honest than a Sagittarian. You may be honest to a fault in that you give voice to your thoughts before thinking of their potential effect. While there are virtually no circumstances in which one can be *too* honest, it also is important to think about the reaction of the person who hears your message so you may make your point as effectively as possible. Your perceptions are indisputably correct. You deploy humor, tact, diplomacy, and subtlety to most efficiently reach your target.

Your idealism and candor are beautiful gifts if you are fighting for a cause or for the rights of the downtrodden. There is no greater spokesman for a cause you believe in. You will feel quite satisfied with your life if you channel your enthusiasm for your ideals toward an altruistic cause. Like the archer for whom your sign is named, you are most comfortable when you can see your target, and aim your bow and arrow at the bull's eye rather than turning in many directions in search of a target that is eluding you.

The goal of your journey is to bring pieces of knowledge together to construct a philosophy of life. Ultimate meaning comes from uniting diverse experiences to reach a higher plane of wisdom—the target. Information is gathered in the sign of Gemini, the sign opposite your own on the Zodiac wheel. By the time the wheel turns to Sagittarius, the diverse pieces of the puzzle become the big picture. Your greatest joy comes from discovering a pattern in seemingly unrelated pieces of information or events. While you may be adverse to details, the constant work of synthesis makes you a master of meaning, a greater level of understanding to which you aspire.

While other signs may meander along blissfully unaware of the wisdom lurking within and around them, you prefer to ask questions so you may discern truth. You have incarnated to garner understanding and meaning from life experience. That is why you are so open-minded and curious. Your goal is to collect as many experiences as possible, with as many people, in as many places, as possible. That is why freedom is so important to you—so you are free to explore expanded horizons. Give yourself as much latitude as possible to explore the peaks and valleys of human experience through people, places, literature, religion, spiritual experiences, travel, and finally, by asking a lot of questions. You cannot get answers if you do not have questions. You already have won half the battle, because the realm of questions is abundantly yours. As life unfolds, the answers will come. So too will the sense that there is an important reason for your sojourn on Mother Earth.

RELATIONSHIPS

You have more friends than you can count and you might even be married. But one theme rules your relationships—you love your freedom. Limitations on your freedom could deal a death-blow to a relationship, and you certainly would prefer to be alone than have your wings clipped by another person. If a relationship limits your freedom, you may seek to experience your freedom through your mind. To overcome a restrictive relationship, you may read, watch travel or adventure movies, or escape into your own fantasy world as a way of maintaining your independence from mundane reality.

The charming, footloose quality you possess attracts many people to you, and attracts you to many people. You probably have had no shortage of partners and friends. You are most attracted to, and get along best, with other curious, adventure-seeking souls. You feed each other's passion for excitement, exploration, and discovery.

Sagittarius and Sagittarius

Two Sagittarians in partnership create more comedy than three comedy clubs put together. You enjoy each other's company, and strengthen each other's ability to see the irony of life. Together, you discover the answers to many existential questions. There is nothing boring about your conversations—except when you two philosophers have to ask whether someone has paid the rent. If you two commit to sharing a few practical tasks in the world, there is nothing to stop this from being an enduring relationship of the highest quality.

Sagittarius and Capricorn

A partnership between you and cardinal, earth sign Capricorn heightens the ambition of both signs, creating an empire rather than a relationship. You both are strategic-thinking visionaries who fuel each other to create more ... and more ... and more. There is no end to the creative ideas you will think of, and there is no lack of creative energy to manifest your ideas. This may not be a relaxing relationship, but it certainly is productive. Emotionally, you have very different make-ups. Sagittarius is hopeful, optimistic, expansive, and rarely feels defeated. The hard-working, ambitious Capricorn can be pessimistic, fearful, shy, and contracted. On a good day, you balance each other. On a bad day, you do not understand each other. In a deep relationship, you may find Capricorn lacks the spontaneity you would like in a partner. As a friend or a business partner, however, you and Capricorn are a dynamic team. You have many practical lessons to learn from a relationship with Capricorn. Once your lessons are learned, you may consider a more fiery personality to join you in your life journey.

Sagittarius and Aquarius

You and fixed, air sign Aquarius are a highly compatible couple who want to reform as many people as possible with your *avant-garde* ideas—first your neighborhood, then your city, then your country, then the world ... and maybe the universe. You are high-minded individuals who share philosophies and solutions. You may fear the great ideas you create in this relationship will become imprisoned in your minds. You both must be aware to build a bridge between the conceptual models you live by in this idealistic relationship, and the physical reality with which you would like to interact. Aquarius will inspire you, and provide perspective to help you see more clearly the direction you would like to take. You may be the one to take the initiative to bring your heavenly ideas to earth.

Sagittarius and Pisces

The dreamy, spiritual nature of mutable, water sign Pisces fascinates you. Your hope and optimism dovetail with Pisces' similar trust in Spirit. Pisces and Sagittarius see eye-to-eye on issues of spirituality, idealism, altruism, and faith. You both are dreamers who feel nothing is impossible. While you and Pisces implement your ideas with different tools—Sagittarians through bold actions and projecting positive energy, and Pisces through projecting deep feelings and thoughts—you both successfully manifest your ideas, albeit in unconventional and unexpected ways. You have a happy partnership, and only occasionally will someone have to think about who is paying the bills!

Sagittarius and Aries

You enjoy the company of cardinal, fire sign Aries because this sign is not afraid to speak the truth, strike out on its own, or overturn the status quo. These qualities enormously appeal to you. Aries cherishes your sense of humor, your ability to see the big picture, and think strategically to create positive results. Every once in a while, your impulsive Aries partner may take off without consulting you and your storehouse of wisdom. You treasure the companionship of your fiery, energetic mate nonetheless. The enthusiasm of Aries, the first fire sign of the Zodiac wheel, sparks positive energy in you that leaves you feeling nearly intoxicated. Together, you have a dynamic relationship in which both can support the vision of the other.

Sagittarius and Taurus

You are drawn to the down-to-earth stability of fixed, earth sign Taurus. Taurus is attracted to your idealistic, truth-seeking, fun-loving nature. You appreciate Taurus' common sense, predictability, and manual dexterity. Taurus appreciates your ability to see the big picture, and find meaning in patterns. You are a philosopher who creates with your mind. Taureans are artists who create with their hands. You each appreciate the gifts of the other. But a steady diet of each other may jangle the nerves of both the earthy Taurus and fiery Sagittarius, the way fire burns earth in its path. Sagittarius may feel encumbered by the slow, deliberate, methodical Taurus. Taurus may feel jangled by the spontaneous, non-detailed, non-linear, enthusiastic Sagittarian. This combination easily creates a warm friendship, but may create a lot of wear and tear in an intimate relationship.

Sagittarius and Gemini

You are fascinated by Gemini, the mutable, air sign opposite Sagittarius on the Zodiac wheel. Opposites attract, and a relationship between Sagittarius and Gemini is no exception. Gemini is a master of knowledge and Sagittarius is a master of wisdom. Gemini gathers bits of information, for reasons it does not always know. And Sagittarius steps back to look at the big picture to discover patterns and meaning in seemingly chaotic bits of trivia. Gemini provides information and Sagittarius provides form and context to the facts. Together, you have more knowledge than a library, and an endless stream of theories and ideas to fill your days as you travel the path of life together.

Sagittarius and Cancer

You have a warm place in your heart for cardinal, water sign Cancer. You appreciate Cancer's domestic flair and loyalty to family and traditional values. Cancer is spellbound by your sense of humor, capacity for adventure, and ability to make the best of seemingly difficult situations. You are friends who are fascinated by your differences. Cancer marvels at your ability to pick up and make change at a moment's notice. You marvel at Cancer's ability to maintain a stable home and routine for a seeming eternity. You contemplate the future while Cancer feels nostalgic about the past. You are thinking about your next overseas journey while Cancer is thinking about what color to paint the walls. Your orientations to life are quite nearly opposite. You respect each other's ability to do what the other feels he or she could never do. But your diverse paths may clash in an intimate situation.

Sagittarius and Leo

You are drawn to the radiant and theatrical personality of Leo, a fixed, fire sign. You appreciate the warmth and generosity of your Leo partner. Leo is inspired by your vibrant optimism and witty humor. Leo is the romantic partner you have always dreamed of. Sagittarius is the exciting companion Leo has always imagined. Together, you will fulfill many desires to meet new people and explore new places. Still, you each challenge the other to become better. You will challenge Leo to bring meaning to his or her social interactions. Leo will challenge you to slow down and enjoy life rather than run from place to place in search of meaning. Leo may act from a sense of passion without fully calculating consequences. You may act from a sense of meaning without fully considering passion. A thoughtful Sagittarian will give Leo's path meaning and direction without dampening Leo's zeal. A fun-loving Leo will help Sagittarius relax, and take a momentary break from a lifelong quest to discover the meaning of life.

Sagittarius and Virgo

You appreciate the bright-eyed, witty quality of Virgos. You are grateful for Virgo's eye for detail and ability to handle small matters. Your expansive vision and Virgo's attention to fine points could create a winning team in a business or professional endeavor. Yet, in the realm of the heart, you see the world from such different perspectives that you both may feel it is impossible to find a middle ground. Sagittarius feels only the big picture matters, and the details will naturally fall into place. Virgo feels that only the details matter, and the big picture will build upon the orderly structuring of the small pieces. The truth is a combination of the two philosophies. A large vision is needed to determine direction. Refinement and details also are necessary to manifest the vision in physical reality. Virgo and Sagittarius feel happiest when they blend the skills of the other. A relationship entails spontaneous reactions. There may be too much attachment to competing philosophies in this relationship for a rapid, smooth, flowing meeting of the minds on a daily basis.

Sagittarius and Libra

You appreciate the fine tastes and elegant demeanor of cardinal, air sign Libra. Libra appreciates your candor, wit, and humor. You cherish Libra's demure elegance, and Libra relies upon your can-do spirit to push through obstacles Libra may prefer to avoid. You are driven to speak the truth. Libra is skilled at framing the truth in diplomatic ways so others can hear what you have to say. In a professional relationship, you will accomplish positive change without ruffling feathers. In a personal relationship, you share a refined, peaceful home and many cultural and artistic activities. Your shared sensibilities and values support each other's continual growth.

Sagittarius and Scorpio

The fixed, water sign Scorpio may be a bit clandestine compared to your personal policy of openness and honesty. But you honor the deep insights expounded by the Scorpio soul. This is a relationship that will fascinate or repel you. You and Scorpio can be extreme in your personal reactions. The combination of two intense personalities polarizes the strongest elements of both people. You will loyally commit yourself until your dying day, or you will not want to speak to a potential Scorpio mate. Either way, the Sign of the Scorpion elicits strong feelings from you. If you have a mutual goal, or an outlet for the strong energies created by this union, you and Scorpio can surmount many obstacles. Without an outlet, you are a fire and water sign who may create a lot of steam.

Sagittarius, it is your nature to see the best in everyone. This is why you are so easy to get along with. It is hard to find someone you truly do not like, except if the person is not honest. You have little patience for people who do not tell the truth. As far as you are concerned, it is far easier to tell the truth and take the consequences than tell a lie and try to remember what you said to whom. You cannot understand why people behave otherwise. So, while you are friends with everyone, even people you have never physically met, you will never tolerate a liar. And you probably will never be one either.

Chances are good that you have had warm relationships with nearly every sign of the Zodiac. If you have not, it might be a good idea to explore relationships with signs to which you are not accustomed. The greater your exposure to choices, the more you will feel you have fulfilled your soul's mission of having a wide range of life experience. Your mind and heart are flexible, open, loving, and accepting of every person and experience that crosses your path.

SPIRITUALITY

You are a highly spiritual soul who has incarnated to learn about spiritual teachings, philosophy, and ideas. Your curiosity is endless, and you are willing to put your curiosity into action. Sagittarius is the sign of the seeker, and you are willing to go to the end of the earth in one way or another to find what you are seeking. Ultimately, you are seeking an answer to the question of the meaning of life. You may find many answers to such questions through spiritual study and practice. The Sagittarian soul finds his greatest solace in one answer—the meaning of life is to experience the presence of God. Wherever you are, there He is. While it is innate to your nature to travel and seek answers to your myriad questions, you ultimately find the richness and meaning you are seeking through the experience of the divinity within yourself.

You are like Dorothy in *The Wizard of Oz* who went all the way to the Emerald City to find a wizard who tells her that she already possessed the "soul-ution" to her problem, symbolically the red shoes that could take her home. And like Dorothy, your spiritual quest will show you "there is no place like home," within yourself, where love and God abundantly reside.

As a child, you had many questions, everything from who made God, to where He lived, and how He created you. You had a lot of questions about many things and the number and scope of your questions has multiplied with time. If you were asking about God as a child, imagine how far your mind has expanded by the time you are an adult! To satisfy your innate curiosity about Spirit, God, and religion, read the sacred teachings of the spiritual path of your choosing. Eventually, your spiritual quest will take you deeply into yourself and the teachings of one path.

Your thoughts may be peripatetic at times, and the choice of a spiritual path will help you work with an innate trait—the love of freedom—that could hamper your spiritual progress. While your freedom-loving nature is beneficial to help you experience many facets of life, it also is a quality you may desire to narrow as you travel the spiritual path. Guidance from the biblical Book of Psalms sums up the essence of your spiritual work: "Be still and know that I Am God." As a result of inevitable discipline to your curious nature on the spiritual path, you will develop precious spiritual qualities such as loyalty, endurance, perseverance, devotion, and love, which will help you experience a Divine presence within. This discovery will give meaning to your experiences on earth.

HEALTH

Sagittarius rules the thighs, the liver, and gall bladder. Your thighs may be your strongest asset, and your greatest vulnerability too. Like the centaur, the mythical creature associated with Sagittarius, you have strong thighs to carry you from place to place in your quest for higher knowledge. In Greek myth, centaurs wandered from village to village, seeking adventure. They engaged in sporting events with local villagers for the sake of competition. In one such contest, a centaur named Chiron was mistakenly hit in the thigh by a poison arrow shot by Hercules. Try as he might, Chiron could not heal himself from this painful wound. In the course of trying to heal himself, he became a brilliant counselor and healer. Even though he could not completely heal himself, Chiron gave invaluable assistance to countless souls on their path to enlightenment. He learned from his experience that his only sustenance came from a spiritual source.

The myth of Chiron the Centaur holds many lessons about the archetype of the wounded healer. It also carries great import to the people born under the constellation of Sagittarius. Like the centaur, you are a brilliant marksman who can hit virtually any target with your bow and arrow, symbolically your mental and verbal capabilities. Yet in the course of life, it is possible you will suffer a physical or psychological wound that is difficult to heal. In the course of trying to learn, grow, and heal, you will learn many lessons that will enable you to generously share with others, which is why Sagittarians have a strong reputation for being gifted counselors, consultants, and healers. You will go through a quest for knowledge, and through advising and helping others, you learn that healing comes through communion with Spirit.

On a physical level, your thighs may be vulnerable, or remarkable in some way. Even though most people take their thighs for granted, thighs are an important linchpin between the upper body and the knees, lower legs, and feet. Thighs carry the bulk of the body weight as one travels from place to place. On the Sagittarian body, the thighs may be extraordinarily long, heavy, or thin. The Sagittarian thighs also are vulnerable to tight muscles, broken blood vessels, or blocked energy meridians that affect the vital organs, particularly the liver and gall bladder. Blocked energy in the thighs can lead to diminished vitality in the organs of detoxification. The Sagittarian liver and gall bladder often are strong because of your passion for living and desire to rid your body of anything that is negative or toxic. Yet, under stress, these organs are the first to feel the pressure.

Health & Food

The antidote when you are tired or gaining weight is to support your liver and gall bladder. You can begin by limiting the amount of fats and oils in your diet, at least temporarily, to rest your usually active liver and gall bladder. Foods that support your liver and gall bladder include root vegetables such as beets, burdock, rutabagas, leafy greens, fennel, and berries such as strawberries, raspberries, blackberries, and blueberries. Lemons in hot water also stimulate the liver and gall bladder. Anything that supports your generally strong circulation also will remedy sluggishness. Aerobic exercise, walking, running, hiking, biking, swimming, and yoga all enhance your physical vitality, and satisfy your sense of adventure, especially if these activities take you to new places.

Flower Essences

Flower essences, which are distillations of the high vibrations in flowers, also help you. Dill calms your senses if you feel overly active. California Poppy focuses you so you do not scatter your energies. Sweet pea settles a restless mind.

FINANCES

You are not one to hold on to money, and you can be generous to a fault. Your perpetual belief that the universe provides holds true even in the realm of finances. And one way or the other, the universe provides you material, financial, and even emotional support. Whenever you find yourself in need, help always materializes to restore your faith—even in the 11th hour. You are highly resilient, so a bump in the road barely registers on your buoyant radar screen.

Nonetheless, you are human and your faith may be tested in the realm of finances. If this happens, visualize what you would like to receive, and imagine the universe abundantly responding to you. Take the necessary material steps to make space for your vision to unfold. Pray, do charitable work, and continue to give your time, energy, advice, listening, understanding, and personal resources. Eventually, the universe will respond in ways that are in the highest good for yourself and others.

Another avenue of healing for you in the financial arena is through the reconciliation of ideal with reality. You are a highly, highly, highly idealistic soul. You imagine what is possible, and often you manifest what you have envisioned. But if you cannot, there is no one more dejected. This is because you believe so strongly that everything works out for the best and that the universe is basically good. So, what happens when your ideas do not work? Either your idea was not aligned with your soul, or with the highest good of yourself and others. Or, your idea simply was not realistic. The necessity of melding ideal with reality may afflict you in the realm of finite financial resources. You have figured out ways to make your resources elastic in almost every other domain, particularly time and space. But money? That's another story. And even though you are able to make your money stretch farther than the average human being, your funds may eventually be a finite commodity. You often find a way around financial constraint, either by juggling demands, finding a bargain, setting up an exchange, taking a loan, or using your charm and wit to get what you need, or where you need to go. But every once in a while, you hit a proverbial wall.

While prayer is the antidote to obstacles on the path of life, financial resources may occasionally be blocked to the Sagittarian soul for good reason. The reason? The lesson of boundaries and limits. If you have tried everything from prayer to affirmations to visualizations to every other creative idea you can conjure, try reviewing the situation to see where you can scale back, where you can better observe limits, where you can revise your expectations, or where you can align with earthly reality, or the true desire and direction of your soul. By doing this, the financial limitations may melt away, or you may find you really do not need what you initially thought.

CAREER

You are a brilliant teacher, counselor, healer, travel agent, artist, athlete, writer, speaker, actor, preacher, spiritual leader, professor, communicator, and consultant. You are multi-talented and multi-faceted, and your enthusiasm enables you to do well at almost anything you undertake.

Chances are good that you do more than one thing well. And chances are equally good that whatever role you fulfill, you do it enthusiastically. You do best when you believe in the people, the cause, or the product you are working for. Honesty is important to you, and you do much better when you honestly feel the value of the endeavor you are promoting. If you feel less than passionate about a pursuit, you either will not pursue it, or you will not pursue it well. There are few ways to dampen the Sagittarian spirit than to give your energy to something in which you do not believe. When you believe, your energy is boundless. When you do not believe, you lose the inspiration that makes you such a magical soul.

Take a searching inventory of your life. Make sure you believe in what you are doing. If do not have faith in something, re-commit to things that excite your passion and your sense of limitless possibilities. When you devote your energy to a cause that matters to you, you discover energy, resources, and inspiration beyond your wildest dreams!

♑ CAPRICORN (December 22–January 19)

♑ CAPRICORN (December 22–January 19)

PERSONALITY PROFILE

Capricorn is a cardinal, earth sign symbolized by the goat.
Your key motivations are achieving success and recognition.
Your outstanding attributes are ambition, concentration, determination, practicality, a methodical style, administrative, organizational and leadership skills, and willpower.
Your karmic challenge involves feeling your feelings, while simultaneously feeling and considering the feelings of others, to find balance.
Capricorn rules the knees.
Saturn rules the constellation of Capricorn.
Capricorn is associated with the Greek god Cronos and the Roman god Saturn.
Capricorn is associated with the color violet, the crown chakra, and the pituitary gland.
Best Day: Saturday
Best Number: 8
Healing Gemstone: Celestite

The karmic planet Saturn rules the demure Sign of the Goat. Your decision to incarnate in this lifetime is based on a strong sense of karmic responsibility, a desire to work hard to prove your value to yourself and others, and a desire to accomplish something of note during the span of your years. This is true if you were born with a Capricorn Sun, Capricorn Moon, or Capricorn Rising.

The sign of Capricorn may feel like a blessing or a curse. You were born in the hours, days and weeks after the annual Winter Solstice. While you entered the world at a time of physical darkness in the northern hemisphere, you also entered the earth plane at a time when the light is growing. The days are beginning to get longer. You were born at a time of tremendous hope—hope for greater light, consciousness, and awareness. Your life is part of an earthly imperative to bring greater light to darkness, from a metaphysical perspective.

You chose on a soul level to work off much karma in this lifetime. While this is not easy, and you may feel you encounter more trials and tribulations than the average person, you also have the potential to grow more quickly, to become stronger through your tests, to work off negative karma, and to accrue much positive karma. As a soul, you set up many challenging circumstances prior to your incarnation, through the family you chose and the physical body you created. You designed these challenges to make yourself stronger, wiser, more resilient, loving, compassionate, and patient. These challenges were meant to help you draw to the fore wisdom, strength, compassion, and love you had cultivated in previous lives.

Life will present you with many difficulties that will call you to blend, balance, and express the myriad qualities you have developed in previous incarnations. These qualities include a mix of spiritual awareness with an innate common sense and instinct for survival. Not everyone is called to bring spiritual wisdom to bear in even the most mundane situations—but you are! You are a bridge between the spiritual world and the practical, physical world. Nothing less than an integration of both realities will satisfy you. Too much concentration on spiritual practice will make you feel spacey and as if your life has no practical value. Too much focus on material gain will bring out a latent opportunistic streak that will block spiritual vibrations from your soul. Your task is to balance your strong spiritual inclinations with your practical, material skills to achieve something of merit in your eyes.

You also have a strong sense of the karmic consequences of your actions. You will meet with many opportunities to balance the karmic scales—and rebalance them in your favor. Take precautions and care in every situation to ensure that you do the right thing, give back what was given to you, or treat others as you would like to be treated. Ultimately, over the course of a lifetime, this kind of behavior earns plentiful good karma.

Capricorn is a sign that may experience delays in reaping positive karmic rewards until after 30, or even after 42. This is a condition designed by your soul to help you develop faith in the Divine, and faith in the inexorable and exacting laws of karma. The rewards will come. You may feel you need endless patience as you wait for the hand of God to reach down and lift you up. It will.

The spiritual qualities you chose to develop as a soul include surrender, patience, endurance, perseverance, and loyalty. You will receive the rewards you have earned. The rewards include a solid foundation for your life, a high degree of achievement, the ripening of mental and emotional qualities that engender success, a strong spiritual compass, and a sense of confidence that was lacking in your younger years.

From a spiritual perspective, your life is a success because you are becoming a highly advanced disciple of the Creator due to the circumstances you have faced or surmounted. Even though your life may not be exactly what you want at times, take heart. You are making progress! I can hear all of your Capricorn voices saying you do not feel like you are making progress. But you are. You would not have incarnated as a Capricorn if your soul did not have an impeccable plan for your advancement and ultimate salvation. It may not look that way from a human perspective, but it is infinitely true from a spiritual point of view. A disproportionate number of Capricorns, for example, have trouble with their legs or with their physical bodies. It would seem that Capricorn is either an accident-prone, sickly, or bad luck sign. This is not the case. Capricorn souls have chosen to take on pain while in physical form to burn off karma and thus advance more quickly on the spiritual path. It is mathematical law that one's quest for God—and arrival at the feet of the Divine—is often stronger when one is suffering the most. So it is with Capricorn.

In the midst of burning off negative karma, you also have the wherewithal to accrue much positive karma that will serve you in your earthly sojourn and in your subsequent astral incarnation. Positive karma comes to you when you contribute something of lasting value that emanates from the vision of your soul. You will do best if you align your life with the design of your soul. You are a particularly good organizer, administrator, and leader. You have a lot of ideas. You have a lot of stamina for hard work. And you have developed faith, patience and surrender so you may partner with the Divine to accomplish your goals. Your goals can be anything from having a loving relationship, a beautiful home, or a thriving business, to running a charitable organization, or traveling the world. The only prerequisite is that the "goal" resonates with a longing in your soul.

When you stand on a mountaintop and look at your life, what do you see? What do you want to see yourself doing? This is the view of your soul. What you see yourself doing is the mission of your soul. Pursue it! It does not matter whether you succeed or fail in human terms. It simply matters that you have tried to manifest your soul on the earth plane. Your soul's vision is driving you more strongly than many other signs. It is what makes you feel as if you have an overly active conscience. So, you must contemplate and meditate on what your soul wants, and follow its gentle guidance, which comes through intuition, dreams, and your senses.

Your success, as a Capricorn, is not measured in earth plane terms. Success for you is measured by the amount of soul energy you bring through your body. Your soul is judging your success based on the lessons you learn—which can take place even in the midst of an apparent "failure." So please, dear Capricorn, judge not your success or failure with limited earthly eyes. You are the mountain goat who eventually reaches the summit of the proverbial mountain. Keep climbing. Even though it may seem you are still stuck in the thicket of a mountain pass, you inevitably are higher than you were when you began your journey. You will eventually reach the top!

A drive to leave a legacy has motivated you to make highly ambitious decisions to fulfill your soul's mission. The need to accomplish something—the mission of your soul—supplies a thought form that you feel prodding you throughout the days of your life. It is as if you have a persistent voice in your head that pushes you to do better. The standards you set inside your mind are continually rising. Even if you meet your standards one day, you are in a quandary the next—because you raised your own standards!

As a Capricorn, you are destined to surmount obstacles and meet high standards. A disproportionately high number of Capricorns have overcome enormous obstacles. Among them are the Reverend Martin Luther King, Jr., Anwar Sadat, Paramahansa Yogananda, and Jesus Christ, if you take December 25 as his date of birth. Other notable Capricorns are Muhammed Ali, Humphrey Bogart, Elvis Presley, Howard Stern, Rush Limbaugh, Marelene Dietrich, Mary Tyler Moore, and Dolly Parton.

There are several solutions to the challenge of meeting the high standards you set for yourself. No matter what the fear, the worry, the self-doubt, the trepidation, or the potential disaster, just keep going. Even if the worst happens, it will not be as bad as being stuck and going nowhere. Also, try to limit the negative scenarios running through your mind. The world is made of energy and it responds to pictures. If you transmit pictures of negativity with your thoughts, the negative pictures will return to your life. Imagine your soul as a luminescent ball of light hovering over your head. This light is guiding you and illuminating your way. If you ever question your way, follow the light you sense coming from your soul as it shines on your path.

PERSONAL GROWTH

You have a persistent personality that can face any challenge in the outside world. It is vitally important to attune your will with the will of the Divine. Many Zodiac signs are extremely flexible and receptive to the silent but present voice of the Divine. Yet, they lack strong willpower to put their awareness into action. In contrast, you have a strong will that is capable of putting your divinely inspired awareness into action. But you are not known for your flexibility, and therefore may resist Divine guidance you receive through intuition. This resistance creates rigidity in your body. And it also contributes to frustration on a psychological level, which may eventually lead to depression when you are unable to exercise your will and achieve the state of affairs you desire.

Letting go of a course of action to which you have committed is difficult. In fact, it may feel virtually impossible. The only solution when you face a dilemma—my will versus Thy will—is to imagine yourself surrounded by Divine light, and pray to be given the power to follow the light.

For a Capricorn, a pattern is a pattern … is a pattern. Allow the Divine pattern, in its infinite yet inexplicable wisdom, to silently guide you. You probably are already doing this. But if you are a Capricorn, you might also have some set patterns in your personality, and there probably is at least one pattern you have secreted in your private fiefdom, where you have not allowed the Divine to enter. Do a searching and honest inventory. See where you may be stubbornly refusing Divine assistance. Open a door or even a window, metaphorically, in this corner of your life. You may find little by little that the situation—and you—change.

Finally, try to love and accept yourself exactly as you are. Even if you find a flaw, love it, and accept it. This is the easiest way to let it go. In fact, this is the solution to many dilemmas you face. Love the problem, watch it dissolve in the light of your love, and let it go. You may categorize the world and put it in boxes, particularly if there is a problem. This means that over time, you accumulate many unopened boxes of problems. The simplest way to let them go is to acknowledge them and send them love rather than pretend they do not exist. As you systematically do this with every problem, you eventually will have nothing left but a life filled with love and a positive sense of yourself. This alone will do more to allow in the Divine than any other system you may deploy.

RELATIONSHIPS

If you are a true Capricorn, relationships are not a top priority unless you share a mutual goal with another person. Your goals are hard work, achievement, and advancement. If a relationship happens to come along that supports your endeavors, then there is no one more loyal than you. But if a relationship does not serve a long-term purpose, there is no one better at going it alone, like a mountain goat diligently climbing to the top of the mountain whether he has a companion or not.

Your diligence and perseverance are your greatest assets. Relationships are only vital to you if your partner can accompany you on your infinite climb. You are eternally trying to get to a higher place, whether you seek more money, more status, more knowledge, more spiritual progress, more achievements, more physical power, more recognition, more possessions, or more of anything that you set your sight upon. But unless you set your sight upon a harmonious relationship from early in life, you are unlikely to devote enough energy to this facet of living to achieve the level of contentment in domestic life to which you may aspire.

If you make it a goal early in life to achieve something, your persistence and determination will enable you to reach your goal. Therefore, if marriage and a happy family have been your goals all along, you will get them. But if marriage and family are afterthoughts, you are unlikely to achieve this goal because you are so focused, and your energy is devoted to work goals.

Capricorn and Capricorn

With a fellow Capricorn, you feel a sense of security you rarely experience. You and your Capricorn mate understand the need to create systems and order. You support each other's goals, and try to bring as much success to the relationship as you do to your ambitious endeavors in the world ... unless you are a competitive Capricorn. If you are unable to support the success of another because it makes you feel less about yourself, you may feel threatened or challenged by this industrious relationship. Capricorn is a sign that values achievement. If your definition of achievement is limited to yourself, you may feel frustrated by an ambitious Capricorn partner. You may feel more comfortable with another sign more inclined to support your upward climb. In a business, where you have a defined mutual goal, two Capricorns are a dynamic pair who can accomplish almost anything. Please note that Capricorn enjoys being the boss, even if quietly, behind the scenes. Make sure you and your Capricorn business or relationship partner take turns running the show.

Capricorn and Aquarius

You are impressed with the Aquarius' far-reaching mind and ability to remain objective about almost anything. You admire Aquarius' ability to remain unruffled by the kind of dire news that could send you into a downward spiral. You wish you could emulate some of Aquarius' cool and detached qualities, and this could attract you to a friendship with the Sign of the Water Bearer. Yet in an intimate relationship with Aquarius, you may feel dismay at the Aquarian's lack of concern about issues that totally transfix you. While the cool demeanor of Aquarius is something you may emulate, it may not be something you wish to live with. You may feel too immersed in worldly concerns to enjoy the luxury of the breezy attitude of the sign following your own. While Aquarius may have a few ideas you would like to borrow, you may not understand the *laissez-faire* attitude of this liberal-minded sign.

Capricorn and Pisces

Capricorn is organized, ambitious, and strategic-thinking. Pisces, a mutable, water sign, is flowing, spontaneous, spiritual, and emotional. Pisces relies upon instinct and intuition while Capricorn relies upon formal logic and systems. Pisces feels compassion for others while Capricorn calculates how he or she can get people to cooperate with his or her ambitions. Pisces and Capricorn could easily come from different planets, although the two may find common ground upon which to build a partnership. Pisces is attracted to the managerial and executive qualities of Capricorn, and feels secure with a Capricorn mate. You may enjoy taking a break from your serious, worldly concerns to experience the flowing, spiritual energies of the Pisces soul. If Capricorn and Pisces are highly independent, and understand they approach life from opposite perspectives—tangible versus intangible—these signs will have a high degree of success in creating a life of balance between heaven and earth.

Capricorn and Aries

You are attracted to the drive and confidence of entrepreneurial Aries, the first sign of the Zodiac wheel. You admire the ability of cardinal, fire sign Aries to get up before dawn and accomplish as much in reality in the first hour of the day as you may accomplish in your mind. You were born just after the winter solstice, when the light of the Sun is so diminished you feel you have to conserve your energy throughout the day. You are slow to warm up, and you appreciate the fiery enthusiasm of the Sign of the Ram. This is a highly productive business combination, but could cause problems in the realm of the heart. Capricorn wants a partner who will support his or her upward climb, while Aries wants to be independent, and free to pursue his or her dreams spontaneously. This is a dynamic combination if you have similar goals, but you may go separate ways if your lives take you in different directions.

Capricorn and Taurus

The warm sensuality of fixed, earth sign Taurus will appeal to your tactile, sensitive, sensation-oriented side. The stable, committal, and security-driven Taurus will enable you to feel a deep level of inner safety. Taurus shares your love of material security, schedules, routines, and physical comfort. Taurus delights in your accomplishments in the world, and has a few practical suggestions to lighten your load. You appreciate Taurus' sensible approach to life, and concern for culinary pleasures. You and Taurus enjoy fine meals, luxurious surroundings, and trips into nature. With no more than a little convincing, you usually see eye-to-eye.

Capricorn and Gemini

A relationship between spontaneous Gemini and systematic Capricorn may seem awkward, and may resemble a friendship more than a romance at first. Yet the greatest love springs from the garden of friendship, and with mutual goals, Gemini and Capricorn may find they are willing to compromise to accommodate the other. At first, however, Capricorn's rigidity and discipline may seem unnecessary to Gemini. And Gemini's total lack of planning may seem anathema to Capricorn. But gradually, you two will learn to see the wisdom of the other's ways, and what at first seemed foreign may eventually be endearing. While this is a relationship that will require compromises to accommodate the diverse styles of the partners, neither partner will interrupt the rhythm of the other, and both will offer sincere logistical support to help the other realize his or her dreams.

Capricorn and Cancer

Your complementary opposite on the Zodiac wheel is Cancer, an emotional, sensitive water sign dedicated to nurturing the people he or she feels close to. Even though you have the air of an accomplished executive, underneath the surface, you nurture a secret desire to be taken care of. The mothering, nurturing qualities of a Cancer man or woman are just what you need to give you the sense of security you so deeply crave. Outwardly, you seem less emotional than your Cancer mate. Yet, this is only because you are less likely to express your feelings than because you are not feeling. You feel comfortable expressing your feelings with precious few people, and Cancer is one sign of the Zodiac with whom you feel comfortable showing your vulnerability. Underneath your responsible, managerial veneer lies a sensitive soul waiting to express itself. Conversely, underneath Cancer's sensitive, moody exterior is a capable parental figure waiting for someone to take care of. This relationship may help you open and be yourself in ways you never imagined. The balance of Cancer and Capricorn is a healing experience for you.

Capricorn and Leo

Leo is magnetically drawn to relationship with the hard working Capricorn, a cardinal, earth sign. Leo and Capricorn enjoy being the boss, but in markedly different ways. Leo likes to lead in a theatrical, fiery way. Capricorn is not concerned with being the one who appears before the crowd. Capricorn would prefer to be the mastermind who controls the situation from behind the scenes, and who appears very little before other people. Together, Capricorn and Leo may create a successful company, corporation, or thriving organization. As long as you two run your relationship and family as a business, this is a relationship destined to endure.

Capricorn and Virgo

You are naturally compatible with mutable, earth sign Virgo. Although you may find the Sign of the Virgin to be more peripatetic than your conventional mind may have planned, you will find that you and Virgo consistently support the goals and desires of the other. A natural sympathy and understanding flow between you and Virgo, creating a mutual sense of loyalty and a desire to please the other. You each understand the importance of earth plane constraints, such as financial security, organized paperwork, being on time, and keeping your word. Whereas other people misunderstand many aspects of Virgo and Capricorn, you two naturally harmonize in your daily affairs. Make sure you take a moment from your industrious endeavors to enjoy emotional communion so possible in this celestial combination. Chances are good that you will responsibly undertake many endeavors together. Success is bound to come from this harmonious union.

Capricorn and Libra

You appreciate the poise, balance, and sense of fairness of Libra, the Sign of the Scales. You and Libra, a cardinal, air sign, have a strong sense of justice and desire to do the right thing. You are excellent business partners, and share a mutual respect for systems, hierarchy, protocol, and procedure. But what fun is this in a romantic relationship? While both Capricorn and Libra have the ability to conduct a fair and equitable relationship, neither sign possesses a naturally romantic inclination toward the other. It is as if the mutual respect, deference, and formality that reigns in this relationship precludes a relaxed, flowing affair of the heart.

Capricorn and Scorpio

A relationship between you and fixed, water sign Scorpio is bound to provide what you are looking for in the realm of relationship. You appreciate the focused intensity of Scorpio, and the ability of this insightful sign to listen to everything you say, and even to the things you do not say. The piercing eyes and penetrating mind of Scorpio make you feel accompanied on the journey of life in a deep way you rarely experience. While your confrontations may be equally intense, you feel it is a small price to pay to be with someone who has such penetrating eyes that see all of who you are, and even things you may not see yourself. Being in a relationship with a Scorpio is like having an extra pair of eyes. You see more than you ever perceived in the past, and you gain a wealth of understanding from your new perceptions.

Capricorn and Sagittarius

A partnership between you and mutable, fire sign Sagittarius heightens the ambition of both signs, creating an empire rather than a relationship. You both are strategic-thinking visionaries who fuel each other to create more … and more … and more. There is no end to the creative ideas you two will think of, and there will be no lack of creative energy to manifest your ideas. This may not be a relaxing relationship, but it certainly is productive. Emotionally, you have very different make-ups. Sagittarius is hopeful, optimistic, expansive, and rarely feels defeated. Capricorn can be pessimistic, fearful, shy, and contracted. On a good day, you balance each other. On a bad day, you do not understand each other. You have much to learn in a Sagittarius-Capricorn partnership. Once your lessons have been learned, you may consider a more placid earth, water, or air sign to support your worldly goals.

Remember, you are a goal-oriented person. Make sure your goals are *completely* respected before you commit to a long-term partner. Your goals may be more important to you than your partner as the years pass. Be honest with yourself and your partner as you make decisions about the future course of your life. Your power of concentration is so strong that your life may lead you to do only one thing at a time rather than many things at once. As a result, you may either need a controlled environment to reach your goal, or you may not be able to spread yourself thin enough to have a happy marriage and family, and a fulfilling career. You may have to make a choice because of the intensity with which you approach everything. There just may not be enough of you to go around.

SPIRITUALITY

Your spiritual tests are many. Unlike the air, fire, and water signs of the Zodiac, gratification of your desires is often delayed. Capricorn is the 10th of the 12 Zodiac signs, serving as a bridge between the relatively greater material consciousness of the first nine signs and the more purely spiritual consciousness of the last two signs. The Zodiac wheel represents the evolution of consciousness in the human being, and you represent the 10th rung in the ladder of ascension to the Divine. Thus, in choosing Capricorn as your birth sign, your soul chose the complex issue of navigating the passage between materiality and divinity.

As a result of the juxtaposition of material and spiritual consciousness in equally strong proportions in your psyche, you have developed a strong will to hold both forces at bay, as if to keep both the earthly and heavenly pulls under control so neither could completely take you over. This theme of inner strength will be constant throughout your existence. It has been a survival tool in many incarnations, which is the reason this strength comes so easily to you. Yet, this inner force can be used either to your benefit or detriment. You can use your strong will to comply with the will of the Divine, or you can create a block. Ultimately, a balance between the two must be found in the life of every Capricorn. It may seem as if you already have surrendered your will to the Divine. As mentioned earlier in the Personal Growth section, even if it may feel true that you have surrendered to the Divine, there may be a secret inner sanctum in every Capricorn where the Divine has yet to enter. This does not mean that you need to go to extremes and give up your quest to do what you believe is right. On the contrary, as an active, work-oriented earth sign, your mission is to continue to work and create—but in collaboration with the Divine, rather than as a separate unit. Your mission is to tune your will with the will of the Creator, so that two may become one.

Your spiritual inspiration and direction from the Divine will come through intuition, common sense, natural patterns that unfold in your everyday life, or more formally, through scriptural injunction, spiritual counseling, or meditation. In whatever way you receive your spiritual direction, follow it! Use the rich gift of spiritual inspiration awarded abundantly to you. It is your birthright—one you have earned and karmically paid for through many trials in life. Open up your big, beautiful heart, and receive the spiritual blessings all around you!

Finally, consider a daily practice of meditation and a weekly period of self-imposed silence and contemplation as methods to promote your spiritual advancement. It is not easy for you to sit, and sit quietly at that, without doing anything, and without receiving affirmation that you are okay. Try affirming to yourself when you meditate that you are okay, and that everything else is okay too. You will be amazed at the sense of peace this affirmation brings to your tired psyche, tired of fighting for achievement and perfection.

Experience the peace that naturally surrounds you. This feeling may at times elude you as you busily go about managing your life. But this peace is always there. You simply need to stop and breathe it in. Ultimately you will realize you always had more control than you thought. This simple, quiet moment will give you the sense of mastery you have always longed for.

HEALTH

You have always looked younger than your years because of the crystallizing power of your ruling planet, Saturn, which delays the aging process. When you were younger, you may have felt that you were not growing or maturing as quickly as your peers. This is because the power of Saturn creates delays. The delays are not imposed to create frustration, but to give you time to work out physical, emotional, and mental glitches. Saturn rules time, and your relationship with time may diverge from that of others. You may feel as if it always takes you longer to do things—be it reading a book, walking from Point A to Point B, being ready for a relationship, or getting ready to go out. The maturing process is no exception. You like to do everything methodically. You tend to details. And you complete one step at a time before moving to the next. This process applies to your physical body as well. It likes to do one thing at a time. It moves slowly. Its processes are methodical. It is thorough. It takes care of every detail.

While the crystallizing power of Saturn can slow the growth and aging processes, it also can constrict blood flow and muscular flexibility. The sign of Capricorn may predispose one to stiffness of the joints, rigidity of the spinal column, and in old age, arthritis. The antidote to these crystallizing affects is to drink water to eliminate toxins, stretch to increase blood flow through joints and muscles, do aerobic exercise to stimulate circulation, and eat healthy foods that are free of chemical additives to lessen the toxicity and acidity in your joints, a major contributor to arthritis.

Capricorn rules the knees, a particularly vulnerable point. During the course of the karmic learning process every Capricorn must face, your knees may be susceptible to the continual wear and tear of mental and emotional resistance to the spiritual lessons your soul continually attracts to you. Your knees stiffen to resist the pressure of the Divine will. At some point, you may have refused to surrender ... and get down on your knees. The result is stiffness of these pivotal joints. The solution to any lack of flexibility in your body is to ask yourself whether there is currently a situation in which you are too rigid. The way to surmount any inflexibility in your body, particularly in your knees, is surrender to the Divine will without surrendering to your own negative thoughts. This is a reminder of the narrow path you have chosen to walk as a soul. If you believe you have chosen your moment of birth, your soul has chosen a highly karmic and exacting path toward liberation.

Exercises, Herbs, and Food

Yoga and gentle stretching are helpful antidotes to the rigid patterns that beset the Capricorn musculature. Your body responds well to massage, deep tissue work, shiatsu, acupressure, or any healing technique that facilitates a smoother flow of energy through your tissues and the energy meridians. Cayenne or chile peppers heat and move your blood. Beets and strawberries also speed the flow of toxins through your liver and blood. Calcium, Vitamin D, and Magnesium are important to strengthen bones, but can be detrimental to Capricorns with joint problems as these elements and minerals may collect in the body. Minerals should be taken in moderation. All herbs and spices that warm your system are beneficial, including garlic, ginger, cinnamon, cumin, and cloves. Environments, exercise, and foods that promote warmth, calmness, and a balance between expansion and contraction are best for you. For example, salt promotes physical contraction and sugar promotes expansion. A balance of both white crystalline substances is best for you. A good source of salt, and related minerals and trace minerals, is sea vegetables. A good source of sugar is fruits and natural sweeteners, such as molasses, maple syrup, date sugar, rice syrup, or barley malt.

Flower Essences

Flower essences, which are distillations of the high vibrations in flowers, also may help you. The flower essence Baby Blue Eyes counteracts pessimism. The flower essence Blackberry helps overcome inertia. And the flower essence Angelica helps you feel assistance and protection from the angelic realms—which you deserve!

FINANCES

Of all of the signs of the Zodiac, you are most able to practice austerities and self-denial. You are a born ascetic. So, the ability to save money, follow a budget, or limit expenditures is not a problem for you. Bringing in money in the first place could be a little more difficult. Your concept of what is possible can be limited or circumscribed because your organizational mind tends to think in boxes. And potential results or financial possibilities may be one of those boxes, keeping financial prosperity limited to the size of the conceived box, which may be smaller than what the Divine has in mind. Here is an example of where your will may overrule that of the Divine.

You also may suffer at times from self-criticism and a potentially over-bearing inferiority complex. You may limit your conception of what is possible. These thoughts, feelings, and subconscious pictures are telegraphed to the universe, and limited results may ensue. The solution is to break open the mental box in which you keep your financial goals. Even though you are good at earning money because you work hard and are good at saving what you earn, you also may want to allow the will of the Divine to flow abundantly into this sphere of your life so you may receive all that is karmically flowing to you.

Finally, you may consider the biblical concept of tithing, which involves giving 10 percent of everything you earn to uphold a spiritual cause. You probably already do this, but there are other forms of tithing that you may not have considered. Tithing may also come through giving your time, your life energy, a listening ear, or your love.

The universe is committed to giving back everything you give—times 10. If you already give money, then consider giving emotional, mental, or physical assistance to someone in need. Even if no one knows about it, it will come back to you. This is the unalterable law of prosperity. At every opportunity, give, give, give, and then give some more, of course, without any expectation of receiving anything in return. This lack of expectation will open a channel for the universe to give, give, give, and give some more—to you!

The idea that you would give without receiving compensation is simply untrue. *Everything* is equitably compensated in this universe. You may not always be aware of prior karma that is requiring you to give more than you are apparently receiving in the moment. Nor are you always aware of the positive rewards that are coming in the future as a consequence of your efforts. Since you never know the effects you are creating in the future as a result of your present efforts, it is always good to give as much time and energy as you can, knowing that only good will return to you as a result of your efforts. This attitude will richly reward you in all of your financial undertakings so the outgo of your material wealth does not exceed your income.

CAREER

You are a cardinal, earth sign dedicated to the achievement of solid, concrete, earthly goals. You have many talents cultivated in previous incarnations of hard work. You have mastered many facets of business, organization, technology, and systems. You have a focused mind, you are self-disciplined, and you have strong powers of concentration. You can accomplish anything you set your mind to. Now, the challenge is believing that—every moment of the day!

Again, there is no shortage of talent within your body and your mind. You truly can achieve *anything* you set your mind to. Of all signs of the Zodiac, you are the most disciplined, ambitious, and achievement-oriented. You simply need to believe these words. Again, you like repetition.

You can succeed at any form of business you choose because your determination to succeed is so strong. You thrive in an office or a systematized setting. You think in organized boxes, and you like your environment to be the same—organized, standardized, predictable, and neat. When that orderly state of affairs has been achieved, you can accomplish almost anything. Your talents are best applied in corporate environments, organizational structures, and entrepreneurial endeavors. You do best when you are in charge, because you are a visionary who sees how to delegate work to get a job done, and because you prefer to manage than be managed. Thus, you make a much better manager than subordinate. Although many happy Capricorns are in middle management, one often finds these happy people have carved out a domain, so they effectively are in control. If a Capricorn is forced to be subservient too often, it will crush the spirit of the independent goat for which the sign is named. Eventually, the Capricorn who is being dominated will silently or not-so-silently rebel. This is the kind of Capricorn one often sees going out to start his or her own business, and he or she is often highly successful on his or her own. If you are working in an organizational structure and you feel you are not able to carve out your own domain, consider starting your own enterprise. Capricorns have a long history of running successful ventures that survive long into the future. Consider that you incarnated to leave something of lasting value. This may be a business, a work of art, a piece of writing, a building, or a charitable organization. Consider how satisfying any of these ventures might be. Think about your own particular personal interests, and do what you do best—create a lasting system from a brilliant idea, one of the many you carry around in your head!

♒ **AQUARIUS (January 20–February 18)**

♒ AQUARIUS (January 20–February 18)

PERSONALITY PROFILE

Aquarius is a fixed, air sign symbolized by the water bearer.
Your key motivations are friendship, discovery, perspective, group activity, and community.
Your outstanding attributes are objectivity, idealism, humanitarianism, innovation, understanding large concepts, acceptance of others without judgment, non-attachment, and facility with electronic and computer technology.
Your karmic challenge involves using your inventive mind to reform rather than rebel.
Aquarius rules the ankles.
Uranus rules the constellation of Aquarius.
Aquarius is associated with Ouranos in Greek myth and Uranus in Roman myth.
Aquarius is associated with the color violet, the crown chakra, and the pituitary gland.
Best Day: Saturday
Best Number: 4
Healing Gemstone: Amethyst

As a soul born under the constellation of Aquarius, you have incarnated to build a bridge between heaven and earth. You live in a highly expanded state of awareness. You may feel compassion for someone a world away as easily as you may feel for yourself or someone in your home. You consider the effects of your actions globally. It would not occur to you to consider someone less if they did not live nearby, or in your country. You are a global citizen who believes that all members of the global village have the right to be treated as equal neighbors. Anyone qualifies as a neighbor in your altruistic view. Distance is no barrier. You may even be uncomfortable when something is too close to you.

You are an open-minded individual who embodies the quality of universal acceptance so often ascribed to the Divine. You believe every soul carries a seed of divinity within. You cultivate the seed through understanding. Your divine seed is your ability to unconditionally accept anyone from any place, any orientation, any walk of life, and any intellectual, financial, or physical status. You do not judge others, and accept everyone and everything with an even mind.

Your expanded state of awareness comes from a decision by your soul to incarnate in a form that could serve humanity and embody the qualities of your advanced soul. You made tremendous spiritual progress in a prior incarnation. But at the level of your soul, you were disappointed for not having focused on the needs of others. This perspective shows a high degree of soul evolution. You may not be aware of how elevated is your perspective because it is so innate to you. Yet, precious few souls currently on Earth can equal your level of understanding. Other souls may have incarnated for self-serving reasons while your developed soul has more lofty objectives. You may wonder why you feel compelled to take the high moral road when so many others take shortcuts. How can you do otherwise when your soul continually whispers in your ear? You have an active conscience due to a strong conscious or unconscious connection to your soul, which has a strong alliance with your guardian angel, etheric spiritual teacher, Guru, or God.

Your evolved spirituality is reflected by your position on the Zodiac wheel. Each astrological sign represents a stage of human consciousness, from self-oriented Aries in the first sign to other-oriented Pisces in the 12th sign. As Aquarius is the 11th sign, you are a people's person, ready to take a step away from awareness of the limited self to awareness of your connection with humanity. After Aquarius, the next sign of Pisces has expanded its consciousness one more step beyond humanity to unite with the Divine.

You view the scenes of life from a detached perspective because you see how small every individual is compared to the vastness of divinity. As a result, you do not participate on an emotional level because many things seem small to you. You feel like a spectator or daydreamer. The drama of your life appears as a series of pictures rather than as experiences that are part of you. Events around you form a vast and distant panorama. This is an evolved perspective that enables you to align with your soul rather than the melee of earthly life. You have mastered important spiritual lessons about the ephemeral nature of physical reality versus the permanent nature of the Divine. Consequently, your sense of "we-ness" is stronger than your sense of "I-ness." As your ego dissolves in the sea of humanity, you feel more "at one" with scenes of distant reality than you feel with your own life, knowing all is part of God, therefore related, and anything but separate!

As a result of your comprehensive perspective, physical reality is not always comfortable for you. You feel a weightiness slowing you down. You wonder is life real, or is it a fantasy? You are not sure whether to participate or whether to wait for the movie to end. Yet, if you do become involved, there is no one better equipped to fight for right action. The ability to wisely discern when to step in and when to step away represents a critical stage in your evolution. Once you choose to contribute, you are a reformer who revolutionizes the status quo, no longer a rebel on the sidelines. When you are committed to a course of action, you are thoughtful, considerate, involved, and dedicated. You have a magical ability to step back and see all that is needed so you may implement the correct course for as many people as possible. You gather groups of people quickly and efficiently, and see the strengths of each member, and coordinate all participants so they function harmoniously. You are a selfless leader who works tirelessly to serve the greater good. You are an egalitarian who believes in treating team members as peers who deserve respect. You would not ask anyone to do anything you would not do yourself. You are a good listener, organizer, and manager. You anticipate the future and react accordingly. You simultaneously consider the big picture and the details. You are open, adaptable, and fair. You have the qualities of an enlightened leader.

Yet, without an ideological commitment, you can become apathetic, aloof, distant, and undecided. Your neutrality may translate into passivity that enables other people or forces to take power over you. The result may be circumstances beyond your control. It is easy for you to give up because you do not experience strong emotional reactions to events, even if they are close to you. Yet, you have an ideological commitment to right action, and when you perceive a transgression, you only need to marshal your physical forces to follow your principled mind. But be aware that your expanded mind may create an internal debate. "How wrong does it have to be for me to get involved?" "Will a good outcome come to pass if I participate?" "Isn't this all karma?" "Will the outcome be the same if I don't join?" The truth is that your perspective is so expanded that you grapple with the significance of earthly events when you compare them to an expanded reality that seems more real to you.

The lack of strong emotional reactions also renders decision-making elusive because you do not feel strongly, or on a personal level. How do you decide when to act? Given that you may have trouble perceiving personal feelings, you must rely on mental constructs to make decisions about what is right, when to act, and what to do. Your mental acuity gives you objectivity and good judgment. If you are aware of your natural cerebral approach, you will be better able to interpret your impulses and inclinations, and choose the right course. You may envision an avatar, Guru, spiritual teacher, or someone you admire, and think of what they would do. You might imagine that you are the other people in the situation. How would they benefit from your involvement? What would happen if you did not participate? Is this outcome palatable to you? Is the outcome consistent with your moral values? If it is not, it is time to act. Disregard hesitations or philosophical wrangling about the existential meaning of your participation. If you see something wrong, become involved.

A great deal of your life energy is concentrated in your mind, enabling you to think more quickly—and from more angles—than most people. This is good news and bad news. The good news is that you conjure up more creative solutions than the average person. The bad news is that you create an internal debate between all the ideas, and you are an expert at rationalizing any number of solutions. How do you sort creative inspiration from impractical idea from excuse to avoid action? One antidote to the accelerated speed of your cognitive process is to periodically stop and take a deep breath. Feel your body. Experience yourself and your feelings. Take an inventory of your thoughts. If you sit quietly for a few moments, you may feel a higher vibration ordering your thoughts. Allow this process to unfold. You may feel as if you are untangling internal circuitry.

Speaking of circuitry, you have an extraordinary facility with electronic and technical devices. Are you beginning to understand why? Electronic and technological devices are designed to move more quickly than mechanical equipment. And due to an invisible source of energy—electricity—technological devices are able to process energy or information more quickly than average machines. You are like an electronic device processing large quantities of electromagnetic energy while other people are like a mechanical device. Now you see why you move more quickly. And you see why you are more prone to the confusion caused by bombardment from so many sources of electromagnetic energy inundating the planet. There are planetary, psychological, informational, electronic, technological, mechanical, and evolutionary influences simultaneously energizing your mind. You are more susceptible than any sign to electromagnetic disruptions because Aquarius is the Sign of the Water Bearer. And moving water produces electricity, and electricity produces magnetism, creating the strong electromagnetic field around the Earth, to which you are so sensitive.

Aquarius also is ruled by the planet Uranus, which is associated with electricity. Uranus was discovered in 1781, coinciding with the discovery of electricity. Uranus is a planet that orbits at a right angle to the axis of Earth. You constantly feel disynchronous vibrations from the planet with which you resonate. This alone is enough to make you feel a bit out of step. But it also is what makes you able to see the world from a wider angle. Knowing your wider perspective is a natural talent, you now understand why you comprehend aspects of life others have yet to grasp. You are ahead of your time, and with the passage of more physical time, others eventually will catch up.

PERSONAL GROWTH

You are an idealistic soul who may suffer when you perceive wrongdoing, injustice, and inequality. You live by your ideals, and expect others to do the same. You may detach yourself from the troubled scenes of the world in order to cope. But in a quiet moment, when you slow down and feel your feelings, you feel pain about the condition of the world. You try to make a difference, yet there is still suffering. What do you do? If you are a typical Aquarian, you either work harder to find a way to help everyone, or you shut down, overwhelmed by the vastness of it all.

The solution is to find a middle ground, so you may help to the extent you are personally able, and draw a boundary at that point. If you allow yourself to participate in solutions and understand that partial reform is the most realistic expectation, you will feel far more satisfied than if you expect 100% perfection. Otherwise, if you become overwhelmed by the immensity of others' problems, you may become paralyzed and unable to make a contribution. It is true that you see the perfect solution in your mind's eye. But the minds of other people work more slowly than yours, and you are often constrained by groups to move as slowly as the slowest member.

You may grapple with the immeasurable distance between what you envision is possible, and what happens. Your challenge is to balance between doing the best you can with the people and materials available, and staying true to your ideals. You may reconcile yourself to the chasm between your vision and the limits of reality by maintaining faith in the invisible workings of a higher power. Not only is the higher power continually creating balance through the inexorable law of karma, but your attempts to create a better world create positive karma for you.

Your spiritual status is based on the purity of your intentions and the integrity of your actions rather than on the outcome of your efforts. It is spiritual law that you are responsible for right action, not for the fruits of your action. You certainly are not responsible for righting *all* the wrongs in the world, and you are not responsible for retribution in the case of a wrong. That is where knowledge of the law of karma, cause and effect, can be so helpful to you. You are responsible for your own correct actions only, not for correcting the actions of others. Contributing to the betterment of others is your karmic destiny, so it is beneficial to try to right the wrongs you perceive. But it is not important to be attached to the results. You are equipped to live the life of a reformer, and you have all of the vision and equanimity you need to remain steadfast on the noble path you have chosen. As you practice nonattachment, tolerance, and acceptance, you will feel a growing sense of inner peace and contentment. This is the ideal equilibrium of the Aquarian soul who lives in the balance between what is possible—and what is.

RELATIONSHIPS

You believe in being friends with everyone. Picking a special person with whom to be in an intimate relationship is as perplexing as choosing your favorite candy in a candy store. And if someone chooses you, it is hard for you to turn that person away, even if you feel the relationship is not of the highest quality. Yet, as tolerant as you are, you will not allow anyone to limit your idealistic, independent, unorthodox thinking. If anyone tries to restrain you, you will find a way to escape—even if you leave in your mind. There is a hidden or not-so-hidden part of every Aquarian that abhors the experience of restriction. If you agree to collaborate in a restrictive partnership, you will probably develop passive-aggressive, or aggressive means for achieving psychological freedom. While some signs run from the unknown, you run from the known. There is nothing more limiting to you than a relationship that is predictable. If this happens, you will go along for a while, then pick up one day—at least in your mind—and seek expanded horizons. A quirky or unusual partner will hold your interest longer than a partner who is conventional.

Aquarius and Aquarius

You will experience harmony with fellow Aquarians, who resonate with your fast-paced mind and unconventional lifestyle. A fellow fixed, air sign, Aquarius understands your altruistic outlook and preference for impersonal deliberations rather than discussions of matters of the heart. Aquarians above all, believe in being friends. If you choose an Aquarian partner, you may not have the most romantic mate, but you always will have a best friend. Your Aquarian partner will never judge you. He or she will always accept you. And he or she will be willing to put you ahead of him- or herself.

Aquarius and Pisces

The emotional nature of the mutable, water sign Pisces may befuddle or fascinate you. You may be attracted to this water sign as a way of healing your emotional life. You are tolerant of others' feelings, but you may not be prepared for the subtle and not-so-subtle waves of emotion expressed by water sign natives, such as Pisces, Cancer, and Scorpio. Aquarians often team up with Pisces because of shared compassion, global perspective, and spiritual values. Yet, in an intimate relationship, the Pisces partner often reports feeling emotionally neglected, because of the Aquarian's emotional detachment and unpredictable reactions to electromagnetic influences. While Pisces, a mutable, water sign, also reacts to energetic influences and enjoys an expanded perspective that enables him or her to feel more for others than for him- or herself, Pisces also experiences compassion through feelings rather than thoughts, whereas Aquarius experiences compassion primarily as a thought. Pisces also seek emotional communion from a mate, while Aquarius seeks a meeting of the minds. This disparity can lead to misunderstandings of a subtle and not-so-subtle nature. If your Pisces partner is highly independent, or has many planets in Aquarius, you may have a meeting of the minds.

Aquarius and Aries

You will experience tremendous movement and change in a partnership with Aries. Aries is an innovative, cardinal, fire sign, and will introduce you to many new people, places, and ideas. Do not depend upon Aries to bring to fruition the projects he or she introduces to you. Aries gets the ball rolling. Aquarius keeps the ball in play, and decides where it will land. In this relationship, you will be the one who takes responsibility for your partner when he or she lets go of the ball. You are the one with the ability to follow through in this relationship, and you may feel like an old soul in comparison with the youthful enthusiasm of your Aries mate.

Aquarius and Taurus

A partnership with fixed, earth sign Taurus may provide financial or material security, but may do little to further your idealistic vision. Taurus is happy to provide logistical support, but may provide little in the way of ideological inspiration. If you are seeking a relationship that is more practical than ideal, this could be the answer to your prayers. But typically, Aquarius finds security in freedom and movement. If this is true for you, an association with the Sign of the Bull is best kept at a professional distance.

Aquarius and Gemini

Gemini, a mutable, air sign, appreciates your mental prowess, and you appreciate Gemini's ability to live his or her own life and give you mental, emotional, and physical space. You share many enchanting ideas with the mentally versatile Sign of the Twins. But be mindful to take action on all of the brilliant ideas spawned by your union. Otherwise, you will feel as if your relationship is more talk than action. Your Gemini partner will excite you with never-ending enthusiasm for developing new theories. There are many ideas to discuss and places to explore in this peripatetic relationship. You may find this relationship works better as a romance than a marriage, not because you are not compatible, but because a loose association better fits the restless natures of Gemini and Aquarius.

Aquarius and Cancer

You may be lucky in a relationship with Cancer, a cardinal, water sign, ruled by the Moon. Although you are not known for your affinity with the feeling nature of the Moon, the gentle, home-loving qualities of the Sign of the Crab, are compatible with your basic values. You may lead a more extroverted life than your Cancer companion, but you appreciate the stability and loyalty the Cancer brings to your relationship. As long as your Cancer mate respects your freedom, you will support the Cancer's need for domestic harmony and stability. You may make compromises in this relationship, but the compromises will be ones you both can tolerate.

Aquarius and Leo

Leo is a fixed, fire sign directly opposite Aquarius on the Zodiac wheel. Opposites attract, and this is a highly magnetic astrological pair. You will be dazzled by Leo's buoyancy and dramatic flair. Leo craves an audience as much as you enjoy being a spectator. You could be just what a Leo needs to bolster his or her sometimes-sagging self-esteem. While Leos are masterful at establishing their personal identity, you are masterful at harmonizing in a group. You have much to teach Leo about how to expand his or her awareness to encompass awareness of others. Conversely, Leo has much to teach you about deepening your relationship to yourself.

Aquarius and Virgo

A relationship with mutable, earth sign Virgo could be a panacea for refining your ideas. Virgo is as mentally versatile as you, and enjoys perusing details to reach perfection. A relationship with a Virgo may well free you to focus on the big picture while your Virgo companion focuses on the details. If this is a combination you seek, Virgo could be a productive mate for you. But be aware that Virgo also cherishes neatness, order, and often, healthy food. These are not important accoutrements to the footloose Aquarian. If you have a taste for a few alfalfa sprouts with your otherwise utilitarian meals, and you do not mind organizing the papers on your desk, you and Virgo are a compatible team.

Aquarius and Libra

You appreciate the measured, refined quality of Libra, a cardinal, air sign, represented by the Sign of the Scales. Libra brings balance and harmony to your life. Librans are endlessly patient and able to listen to your far-out ideas, but less likely to contribute innovative ideas about the world to the conversation. Libra is more likely to confront you about the quality of the relationship and ask you to pay more attention to the exchanges between the two of you than between you and the world. Although this may be a more personal interaction than you prefer, Libra knows when to back off to give you the freedom you need. With very few compromises, this relationship will teach you a lot about the art of relating. This relationship could generate much positive energy for you and the people around you.

Aquarius and Scorpio

A relationship between Aquarius and Scorpio, a fixed, water sign, could lead to power struggles you may prefer to avoid. In fact, power struggles are so alien to your nature, you may not notice when a Scorpio is having a power struggle with you. You simply are not tuned into this level of human relating. So, your Scorpio partner may try harder to entangle you in an emotional web that will lead to a test of your desire to stay in the relationship. Unfortunately, you do not believe in being tested to qualify to be in a relationship, whereas the sensitive Scorpio believes he or she can only trust you and be open, if you pass the test. You want people to take you as you are. A Scorpio wants to find out who you are under pressure, not how you react to average, daily experiences. This relationship does not ultimately create lasting harmony, even if it appears to be complacent at first. Over time, the divergent needs of the two signs—Aquarius for expanded consciousness of the world, and Scorpio for in-depth awareness of the Self and the relationship of the partners—pulls Scorpio and Aquarius in different directions. A stable middle ground is difficult to maintain.

Aquarius and Sagittarius

The mutable, fire sign of Sagittarius is as concerned about making positive contributions to the global village as are you. You and Sagittarius are a highly compatible couple who want to reform as many people as possible—first your neighborhood, then your city, then the country, then the world ... and maybe even the universe. You both are high-minded individuals who enjoy sharing philosophies and solutions. If you ever fear your great ideas will become imprisoned in your mind, find a can-do Sagittarian to help you bring your creative ideas into physical manifestation. Sagittarians also will inspire you, and provide a direction around which to orient your life. Fiery personalities bring warmth to your cool, airy nature and encourage you to take action in situations where you might otherwise remain ambivalent. You bring stability and perspective to the fire signs' impulsive, hot-headed approach. You may change your life direction under the influence of a fire sign partner, which you may be less prone to do under the influence of earth, water, or fellow air signs.

Aquarius and Capricorn

If you enter a relationship with a stable Capricorn, a cardinal, earth sign, you may wonder if you are in a relationship or a business. Capricorn is serious and business-minded, and this tendency is magnified in a relationship with an idea-oriented Aquarius. All you have to do is mention a concept, and your Capricorn partner will have the trademarks, patents, and copyrights lined up before you realize your partner was taking you seriously. This partnership works better in business than in romance. But if you have much to accomplish, there is no one more loyal to you than the Sign of the Goat.

As an Aquarius, you have the ability to accept nearly any sign because you are so non-judgmental, accepting, and accommodating. You understand everyone, but it is not always easy for others to understand you because your perspective is so advanced. You may feel as if you have a satellite dish on your head, receiving thoughts and innovative messages from higher realms. Consequently, your natural frequency pattern may be erratic. You may be passionately warm if the cause excites you, particularly if the cause is world hunger, global warming, or nuclear proliferation. Or, you may be blind to the feelings of others if you perceive their needs as petty. Why the discrepancy? You think big. Many souls cannot keep pace with your far-reaching thoughts. Or they may not be able to comprehend your alternating currents of passion and dispassion. Perhaps it would help if you supplied an owner's manual to prospective partners before they make a long-term commitment to you.

Be patient with you partner as he or she struggles to understand your big thoughts from a potentially more limited perspective. You do not have all the solutions to human relationships, but you do have all of the wisdom you need to solve life's big questions. If you choose to enter a long-term love relationship, be prepared to narrow your perspective, and warn your mate you will need periodic breaks to commune with the higher states of consciousness so innate to you—and sometimes difficult to share in a conventional relationship.

SPIRITUALITY

You have a naturally spiritual outlook as you feel brotherly and sisterly love toward all humans, animals, plants, and even intergalactic beings. It is easy for you to feel at one with the universe, which is the essence of spirituality. But participating in spiritual rituals or routines is a different story. You can at times feel like a rebel without a cause, and there is nothing quicker than a spiritual rule or rigid ritual to spark your rebelliousness. You shy away from organized religion or relationships with spiritual groups. They may make you feel as if your freedom is being curtailed, when in fact, spiritual practice would channel your immense spiritual energies in a way that is beneficial for you. You apply your spiritual understanding and efforts to help the people around you. Yet, you focus less energy on the Creator of yourself and the people you are helping. This may be the one missing ingredient in your spiritual practice—acknowledgment of the Source of the spiritual activity you naturally engage in on a regular basis. You are an altruistic humanitarian. But your relationship with spirituality ends with your relationship to fellow humans, and may not easily extend to a relationship with the Divine.

You may experiment with meditation as a way of tapping the Divine energy that abundantly permeates every particle of your being. Take a deep breath and feel the energy in your body. Breathe out, and feel disharmony and negativity leave your body. Lift your gaze, and focus your attention at the point between your eyebrows. Remain aware of your breath coming in and going out, while silently chanting Om to yourself. Om is the sound of the cosmic vibration present in creation. As you chant this sacred syllable, unite yourself with the vibration underlying creation and feel your oneness with your Creator. This may be the missing link in your spiritual practice, or at least the element that will make worthwhile all of your serviceful deeds and altruistic contributions.

HEALTH

Aquarius rules the ankles, which form the bridge between the human body and Mother Earth. Just as your role on the Zodiac wheel is to infuse heavenly principles into earthly reality, your body serves as a vehicle to bring heavenly light to this world. Yet, if you feel bombarded by too many thoughts or electromagnetic energy, your ankles are first to take the stress.

As an Aquarian, your joints are prominent in some way. You also have prominent angles in your face, fingers, and toes. It is as if God gave you an unusual appearance in some way to remind you that you are not like other mortals. You are fashioned from a higher state of consciousness than many signs of the Zodiac. You may choose to use your awareness at any level you choose.

Your health suffers when you lose your balance between spiritual and physical reality, or between virtual reality and your physical body. This may be a result of psychological imbalance, or from overexposure to electromagnetic disruptions caused by computers, airplanes, cars, or television. As a result of an imbalance, you may twist, sprain, or break your ankle, or feel pain in this pivotal area. These are warnings that you are becoming too immersed in a realm distant from your physical body. As an Aquarius, you may distance your energy from your physical body as you dream of greater possibilities. It is important to integrate your ideas with physical reality so your ankles remain strong. You may experience that your energy withdraws from their contact with earth to enter your mind as a channel to heaven. Consequently, you do not remain aware of your body, and ailments may befall you without your awareness. The solution, of course, is to remain ever aware of your body, particularly your ankles, no matter the state of consciousness you may enter.

Still, it is not easy to figure out when to intervene to heal a physical, emotional, mental, or spiritual imbalance, because you are not overly concerned by your own welfare. You are more interested in the well being of others. And like everything, you simply do not take things personally, even if they are going on in your physical body! You are immune to the healing properties of various foods, and are often as happy eating the same foods on a daily basis, or in eating the foods that are most convenient rather than most nutritious. You derive greater energy from your nervous system than from your digestive tract. As a result, your physical body is more reactive to changes in your thoughts or other electromagnetic influences than to changes in your physical circumstances or diet.

Energy Healing

Medicinal or herbal remedies, therefore, may be unnecessary as you are able to treat yourself more quickly by changing your thoughts than taking a pill. You also are highly responsive to vibrational medicine, including homeopathics, radionics, laying on of hands, the use of energetic healing systems such as "Reiki," chakra healing, or crystal healing. You respond to color therapy too, which mediates the vibrations of color through colored light or water. You imbibe the vibration of a color when you drink water stored in a glass container of the desired color.

Color Therapy

You may consider using the color blue to balance your thoughts and nervous system. You also may wear the color blue, or you may use crystals or gems, which carry high vibrations from Mother Earth. Try placing a lapis lazuli, celestite, sodalite, aquamarine crystal, or sapphire gemstone in your pocket or on a chain around your neck. Wash your crystal or gemstone to remove impurities every lunar cycle (28 days) and place the crystal or gemstone for several hours in the Sun. You are sensitive to the multifaceted energy in crystals and gems, and will benefit by having them near you. Remember that there is a quartz crystal in your computer, and this crystal picks up the energy of your thoughts. Your thoughts about computers are generally positive, and the crystal internal to the computer receives and transmits this positive energy to you, which is why you may have a more compatible relationship with computers than some people. Experiment with a clear, quartz crystal. Imagine that your crystal is healing or balancing you, or sending you love. See how you feel. Think about what kind of physical, mental, or emotional assistance you would like. The effect of your thoughts can be amplified by the use of crystals produced by Mother Earth.

Flower Essences

High vibrations in flowers, distilled in flower essences, help you balance the energies in your system. Rosemary helps you feel comfortable in your physical body. Cosmos slows chaotic thoughts so you may reach more coherent solutions in keeping with the rhythm of the Earth. Aspen helps you form a healthy relationship with the unseen energies of Spirit. Lady's Slipper harmonizes spiritual forces with your body's rhythms.

FINANCES

You are not attached to material possessions, but you are not attached to being impoverished either. You seek comfort, but you are unwilling to compromise your integrity or the well being of those around you to attain financial security. You trust the abundance of the universe, or at least the generosity of other humans, to support you if you are in need. If someone else is in need, you are the first to help. You expect the same from others, which you usually attract, although you may feel you are more often the giver than the receiver. This may be true, because your soul has chosen a life oriented to fulfilling the karmic goal of generosity. You will attract all that you need due to a store of good karma you have built by your altruistic acts. As an Aquarius, you are more likely to give than receive because you are so oriented toward serving rather than receiving. Hence, your true needs are likely to be fulfilled by the universe, even if the same people to whom you gave do not repay you.

Knowing that your material needs will be satisfied, you tend not to worry about your financial health. Unless you have strong earth sign influences in your chart, a financially-oriented partner, or strong financial obligations, you probably do not focus your energy on strictly financial goals. You have an altruistic outlook, and it is far more important to you to perform charitable actions in the world than it is to make extra money for what you perceive as ephemeral material needs. Again, the demands of a family, or society in general, may distort your idealistic outlook, but this is not your underlying nature, and you may remain aware of your natural orientation toward good works rather than large bank balances.

CAREER

You are a broad-minded, symbolic thinker who can discern the difference between important technical information and unimportant details. You can balance the large picture with the small, and have an affinity for things foreign, technical, scientific, electronic, and *avant-garde*. You are a good communicator, speaker, writer, and administrator. You adeptly manage people, and feel comfortable in schools, corporations, the media, and government. Ultimately, you want to serve the public, and although you may be derailed by mundane concerns, you feel happiest when you are participating in public service.

You also have a facility for math, science, statistics, computers, technology, banking, travel, and astrology. If it involves understanding the consciousness or state of mind of large groups of people, you are in your element. You hit your stride when you support public or political causes, and you could be a competent pollster, statistician, lobbyist, political strategist, public interest activist, political action spokesperson, or government official. You particularly support causes that promote equal rights, or better the plight of minorities or the downtrodden. You are willing to fight to alleviate pollution, world hunger, disenfranchisement, or any project that involves coordinating and connecting large groups of people to alleviate suffering.

As you dedicate your life to uplifting others in any avenue you pursue, please don't forget to cultivate your own garden by a spiritual practice that helps you connect with your roots as a way to replenish yourself from your intense involvement in bettering the human plight on Planet Earth.

♓ PISCES (February 19–March 20)

♓ PISCES (February 19–March 20)

PERSONALITY PROFILE

Pisces is a mutable, water sign symbolized by two fish swimming in opposite directions.
Your key motivations are mystical experience, perception of higher dimensions of reality, solitude, devotion, romance, fantasy, imagination, and creativity.
Your outstanding attributes are compassion, sensitivity, perceptivity, intuition, forgiveness, deep feelings, selflessness, musical and artistic ability, and love of God's Creation.
Your karmic challenge involves discerning the difference between your perception of reality and commonly accepted versions of three-dimensional reality.
Pisces rules the feet.
Neptune rules the constellation of Pisces.
Pisces is associated with god of the oceans Poseidon in Greek myth and Neptune in Roman myth.
Pisces is associated with the color violet, the crown chakra, and the pituitary gland.
Best Days: Saturday, Thursday
Best Numbers: 3, 7
Healing Gemstone: Clear Quartz

You are a sensitive soul, ruled by Neptune, god of the oceans. You feel more comfortable with the soothing rhythm of the ocean than with the staccato rhythm of the earth. You crave transcendent experience as a way to escape from the confines of earthly reality. Chances are good that you have discovered a few of methods for coping with the harshness of earthly life, including meditation, listening to music, being by yourself, being in nature, gardening, writing in a journal, sitting by water, swimming, boating, or fishing. Any activity that helps you reconnect with your superconscious spiritual mind, which flows into consciousness through the subconscious, is beneficial to help you connect you with your roots in Spirit.

You are the 12th of the 12 Zodiac signs. Each sign represents a stage of evolution of human consciousness, from the self-orientation of Aries in the first sign to the other-orientation of Pisces in the 12th sign. You are the most spiritually evolved of all signs on the Zodiac wheel, and represent the final step in awareness before humanity returns to its Creator.

One With Spirit

As a water sign symbolized by two fish, you are most ready of all signs of the Zodiac to dissolve your ego in the ocean of Spirit. Your role in God's Creation is to bring spiritual vibrations to your physical body so you may emanate this high vibration to the physical world. This may be a quixotic task. As you become more spiritualized, you may feel more removed from the earth plane. Yet, you only feel at one with yourself when you are one with Spirit. As you become more closely united with Spirit, the transmittal of your spiritual light to Planet Earth flows with little or no effort. If you do not find a way to bring a piece of heaven to Earth, however, you feel like two fish swimming in two directions—one toward Heaven and the other toward Earth.

Send Positive Energy Out vs. Take Negative Energy In

Your designated position in God's Creation may pose a further dilemma. You are assigned to absorb positive energy from Spirit and emanate this positive energy to the earth plane. In reality, however, you may do the opposite. You may absorb negative energy from the earth plane, and you may hold it inside of you if you do not practice a technique for releasing energy that is not of your highest nature. A reversal of the flow of energy you were destined to experience may prove detrimental to your physical body. In fact, you may become disheartened by the negative scenes you absorb from the earthly ambiance rather than heartened by the beauty of the spiritual energies swirling around you with equal vigor.

Your Healing Effect

You have a healing effect on your surroundings by your mere presence. This applies if you have a Pisces Sun, Pisces Moon, or Pisces Rising. You may use your spiritual gifts to alleviate the suffering of others by absorbing their pain through your body the way a fish absorbs "breath" through its gills. If you do this, ensure that you release what you absorb by envisioning a Guru, guardian angel, or spirit guide removing the discordant energy from your energy field. Your greatest service is invisible, and perhaps this is why the deep compassion and emotional healing you provide are often overlooked by you and the recipients of your good will.

You are a compassionate, self-sacrificing, self-effacing person who will do anything to alleviate the suffering of others—because you feel their pain as acutely as your own. You have an energetic vortex naturally spinning in your energy field that has the capacity to pull negative energy, and you have an equally strong power to release this negativity from yourself through your thoughts. You may absorb more than you are aware, or you may absorb so much that you are not sure whether you are feeling your feelings or the feelings of others. You may make an inventory of your feelings at the end of every day so you may know what is yours and what is coming from other people.

You also may consider the value of absorbing others' pain like a sponge absorbs water. You may temporarily relieve the suffering of another and bring yourself good karma. You may also undo yourself by absorbing so much pain! If the relief is to be permanent, individuals must struggle with and overcome problems themselves. You may question whether you can help if you do not absorb the pain. The answer is that you may emanate love, compassion, and goodwill—without absorbing anything! As you become comfortable sending high energy out versus taking low energy in, you also will become clearer about the symbolism of the two fish in your zodiacal mandala. One fish is swimming to you with spiritual light from the heavens, and the other fish, bathed in your spiritual essence, is swimming back to God.

The Pull of Heaven and Earth

The dual pull between heaven and earth forces you to straddle three-dimensional earthly reality and higher dimensional astral and causal realms that transcend time and space. The astral realm is the sphere of consciousness vibrating more quickly than physical creation. The causal realm is the sphere of consciousness vibrating more quickly than astral creation. The higher rate of vibration of each subsequent level of creation makes each level less material, less tied to earthly rules, and more closely patterned after the realms of Spirit. While these worlds are not visible to many people, they are perceptible to you. Consequently, you may try to superimpose a heavenly rhythm upon an earthly cadence, and feel dismay at the inability to transfer higher dimensional astral and causal energy to the dense earth plane. The untenable pull creates a desire to escape. You may choose to escape through spiritual practice, contemplation, meditation, art, or music. Or, you may choose to escape through daydreams, fantasy, lack of participation, or through physical means such as drugs, alcohol, suicidal thoughts, or acts of self-sabotage. All of this in the course of avoiding pain! Once you realize the disappointment at the root of your pain, you may be less inclined to heap more pain or sadness upon your already disgruntled self.

The lack of clear direction posed by the symbol of two fish manifests a series of conflicts you may experience. You may undergo periods of intense solitude followed by periods of intense merging with a person, followed by isolation to recapture yourself. Or, you may experience periods of clarity followed by confusion, followed by lucidity. Or, you may give up everything in a spirit of self-sacrifice, followed by a drive to attain luxury, followed by self-denial. Or, you may feel the depths of compassion followed by feeling so overwhelmed that you cannot feel anything.

Conscious Solitude

The best remedy for your sensitive soul is periods of conscious solitude, where you choose a healthy form of escape to replenish your Self. Movies, literature, art, or music are means to transcend. Or, if you are more financially equipped, you may indulge in a luxurious activity or have someone care for you. Or a healing practice of psychotherapy, massage, or energy balancing will help you dip into your subconscious so you may touch your superconscious spiritual nature. Or, any form of spiritual practice will help you tap into an endless source of spiritual sustenance.

One reason you require periods of solitude is because your energy field is porous when you do not consciously protect it. You pick up the energy of nearby people and environments without necessarily being aware of what you are taking in. Be selective about the people you surround yourself with and the situations you participate in. Practice psychic hygiene by consciously releasing energetic toxins. Be mindful to release other people's energy from your aura, even after brief contact. The energy of others takes the place of your own energy and the energy of Spirit, compromising your ability to experience your own higher nature.

How to Cleanse Your Energy Field

To release the energy of another from your body or aura, imagine a golden tornado spinning at the top of your head. Energy from others may exit from this point, and energy from Spirit may enter through this place, which is the highest center of consciousness in your physical body. When you take in energy from your highest center of awareness, which vibrates at the highest frequency in your body, energy enters in a purified form. Even though you naturally open your higher energy centers to assist others in need, you may want to close your lower energy centers. Your lower centers vibrate more slowly than the higher centers, and the higher centers are able to filter negative energy more quickly. In addition, when you receive energy at a lower point in your body, it must travel farther to exit through your crown, causing greater disruption along the way. Therefore, receive <u>all</u> energy through your crown. Otherwise, you will be the person in need, which often is the case for well-meaning Pisces! To close your lower energy centers, tighten the muscles in your lower body and imagine your energy is close to you. You will feel consolidated when your energy is pulled in, and malleable when your energy is diffuse.

Spiritual Practice vs. Escapism

The higher path of the heavenly fish is spiritual practice. The lower path of the earthly fish is escapism. You feel pulled between higher and lower paths. The goal is to tread as much as possible the preferable path, and as little as possible the less preferable path, knowing the pull is magnetic in both directions. Forgive yourself if the ultimate path you follow is imperfect. Imperfection is the nature of the earth plane you have elected to inhabit. Accepting the imperfection leads to a perfection of the natural flow of spiritual energy into your being and out from your sympathetic, sensitive soul to heal you and your surroundings.

To many, energy and feelings are mystical substances that roll in like the fog and burn off with the Sun. You, on the other hand, are comfortable in the mystical depths of feeling, spirituality, psychic awareness, and healing. Share the precious gifts bestowed upon you by the Creator at your discretion. You have worlds of compassion, love, and healing within you. Let your radiant spiritual energy flow out of you to heal yourself and others. Use wisely your God-given healing talents and unlimited access to the uplifting power of Spirit!

PERSONAL GROWTH

You are a sympathetic, idealistic soul who incarnated to serve others and create a heavenly abode on earth. You may have discovered the earth plane defies the rules of the more flowing astral and causal realms you subconsciously remember. The vibrations of earth are more contracted and dense, and less receptive to the fine, subtle vibrations of love and light you are accustomed to in the serene astral and causal realms. You may contend with the density by removing yourself emotionally or mentally. But there are few viable escapes, and unless you find an outlet, usually through spiritual practice, you feel like a fish out of water. Your greatest drive is to find a more soothing, peaceful, and frankly, heavenly, form of reality.

How to Be Grounded

Your perspective is innately tied to Spirit, so you may easily ascend to higher states of consciousness and transcend earthly reasoning. While it is important to remain connected to the heavenly realms, it also is important to balance by expending energy in your earthly abode. Like the two fish in your astrological mandala, one fish is bringing spiritual light to you on earth while the other fish is returning to heaven. It is easy for you to connect with angels, foresee future events, see auras, sense qualities in people, and merge with Spirit. But you also have the imperative of remaining conscious of your physical body and your present home on Planet Earth. Given your proclivity for Spirit, it may seem paradoxical to ground your energy in earth. Yet, as your earthly foundations become stronger, you will be able to catapult yourself ever farther into the spiritual realms. "Grounding" means sending energy from the crown of your head, down your spine, into Mother Earth. It may seem paradoxical to become rooted in a place you want to transcend. But to reach higher spiritual consciousness, you must have a strong foundation from which to launch yourself.

Transcendence vs. Embodiment

The paradox between being a good citizen of Planet Earth and a participating member of the angelic realms poses the essence of the Piscean push-pull between transcendence and embodiment. The truth is that your path comes through embodying both! You are a courageous soul who chose to incarnate in the most complex of the 12 signs. You may not be surprised to find your mission is the most wide-ranging and encompassing of the 12 astrological signs. Even as a fish, it is as important to have your feet firmly planted on the earth as it is to have your gaze fixed on the heavens. A balance between heaven and earth is the *only* compromise that will work. It is tempting to escape into one realm or the other. But your life experience eventually will show you balance is the only "soul-ution."

Bring Healing Golden Light Into Your Chakras

Reconcile the heavenly and earthly realms by bringing heavenly light into your body. After cleansing your energy field with a vortex of golden light, described above, visualize healing golden light in your chakras. Begin with your crown. Move your awareness to your brow, throat, heart, solar plexus, navel, and coccyx. Bring healing energy through your legs to the earth, to a point 12 inches below your feet. This chakra is called the "earth star" and supplies abundant healing energy from Mother Earth to your body. Once you feel the light of heaven and earth flowing through you, emanate waves of peace and healing from your body to the space around you. A limitless supply of cosmic energy flows through your crown, and a limitless supply of healing earth energy flows through the soles of your feet. Even though you may feel earth energy is inimical to your spiritual roots, you have a physical body. As long as you have a physical body, it is vital to nourish it from your earthly home.

Earth Current & Cosmic Current Running Through Your Spine

As you feel an ever-stronger current of earth energy rising up your spine and an equally strong current of cosmic energy descending down your spine, you will feel more strongly rooted in both the heavenly and earthly realms. Now you begin your true work of simultaneously spanning two planes of consciousness, marrying formless divinity with formed earth. You may do this through service, healing, counseling, writing, singing, acting, parenting, cooking, gardening, or being. Please do not worry about the modality you choose to project your love. Your mere presence is enough to uplift others. Despite the earth plane's judgments to the contrary, you are doing the work you were assigned to do by simply bringing in positive energy.

Inevitably, you encounter resistance from earthly circumstances or people. Practice the following techniques to protect the integrity of your personal energy. These visualizations and practices—"The 7 Ps for Psychic Protection"—are vital equipment in your psychic toolbox to protect your mission of sending spiritual energy to earth.

The 7 Ps for Psychic Protection

1) **Pull in your aura until it is two inches from your body.**
   - This step consolidates your energy and protects you from attracting energy from people and places.

2) **Visualize a pyramid over the crown of your head.**
   - This step brings your energy coherence, strength, and stability.

3) **Visualize a pinhole at the crown of your head. Call your Guru or guardian angel to protect your pinhole.**
   - This step creates a small opening in your aura through which spiritual energy may enter your body.

4) **Pray for protection, guidance, assistance, and love.**
   - This step enables your Guru or guardian angel to act as your gatekeeper, so only positive energy may enter your aura.

5) **Project positive thoughts.**
   - This step surrounds your body with positive energy, and attracts positive energy and events to you.

6) **Practice meditation.**
   - This step enables you to bring torrents of spiritual energy into your body.

7) **Experience peace.**
   - This step enables you to experience your Creator, and express gratitude, which attracts more positive energy to you.

Mirror Techniques for Psychic Protection

If you feel unable to protect your energy field from external energies, try the following two "Mirror Techniques:"
- The Mirror Shield
- The Mirror Box

Mirror Shield

Imagine mirrors, with the mirror-side facing out, surrounding your body. The "Mirror Shield" protects your energy and projects energy sent to you back to the sender.

Mirror Box

If intense energy from an outside source persists, you may use a "Mirror Box" with the mirrors facing inward, toward the subject that is sending negative energy. Place this image around the person or object sending you unwanted energy.

Set Boundaries

Avoid overextending yourself. Implement clear psychological boundaries by stating clearly who you are, and who you are not, and what you can do, and what you cannot do. Stick to these parameters. The result is clear boundaries that you and the other person may respect.

Keep Your Energy in Your Body

As you master the art of traversing the physical and heavenly realms, keep your energy in your physical body. In the black-and-white thinking of Western society, it would seem that if a little (a little energetic exploration of spiritual realms) is good, a lot is better. But this does not work in balancing your physical life force with the energy of Spirit. Rather than go completely out of your body to inhabit the spiritual planes, you will benefit if you bring Spirit into your body. As long as you have a physical body, inhabit it. Even if part of your consciousness is in the astral or causal spheres, a portion of your energy must remain anchored in your physical body.

The reasons are three-fold:
- First, even though it is comforting and pleasant to enter astral and causal realms, a part of your energy must remain in your body to maintain bodily functions.
- Second, when your consciousness is not your physical vehicle, it is open to negative energies, as if there is no one home to guard the castle.
- Third, when your consciousness is outside of your body, it also is vulnerable to negative energy, because you are not fully able to protect yourself beyond your physical vision. Even though you are aware of what is going on around you in the astral or causal realms, the non-physical, higher dimension realities are more complex than those to which you are accustomed in three-dimensional reality. Thus, it is easy to miss something that could be injurious to you.

If you have a Guru, guardian angel, or spiritual teacher, who is capable of protecting you in higher realms, call upon this protection when you ascend to higher states of consciousness. Ask your Guru, guardian angel, or spiritual teacher to filter your energy, so that positive comes in, and negative stays out. You are a special soul with a special mission. Guard your precious energies for the sacred tasks for which you incarnated.

As you learn ways to cope with the energetic challenges of Earth, inimical as the earth may be to your aqueous nature, you will master the art of fathoming your own subconscious depths so you can soar to the superconscious spiritual heights for which your soul incarnated. Consider every experience a chance to learn about the depth and breadth of your awareness. You may learn that you are so expanded that you already encompass every quality you have ever sought.

RELATIONSHIPS

You are a person who can get along with nearly anyone because you are so loving, flexible, giving, accommodating, compassionate, and adaptable. You are able to see the best in people, and many of these people see your loving qualities and want to have a relationship with you.

Equality is a key to harmony in your personal relationships. If you are taking care of your partner, or if your partner is taking care of you, you are entering a scenario in which one of the partners eventually feels stronger than the other. Imbalance ensues. A mutually nurturing, caring, and compassionate partnership is wonderful. But make sure that your sensitivity and compassion do not lead you to carry the weight of another person. This eventually weakens your partner, because he or she loses the ability to stand on his or her own—and you feel depleted. Likewise, if your partner is carrying your responsibilities, you eventually feel weakened because you merge with your partner, and lose the ability to stand up for yourself as a unique individual.

Periodic solitude is another key to healthy relating. Solitude enables you to experience your individuality and recapture your center, which is easy to lose even in the best circumstances. It is easier for you to merge with another person than be separate. When you fall in love, you feel as if you have one foot permanently on a banana peel and are about to slip into an abyss called "love." It feels good going in, and you always feel sure you will regain your footing coming out. But after you are submerged in the sea of love, the process of drying out is more complex than you imagine.

Pisces often surrenders his or her time and efforts for the good of a partner. It makes a Pisces feel as if his or her divine mission of merging heaven and earth is accomplished through the partner, which seems like a noble idea. But the *only* love that ultimately sustains an individual is Divine love. As humans, we can assist each other on the path to reconnecting with the Divine. We can allow Divine love to flow through us. We can provide service. But few of us can *be* Divine love until we ourselves have merged with the Divine. And until we have merged with the Divine, we are not on solid footing when we surrender to, and merge with, each other. So, giving love and support to a partner is noble. But giving *yourself* undoes spiritual growth because it clouds both partners' ability to connect directly with the Divine.

A direct connection to the Divine comes so easily to you that you may take this precious gift for granted, and you may seek it through another person rather than from the Source. The most successful relationships involve two healthy individuals who deeply love, respect, and accept each other, but who carry their own responsibilities, and receive their greatest sustenance from God. Rather than see a partner as God, see the hand of God working through the partner.

In the realm of human love, you are most compatible with fellow water signs Cancer, Scorpio, and Pisces. Water signs relate through the element of feeling, and waters signs are most likely to understand the quixotic realm of each other's feelings. The water signs undergo an evolution in feeling that begins with the self-referential feelings of Cancer. Cancer's emotional awareness is limited to feelings recorded by the conscious mind, particularly related to physical comforts in the immediate environment. Awareness of feeling expands in Scorpio to encompass subconscious feelings and their roots. Feeling extends in Pisces from the subconscious to the superconscious spiritual connection with the soul. Pisceans are compassionate souls who feel *everything*, their own feelings, the feelings of others, and even vibrations emanating from higher astral and causal realms. You are a highly intuitive soul who can fathom the depths of other people. As you evolve in consciousness, you develop even greater skill in fathoming your own mysterious depths, and you are able to use your insights to bring greater understanding to your relationships.

Pisces and Pisces

You will cherish a relationship with fellow Pisces because you both understand the role of deep feelings in each other and in the partnership. You both are willing to temporarily let go of your individuality to merge with your partner. This can be initially satisfying. But, symbolically place breadcrumbs on the oceanic trail you create when you submerge yourself in the relationship, and re-read the section above about the limitations of humans merging with each other before merging with the Divine. When you want to come up for air from this relationship, you may find the watery depths of both partners' psyches have washed away the breadcrumbs that were to have shown you the way out. Awareness of the your state of consciousness and your partner's state of consciousness will greatly ease your ability to co-exist as individuals and as partners.

Pisces and Aries

Traditionally, water signs such as Pisces do not harmonize with fire signs, because water puts out fire—and fire heats the water and causes steam and evaporation. The ethereal quality of Pisces enables this evolved water sign to harmonize with the feelings of any sign, even the fieriest of fire signs. A disproportionate number of Pisces pair up with Aries due to a sense of completeness created by the partnership. Aries initiates action while Pisces brings the action to completion. Pisces enjoys the impulsive nature of Aries. And Aries appreciates the flowing, adaptable quality of Pisces. Pisces and Aries see the world from opposite perspectives, and they create harmony by balancing opposites. Pisces lets go of the Self to unite with others as a way of uniting with the Divine. Aries separates from the Divine as a way of asserting the Self to unite with its own individuality. If Aries and Pisces understand their innate differences, they may create a balance between heaven and earth, a creation others admire.

Pisces and Taurus

If you are seeking a down-to-earth relationship experience, you may choose an earth sign partner such as Taurus to balance your watery nature. You may miss the subterranean depths you share with water sign souls, but you will appreciate the solidity, security, and predictability an earth sign mate provides. Taurus, a fixed, earth sign, is methodical, slow-moving, and materially-minded. You are spontaneous, intuitive, and spiritually oriented. Taurus plans where Pisces flows. The focus of the bull's eye can be extremely narrow whereas the vision of the celestial and terrestrial fish is extraordinarily expansive. Taurus thinks about what's for lunch while Pisces contemplates the fate of the universe, and forgets to eat. Taurus and Pisces make a quaint couple if Pisces does not feel tied down by the earthbound Taurus, and if Taurus does not feel destabilized by the unpredictable Pisces. This relationship may cause you to confront the dilemma of how to marry heaven and earth. A relationship between yourself and a like-minded soul is inevitably heavenly. But without some dry land, the two partners may feel soggy. Yet, a more earthbound relationship may seem slow, superficial, or boring despite its practical merits. A relationship with an earthbound Taurus may create a pull between heaven and earth that is so strong you will be forced to find a comfortable middle ground.

Pisces and Gemini

A Gemini-Pisces relationship may initially seem quite attractive as both parties try to accommodate the other. You both are expert at adapting to other people, and this relationship is no exception. You both must be aware of how easily your basic identities will slip away in a long-term relationship. Both Pisces and Gemini are malleable, meaning that each personality changes to adapt to circumstances. Two people together of this mutable nature may create a situation in which there is no stable center around which the relationship may revolve. This is okay if the partners are willing to stagnate or individually spin in their own orbits. But if you are looking for a dance partner who can dance the same rhythm as you, this may not be the relationship you are seeking.

Pisces and Cancer

You enjoy the Cancer's domestic flair, and are happy to luxuriate in the warmth, peace, and comfort of the domestic situation the two of you create. Traveling or going out in the world may be a bit elusive, as neither has the inclination to motivate the other. Yet, if both individuals are self-motivated, this is a relationship with infinite potential for emotional understanding, shared sympathy, compassion, common values, and companionship. Pisces and Cancer are especially loving, protective, nurturing parents if you desire a family. If this is the case, pray for a soul to enter your family who will appreciate the emotional warmth and nurturing you are able to provide. A child seeking independence or adventure may feel less comfortable in your family than a sensitive, emotional child who could infinitely benefit from the love created by your union.

Pisces and Leo

Although fire and water combinations are not favored in traditional astrology, Pisces and fixed, fire sign Leo can create a harmonious union. Pisces appreciates the Leo's radiant nature. Leo appreciates Pisces flowing, adaptable nature. Pisces forever reflects Leo's solar radiance in its oceanic depths. And Leo forever enjoys beholding itself in the mirror Pisces provides. While Leo's blustery temperament can ruffle the waters of many other signs, Pisces is a calm soul who absorbs the shock waves and experiences Leo's energy as an endearing expression of passion. This is a relationship in which the Pisces surrounds Leo with its watery compassion and support. Leo, in return, provides Pisces with a warm, stable center around which to build his or her life.

Pisces and Virgo

Virgo is a mutable, earth sign, located opposite Pisces on the Zodiac wheel. Opposites attract, and the sign opposite your own traditionally brings you balance and harmony. Pisces is a flowing, feeling, sensitive being dedicated to harmonizing spiritual and human realms. Virgo is a hard-working, industrious, service-oriented sign. While Pisces and Virgo are both oriented to helping others, your methods are quite different. Pisces gives service through feelings of compassion. Virgo gives service through actions of compassion. Pisces feels compassion, while Virgo acts with compassion. But Virgo and Pisces can be so opposite in their earthly versus watery ways that the two signs struggle to understand each other. A conscious effort to understand the other yields luscious fruit of mutual compassion and service to the relationship and others. Without awareness of the natural difference between the flowing depths of the Sign of the Fish, and the organized, methodical, down-to-earth systems of the Sign of the Virgin, each sign may feel as if he or she has encountered a being from another planet! Again, understanding brings awareness that mutually transforms both partners, and brings out the hidden flow in the Virgo soul, and the hidden organization in the Pisces psyche.

Pisces and Libra

Libra, a cardinal, air sign, is a peace-loving soul who has a healthy perspective on life and does not allow small problems to overwhelm an otherwise harmonious relationship. Pisces agrees with this concept, and you and Libra have a solid foundation of shared values to build upon. You both respect the right of the other to pursue a unique path to happiness, and you each do your part to support your partner's path. Yet, you have quite different ways of approaching life. Libra is a cerebral person who is masterful at the art of detachment, objectivity, and perspective. While Pisces has a mature perspective that enables you to detach, you are not a detached person. You are highly emotional and feel deeply the circumstances swirling around you. You may feel if you express your emotional depths, you may unbalance your Libra mate. Or, your Libra mate may feel overwhelmed by your emotional depths, and shut down emotionally to protect his or her sensitive balance. Your chameleon-like nature may lead you to minimize your feelings to stay in tune with your Libra partner. While this may help the relationship, it will not help you be true to yourself. The solution in this otherwise harmonious relationship is for you to find a way to express your feelings so you may be true to your feelings and to the relationship you cherish.

Pisces and Scorpio

You deeply resonate with the magnetic depths of fixed, water sign Scorpio. Both Pisces and Scorpio experience deep feelings and a connection to subconscious feelings. If both signs are aware of the role of the subconscious minds in relationship, this partnership could cause beneficial psychological growth. If the subconscious realms are ignored, and both pretend they are playing house, subterranean feelings may churn under the surface and erupt when least expected. Efforts to develop greater self-awareness will avoid misunderstanding. A conscious relationship between Pisces and Scorpio is romantically, sexually, and emotionally transformational.

Pisces and Sagittarius

The hopeful nature of mutable, fire sign Sagittarius fascinates Pisces. Sagittarians' hope and optimism dovetails with Pisces similar trust in Spirit. Pisces and Sagittarius see eye-to-eye on issues of spirituality, idealism, altruism, and faith. You both are dreamers who feel nothing is impossible. While you and Sagittarius implement your ideas with different tools—Sagittarians through bold actions and projecting positive energy, and Pisces through projecting deep feelings and thoughts—you both successfully manifest your ideas, albeit in unconventional and unexpected ways. You have a happy partnership, and only occasionally will someone have to think about who's paying the bills!

Pisces and Capricorn

Pisces is attracted to the managerial and executive qualities of cardinal, earth sign Capricorn. You feel a sense of security with a Capricorn mate. Yet, you may sometimes feel you are in a business rather than romantic partnership. Capricorn is organized, ambitious, and strategic. Pisces eschews formal logic for intuition. Pisces senses what people are thinking, feeling, and planning. As a result of this sixth sense, Pisces knows precisely what to do, and when to do it, when the moment arrives. But heaven help the person who tries to pin the Pisces down in advance. Pisces simply does not know what it is going to do until it happens, and even then, the Pisces feels as if a greater force has directed him or her. This force is the force of the soul. Unlike many other signs, Pisces responds to the internal rhythm of the soul, and follows a course through life dictated from higher realms, which is a course that may defy earthly logic—and the logical Capricorn. If both Capricorn and Pisces understand that they approach life from opposite perspectives—tangible versus intangible—these signs will have a high degree of success in creating a life of balance between heaven and earth.

Pisces and Aquarius

Aquarians often team up with Pisces because of shared compassion, global perspective, and spiritual values. Yet, in intimate relationships, the Pisces partner often reports feeling emotionally neglected, because of the emotional detachment and unpredictable reactions to electromagnetic influences of fixed, air sign Aquarius. While Pisces also reacts to energetic influences and enjoys an expanded perspective that enables you to feel more for others than for yourself, you experience compassion through feelings whereas Aquarius experiences compassion as a thought. Pisceans also seek emotional communion from a mate, while Aquarius seeks a meeting of the minds. This disparity can lead to misunderstandings of a subtle and not-so-subtle nature. If your Aquarius partner has many planets in Pisces, you may find the communion you are seeking.

As a Pisces, you sometimes detach yourself from immediate circumstances and mentally enter an alternate realm to protect yourself from the flood of feelings you may otherwise experience in yourself, or from another person. This is a defense mechanism, but it is not your natural state. You may be chameleon-like in a relationship by taking on the qualities of a partner, or by taking on opposite qualities in order to harmonize, or you may detach to escape from the mood of a partner. Remember to be yourself when you are in partnership, and continually allow yourself to feel your feelings, and act in concert with the sensations you are experiencing, rather than the feelings and sensations your partner is experiencing. You enjoy the companionship and harmony you establish in any relationship as long as you freely express yourself. No matter whom you choose as a partner, also remember to simultaneously maintain your partnership with the Divine.

SPIRITUALITY

You incarnated to experience spirituality while in a physical body. Your spiritual experiences are as natural as breathing. Even if you are not on a formal spiritual path, your life reflects the embodiment of spiritual principles of compassion, forgiveness, service, and selflessness. You are a self-sacrificing person who is willing to put aside his or her own needs to help others. Your are naturally tuned to the cosmic waves of energy emanating to this planet, and this attunement—even if subliminal—guides you to act in the highest good.

Sometimes the spiritual waves emanating to you feel so overwhelming that you desire to escape, which is a natural defense pattern in your personality. You are sensitive, and often experience events as if they are very close to you, even if they are far away. Rather than confront a situation, you choose to withdraw to lessen the intensity. This is a familiar reaction pattern, and one that you may experience in relation to your own spirituality. You may feel so close to Spirit, particularly in comparison to others, you may run away rather than absorb spiritual energy. Your connection to Spirit comes so easily that you may take it for granted.

Your spiritual muscles may become lazy while others are busily strengthening their spiritual muscles to attain something you already have! While you have the capacity to quickly make spiritual progress, you may notice over time that some other people develop more spiritual strength, determination, and discipline because they are forced to focus to make any progress at all. You also are more open to experience the natural course of events and less likely to push for an outcome than others. The result on the spiritual path may be an unfocused quality that could be one of the sole impediments to soaring to the heights of spiritual enlightenment for which you incarnated.

There are stages on the spiritual path that require forbearance, endurance, concentration, and discipline. While you have all of these qualities in abundance when it comes to helping others, you may have trouble applying your willpower to yourself. This is one of the many paradoxes of the Piscean personality. You have tremendous talent in uplifting others, and great force of will in rescuing them from self-created predicaments. Even though you are infinitely capable of advancing your own spiritual cause, you may not be able to marshal your force of will, or you may even try to help others instead, or look to them for your spiritual salvation. Of course, willingness to surrender to another is perfectly appropriate on the spiritual path if the "other" is God or a Guru whose consciousness is united with the Divine. But as often as not, Pisces are prone to fall under the spell of a false guru, or to devote themselves to a person in lieu of God. Given that you are so susceptible to surrendering yourself, you may want to exercise discernment before giving yourself over to a person or a path to insure your choice will reunite you with God.

Spiritual energy is infinitely available to you, not only because you have karmically earned spiritual access, but because you have developed an ability to resonate with spiritual vibrations through many past incarnations of spiritual practice. It is not possible to incarnate as a Pisces if you have not built significant spiritual aptitude in past lives. Use your spiritual gifts wisely. Like everything in nature, energy seeks movement rather than stagnation. Your spiritual inclination will either increase or decrease depending upon your intentions and actions. If you are determined to maintain and enhance your spiritual status, there is no one better equipped. If you lack the determination, you are as likely to be pulled to material living as to be pulled to higher spiritual planes. Both are acceptable, but know that you are always making choices. When it comes to spirituality, Pisces' fish swim continuously in one direction or the other. Unlike earth or air signs, it is not possible for you to remain stagnant for long. Choose a direction, and notice that the Piscean waters of your mind carry you in the direction you focus your attention upon.

HEALTH

As the wateriest of the water signs, Pisces is sensitive to the movement of water and feelings through the body. Pisces rules the feet, which may be the most sensitive part of your body. These earth-bound extremities are the mediators of heavenly light and solid earth. Your feet may not be entirely comfortable treading the density of earth. Your relationship to your feet is an accurate barometer of the evolving quality of your earthly journey.

Exercise and Food

Your kidneys also are sensitive, and function best when you are well rested, and emotionally centered. You may help your kidneys by taking an equal measure of sugar and salt into your body. Sugar is an expansive crystalline substance, and salt is a contractive crystalline substance. A balance of the two helps water flow most smoothly through your water-sensitive body. Best sources of sugar are natural, fruit, maple syrup, molasses, or honey. Best sources of salt are sea vegetables, nori, kelp, dulse, arame, wakame, spirulina, and chlorella. It also is helpful to drink a lot of water. Water moves positively charged electromagnetic energy through your body. If possible, take salt baths to cleanse your energy, and meditate to bring higher, clearer vibrations to your aura.

Solitude

Solitude, if spent consciously pursuing spiritual practice, is one simple technique that quickly rejuvenates your sensitive system. Time alone helps you replenish your energy, find your center, and reestablish your boundaries more effectively than nearly any practice. Once you rejuvenate your inner Self, you are able to go out and fully give again. Reserve one day a week to go within to fortify your Self. You may also consider practicing healing techniques that reinforce your aqueous nature. These include aqua therapy, where you are massaged or move in water, rebirthing, dream analysis, watercolors, or an isolation tank. Any technique that helps you connect with your superconscious spiritual mind and subconscious depths will help you reconnect to Spirit, to which you feel so close, and with which your soul longs to reconnect.

Flower Essences

Flower essences, which are distillations of the high vibrations in flowers, also fortify your sensitive energy. Yarrow strengthens your aura when you expend too much energy. Golden Yarrow helps you feel your center so you do not have to withdraw or isolate yourself after socializing. Goldenrod helps you maintain your individuality in the face of external or group influences. Willow helps you confront daily experiences with confidence.

FINANCES

You are a generous soul who is more interested in giving than receiving. While you would rather think about spending money on others than on yourself, you also enjoy luxury now and then, for comfort, and as an opportunity for escape. You have a natural aversion to paying attention to the details of money. This pattern has developed in reaction to your sometimes endless access to resources when you need them, and the seeming absence of resources when you do not need them. The reason for this pattern is due to the power of your thoughts. When you need something, your thoughts naturally emit electromagnetic waves that commensurately attract what you need—or at least what you are thinking about! Your faith, hope, and trust create an electromagnetic field that draws you to the right place at the right moment to achieve your goal. You have become so accustomed to this method that more primitive methods such as balancing your checkbook, or budget, may be foreign to you.

You may be aware of your natural antipathy to details. While it may not be necessary to be aware of the minute details of your financial status, it does not hurt to have a general idea either. Many Pisceans say they manage their finances by intuition. This seemingly intangible method for quantifying tangible resources is often quite successful. Yet every once in a while, Pisces' perception of their financial condition may be out of harmony with reality. A periodic financial inventory—of income and outgo—is a tool to enable the Pisces soul to marry material reality with the flowing realms of intuition and Spirit.

Your intuition is an accurate barometer of feelings and thoughts. But this intangible skill does not always translate with 100% accuracy to the physical world. The divergence of perception and reality in the physical world may afflict Pisces souls one way or another. If you discover a discrepancy between perception and reality in your financial situation, you may realign your financial attitudes. Or, you may find this phenomenon affecting other areas. If so, apply the same principle of taking an inventory to gain a clear picture of reality to marry your infinitely accurate spiritual and ethereal perceptions with earthly reality.

CAREER

Your career choice is likely guided by what others need more than by what you want. "Me? Want something?" It is likely that you have flowed, or will flow, into a career that presents itself rather than a career you may have consciously chosen. If you do choose a narrow career path, however, there are several areas best suited to your talents and temperament. You naturally excel in healing, health care, hospital and hospice, charitable giving, community service, writing, art, advertising, drama, film, visual arts, graphic arts, and computer animation. Your health and healing abilities dovetail with the healing energy naturally emanating from you. Your writing flows from your fertile, creative imagination. Your visual arts talent comes from your connection to your subconscious and superconscious spiritual minds, which are permeated by multi-dimensional spatial reality. You have a natural ability to build a bridge between multi-dimensional space and the three-dimensional world.

A number of Pisces also are drawn to financial services and investing. Although Pisces is not a materialistic sign, you have a sixth sense about the movement of unseen energies that characterize the movement of money. With very little training, you may find you have a proclivity for sensing where money is flowing in the collective consciousness. Depending upon your goals, you may tap these collective movements at the precise moment to maximize your profits or prosperity. This sense of timing extends to real estate, banking, and financial investments—and to relationships with people, spirituality, and the natural ebb and flow of energy through the universe. No matter what your career, use your precious gifts to rise above the constraints of physical reality to see yourself—and help others see—the splendorous reality of the Creation of which you are a part.

NOTES

ENDORSEMENTS

"Laurie's astrological predictions speak to your soul. These are not ordinary predictions, but give glimpses into larger forces at work in your life. The insights in this book will shine light on your path, whether your question is about finances, business, health, or relationships. If you are seeking spiritual, emotional, or psychological guidance, this book not only comforts your heart but gives much inner strength at the most important times in your life and serves as a guiding light for your soul to fulfill its purpose."

—*Nalini Sabapathy, Lorenzo De' Medici Institute, Florence, Italy*

"Laurie's teachings have become my spiritual guidance. Her knowledge and perception of our souls gives all of us an awakening call and a chance for change. I often read her astrology report for my sign and am able to capture myself for positive transformation. Her precious gift is ours through her words."

—*Silvia Ichar, Publisher, PARA TODOS, Magazine*

978-0-595-42082-7
0-595-42082-6

CPSIA information can be obtained at www.ICGtesting.com
Printed in the USA
LVOW072044080212

267794LV00001B/62/A